Foreign Currency Trading

Second Edition

by Gary Tilkin and Lita Epstein

ALPHA

A member of Penguin Group (USA) Inc.

To all my friends at GFT, the best forex dealing company in the world!

ALPHA BOOKS

Published by the Penguin Group

Penguin Group (USA) Inc., 375 Hudson Street, New York, New York 10014, USA

Penguin Group (Canada), 90 Eglinton Avenue East, Suite 700, Toronto, Ontario M4P 2Y3, Canada (a division of Pearson Penguin Canada Inc.)

Penguin Books Ltd., 80 Strand, London WC2R 0RL, England

Penguin Ireland, 25 St. Stephen's Green, Dublin 2, Ireland (a division of Penguin Books Ltd.)

Penguin Group (Australia), 250 Camberwell Road, Camberwell, Victoria 3124, Australia (a division of Pearson Australia Group Pty. Ltd.)

Penguin Books India Pvt. Ltd., 11 Community Centre, Panchsheel Park, New Delhi—110 017, India

Penguin Group (NZ), 67 Apollo Drive, Rosedale, North Shore, Auckland 1311, New Zealand (a division of Pearson New Zealand Ltd.)

Penguin Books (South Africa) (Pty.) Ltd., 24 Sturdee Avenue, Rosebank, Johannesburg 2196, South Africa

Penguin Books Ltd., Registered Offices: 80 Strand, London WC2R 0RL, England

Copyright © 2011 by Gary Tilkin and Lita Epstein

International Standard Book Number: 978-1-61564-1-130
Library of Congress Catalog Card Number: 2011904911

13   12   11   8   7   6   5   4   3   2   1

Interpretation of the printing code: The rightmost number of the first series of numbers is the year of the book's printing; the rightmost number of the second series of numbers is the number of the book's printing. For example, a printing code of 11-1 shows that the first printing occurred in 2011.

Printed in the United States of America

Note: This publication contains the opinions and ideas of its author. It is intended to provide helpful and informative material on the subject matter covered. It is sold with the understanding that the author and publisher are not engaged in rendering professional services in the book. If the reader requires personal assistance or advice, a competent professional should be consulted.

The author and publisher specifically disclaim any responsibility for any liability, loss, or risk, personal or otherwise, which is incurred as a consequence, directly or indirectly, of the use and application of any of the contents of this book.

Most Alpha books are available at special quantity discounts for bulk purchases for sales promotions, premiums, fund-raising, or educational use. Special books, or book excerpts, can also be created to fit specific needs.

For details, write: Special Markets, Alpha Books, 375 Hudson Street, New York, NY 10014.

Publisher: *Marie Butler-Knight*	**Copy Editor:** *Cate Schwenk*
Associate Publisher: *Mike Sanders*	**Cover Designer:** *Kurt Owens*
Executive Managing Editor: *Billy Fields*	**Book Designers:** *William Thomas, Rebecca Batchelor*
Senior Acquisitions Editor: *Paul Dinas*	**Indexer:** *Brad Herriman*
Senior Development Editor: *Phil Kitchel*	**Layout:** *Ayanna Lacey*
Senior Production Editor: *Janette Lynn*	**Proofreader:** *John Etchison*

Contents

Introduction

Foreign currency trading gives you the opportunity to participate in the world's largest and most liquid market, known as forex. More than $3.9 trillion U.S. dollars exchange hands daily.

The forex market moves rapidly, with currency prices changing by the second. No single event, individual, or institution can rule this market. It's truly uncontrollable by any single entity because of its large liquidity.

Some traders see very large profits from trading in this market, but always remember that the market is highly speculative and volatile. While you can make a lot of money on a trade, you can also lose a lot on a trade.

Take the time to learn how to research your potential trades using both the fundamental and technical analysis tools we introduce to you in this book. Develop your own strategies for trading and test those strategies using demonstration accounts before you start trading your own money.

Remember, though, you should never trade forex unless you're using money you can afford to lose. *Forex is a high-risk endeavor!*

How We've Organized the Book

You start exploring the world of foreign currency trading by learning how forex got started and how it operates today. Then you explore how currencies differ from country to country. Next, we explore the trading basics. We then introduce you to the tools for trading.

We've organized this book into five parts:

Part 1, Exploring the World of Money, looks at why you should consider trading forex, then delves into how the forex market got started and introduces you to the language of money.

Part 2, Deciphering Money Differences, gives you the opportunity to learn why currency values change and how the foreign exchange markets work. Then we'll take a closer look at the safest currencies to trade—currencies of the developed world. We'll also explore the more exotic currencies—emerging nations whose currencies may be worth considering once you understand the foreign currency market, its risks, and how to trade in it.

Part 3, Trading Basics, introduces you to the basics of technical and fundamental analysis to help you research your potential trades. Then we explore how you develop an investing plan and identify trends and trades. Finally, we explore the various risks you must take in order to trade in the forex market.

Part 4, Tools for Trading, starts with the basic computer hardware and software you need to trade, then goes on to explore how you can develop your own money strategies, as well as the basics for actually placing your trades.

Part 5, Trading Options, starts with how to avoid money fraud, then explores the various ways you can trade forex: with mini accounts, standard accounts, managed forex, and trading systems. We then describe how to set up your trading business and how to find the resources you need to operate that business.

Extras

We've developed a few helpers you'll find in sidebars throughout the book:

DEFINITION

Helps you learn the language of forex trading.

CAPITAL CAUTIONS

Gives you warnings about what to avoid when trading forex.

CURRENCY COIN

Explores interesting facts and other details you should know about forex trading.

WEALTH BUILDERS

Gives ideas on how to set up your own forex trading business as well as suggests tips about resources you can use.

Acknowledgments

We'd like to give a special thanks to Christine Flodin, whose attention to detail and assistance with all the content in this book helped make this a friendly user's guide for our readers. We'd also like to thank our editors at Alpha Books for all their help in making this book the best it can be: Paul Dinas, acquisitions editor; Phil Kitchel, development editor; and Cate Schwenk, copy editor.

Disclaimer

Foreign exchange trading involves high risks, with the potential for substantial losses, and is not suitable for all persons. The high degree of leverage can work against you as well as for you. The possibility exists that you could sustain a loss of some or all of your initial investment; therefore, you should not invest money that you cannot afford to lose. Trading programs or strategies discussed in this book are for educational purposes only and are based on hypothetical or simulated performance results, which have certain inherent limitations. Because these trades have not actually been executed, the results may not have accurately compensated for the impact, if any, of certain market factors, such as lack of liquidity. Hypothetical or simulated trading programs are designed with the benefit of hindsight to illustrate strategic trading concepts, but no representation is being made that any account will or is likely to achieve profits or losses similar to the results being shown. Any opinions, news, research, analyses, prices, trading strategies, or other information contained on websites or in publications mentioned in this book are provided as general market commentary, and do not constitute investment advice. Before deciding to trade foreign exchange you should carefully consider your investment objectives, level of experience, and risk appetite. You should be aware of all the risks associated with foreign exchange trading, and seek advice from an independent financial advisor if you have any doubts.

Trademarks

All terms mentioned in this book that are known to be or are suspected of being trademarks or service marks have been appropriately capitalized. Alpha Books and Penguin Group (USA) Inc. cannot attest to the accuracy of this information. Use of a term in this book should not be regarded as affecting the validity of any trademark or service mark.

Exploring the World of Money

Why trade foreign currency? Who trades it? In this part, you learn the answers to these questions and many more. You'll also take a tour of forex basics.

You'll also learn how foreign exchange trading got started. It's a long story that goes back to Babylon. Today's system of floating currencies is still a work in progress.

The world of foreign exchange trading includes spots (and we're not talking about the type you find on dogs), forwards, options, and futures (and not the reading-the-tea-leaves type). Find out how all these impact the world of forex.

After reviewing the key money terms, compare forex trading to less risky trading options, such as stocks, to determine if forex is right for you.

Why Trade Foreign Currency?

In This Chapter

- Finding out about forex
- Discovering forex players
- Exploring market structure

If we lived in a world where there was only one currency, there would be no foreign exchange market or fluctuating rates; but that's not how our world works. Instead we have primarily national currencies, and the foreign exchange market is an essential mechanism for making payments across country borders.

The foreign exchange market creates a way to transfer funds between countries and to purchase things in other counties. In this chapter, we look at what the foreign exchange market is and who trades foreign currency.

What Is Forex?

Forex is the short way of saying foreign exchange currency trading. Today the forex market is by far the largest and most liquid market in the world. On average more than US$3.98 trillion is traded each day in the foreign exchange market. That's several times more than the daily volume in the world's second-largest market—the U.S. government securities market. In fact, forex trading volume translates to more than US$400 million in foreign exchange market transactions every business day of the year for every man, woman, and child on Earth!

Not only is the total volume hard to fathom for most people, the sheer volume of some individual trades can involve much more money than most people deal with in their entire lifetimes. It's not uncommon to hear of individual trades in the US$200 million to US$500 million range.

It's a fast-moving market, too. Price quotes for a currency pair can change as often as 20 times a minute, or every three seconds. The most active exchange rates can change up to 18,000 times during a single day. Actual price movements tend to be in relatively small increments, which also make this a smoothly functioning and liquid market.

London Time

Foreign currency is exchanged in financial centers around the world, but the largest amount of currency actually changes hands in the United Kingdom. Well, changing hands may not be a good metaphor, because most of the transactions are done by electronic transmission, and paper currency is not really moved from one trader to another. Instead, an initial trade of foreign currency with one dealer leads to a number of different transactions over several days as various financial institutions re-adjust their positions (the open trades held by a trader).

In fact, a foreign exchange dealer buying U.S. dollars in any institution around the world is actually buying a dollar-denominated deposit in a bank located in the United States or the claim of a bank outside the United States based on the dollar deposit located in the United States. That's true no matter what currency you trade. A dealer buying a Japanese yen, no matter where he or she makes the purchase, is actually buying a yen deposit in a bank in Japan or a claim on a yen deposit in a bank in Japan.

CURRENCY COIN

Where do most foreign exchanges take place? About 37 percent of all currency trades are handled through financial institutions in the United Kingdom, even though the British pound is not as widely traded as some of the other key currencies, such as the U.S. dollar, the euro, the Japanese yen, and the Swiss franc. U.S. financial institutions rank second in the volume of foreign exchange transactions handled, but that's a distant second—just 18 percent of foreign exchange transactions are handled by U.S. institutions. Japanese financial institutions rank third, with 6 percent of the transactions passing through their doors.

The United Kingdom is the most active financial trading center because of London's strong position as the international financial center of the world, where a large number of financial headquarters are located. According to a foreign exchange turnover survey completed in the late 1990s, more than 200 foreign exchange dealer institutions in the United Kingdom reported trading activity to the Bank of England, whereas only 93 in the United States were reporting to the Federal Reserve Bank of New York. London has a major advantage over U.S. markets because of its geographic location. Because it is in the center (in regard to its time zone), the normal business hours for London financial institutions coincide with other world financial centers. Its early-morning hours overlap with a number of Asian and Middle Eastern markets, and its afternoon hours overlap with the North American markets.

Around the Clock, Around the World

The forex market is a 24-hour market almost 6 days a week. The markets are closed for only a short period of time on the weekends. As some financial centers close, others open; so the foreign exchange market can be viewed in terms of following the sun around the earth. The 24-hour market means that exchange rates and market conditions can change in response to developments that can take place at any time. This differs significantly from the stock or bond markets, which primarily trade only when the exchanges are open. Although there is some overnight trading of stocks, it's a limited market with a lot less liquidity or volume.

If you learn about major news that might impact a foreign currency in which you trade, you have 24-hour access to act on that news. But if you learn about something regarding a stock you hold after the closing bell, you probably won't find a way to trade it until the next business day. This greatly decreases the chances of market gaps in forex trading that can be found with stock trading.

Although 24-hour access might sound like a great opportunity, it can also create a money-management nightmare. As a trader, you must realize that a sharp move in a foreign currency exchange rate can occur during any hour, at any place in the world. Large currency dealers use various techniques to monitor markets 24 hours a day, and many even keep their trading desks open on a 24-hour basis. Other financial institutions pass the torch from one geographic location to another rather than stay open around the clock.

Trading Flow

As an individual trader, you won't have anyone to watch your trades when you sleep or just want to get away from the computer. The volume of currency traded does not flow evenly throughout the day. Over any 24-hour period, there are times of heavy activity and times when the activity is relatively light. Most trading takes place when the largest numbers of potential *counterparties* are available or accessible on a global basis.

DEFINITION

Every foreign currency exchange involves a pair of currencies traded between two parties. In order to trade a currency pair, you need to have a **counterparty,** such as a dealer who is willing to trade with you. For example, if someone wants to trade U.S. dollars for euros, one party must be holding the euros and one party must be holding the dollars in order to trade.

Business is heaviest when both the U.S. markets and the major European markets are open. That is when it is morning in New York and afternoon in London. In the New York market, nearly two thirds of the day's trading activity takes place in the morning hours before the London markets close. Activity in the New York market slows in the mid to late afternoon after the European markets close and before the Asian markets of Tokyo, Hong Kong, and Singapore open.

Who Trades Foreign Currency?

Although everyone talks about how the world is becoming a "global village," the foreign exchange market comes closest to actually functioning as one. The various foreign exchange trading centers around the world are linked into a single, unified, cohesive worldwide market.

Although foreign exchange trading takes place among dealers and other financial professionals in financial centers around the world, it doesn't matter where the trade occurs. Each trade is still being bought or sold based on the same currencies or bank deposits denominated in the same currencies.

So who is doing all this buying and selling? Only a limited number of major dealer institutions participate actively in foreign exchange. They trade with each other most often, but also trade with other customers. Most of these major players are commercial banks and investment banks. They're located in financial centers around the world, but are closely linked by telephone, computers, and other electronic means.

The central bank for most of these major dealer institutions is the *Bank for International Settlements (BIS)*, which covers the foreign exchange activities for 2,000 dealer institutions around the world. The bulk of foreign exchange trades are actually handled by a much smaller group. BIS estimates that 100 to 200 market-making banks worldwide handle the bulk of all trades.

DEFINITION

The **Bank for International Settlements (BIS),** an international organization based in Basel, Switzerland, serves as a bank for the world's central banks. It fosters international monetary and financial cooperation by promoting discussion and policy analysis among central banks and the international financial community. It also conducts economic and monetary research.

Many different types of institutions and individuals are involved in the foreign exchange trading world. These include commercial banks, governments, broker/ dealers, corporations, investment-management firms, exchange-traded funds, and speculators/individuals. The sections that follow discuss the various participants.

Commercial Banks

Commercial banks handle the vast amount of commercial foreign exchange trading through the interbank market. A large bank may trade billions of dollars daily. Some of this trading is undertaken on behalf of customers, but even more of it involves trading in the bank's own accounts. Most of this trading is done through efficient electronic systems.

Governments

Most governments around the world conduct their foreign exchange trading through their central banks. These central banks control the money supply, inflation, and/or interest rates for their respective countries. In most cases they also try to maintain target rates set for their currencies by the government decision makers. In the United States, the target exchange rates are set by the U.S. Treasury Department working with the Federal Reserve, which actually conducts all foreign currency exchange for the U.S. government.

Sometimes central banks act on behalf of the government to influence the value of the country's currency. For example, if the U.S. government believes the currency is weak, the Federal Reserve starts buying U.S. dollars and even encourages other friendly nations to do so to boost the value of the dollar. If the dollar is thought to be too strong, the Federal Reserve begins selling U.S. dollars on the foreign exchange market or encourages other countries to do so. Governments can also adopt new economic policies to affect the value of its country's currency.

Brokers or Dealers

Retail brokers or dealers act as intermediaries between the banks and individual traders. Individuals and companies who work through brokers or dealers do so because it gives them the ability to trade anonymously through an intermediary. Brokers or dealers also have much lower minimum trade size requirements than large banks, which allow individuals to access the market.

This retail foreign exchange market represents only about 2 percent of the total foreign exchange market. The volume of retail trades through dealers totals about $25 to $50 billion daily. All online trading of foreign exchange currency is done through retail dealers or brokers.

Most brokers do not provide individuals with direct access to the true interbank market because very few clearing banks are willing to process the relatively small orders placed by individuals.

Corporations

Corporations trade foreign currency primarily so that they can operate globally or invest internationally. For example, a U.S. manufacturer may buy parts from a manufacturer in Singapore. When it comes time to pay for those parts, the U.S. manufacturer will need to pay for them with Singapore dollars.

Investment-Management Firms

Investment-management firms, which manage large accounts for other entities, including pension funds and endowments, trade foreign currency for the portfolios they manage, which enables them to buy foreign securities, including stocks and bonds, for their clients' portfolios. In most cases, these transactions are secondary to the actual investment decision; in some cases, however, the investment-management firms do speculate for their clients with the goal of generating profits on the currencies traded while limiting risk. Most investment-management firms place their forex transactions through a dealer.

Speculators

All individuals who participate in the foreign currency market are considered speculators. Although you may hear controversy about the role of speculators in the foreign exchange market, they do provide an important function for the market. They provide a means for companies or people who don't want to bear the risk of foreign exchange trading to find an individual or institution that does want to take on that risk for the reward of future profits.

The largest speculators in the world of foreign exchange currency are hedge funds. These funds trade for a group of wealthy individuals and institutions that want them to use aggressive strategies in the hopes of reaping large profits.

Hedge funds can use strategies not permitted by mutual funds, including swaps and *derivatives*. Hedge funds are restricted by law to no more than 100 investors per fund, so minimum investment levels are high, ranging from $250,000 to more than $1 million per investor. Hedge fund managers not only collect a management fee for their work, they also all get a percentage of the profits, usually around 20 or 30 percent.

DEFINITION

Derivatives are securities whose value is dependent upon or derived from one or more underlying assets. The derivative itself is just a contract between two or more parties. Its value is determined by fluctuations in the value of the underlying asset. The most common underlying assets include stocks, bonds, commodities, currencies, interest rates, and market indexes. Most derivatives are characterized by high leverage.

Forex Market Structure

Every country has its own infrastructure for its currency, including how foreign market operations must be conducted. Each country enforces its own laws, banking regulations, accounting rules, and tax code, and operates its own payment systems for settling currency trades.

The foreign exchange market is the closest market to one operating in a truly global fashion, with currencies traded on essentially the same terms simultaneously in many financial centers. But you must be aware that there are different national financial systems and infrastructures to execute transactions.

In this book, we take you on a journey to learn more about forex and how to trade it successfully. In Chapter 4, you learn how currencies change value. You can find out more about individual countries and their currencies in Chapters 5 and 6. Then Chapters 7 and 8 introduce you to tools for analyzing trading opportunities. Chapter 11 discusses the risks you face as a currency trader. Then Chapters 13 through 16 discuss the tools for trading, including trading platforms, how to place orders, managing your trade, and evaluating your results. Finally, Chapters 17 to 20 look at the various alternatives you can use to trade on the Forex market. Chapter 21 talks about how to set up your trading business and Chapter 22 points you to resources you can use as you build your trading business.

The Least You Need to Know

- The foreign exchange currency market (forex) operates 24 hours a day for 5.5 days a week and is the largest and most liquid market in the world.
- Most foreign currency is traded by major dealer institutions (such as commercial banks or governments), with individual traders making up only 2 percent of the US$3.98 trillion global market.
- If you want to participate in the foreign exchange market, you will be considered a speculator.

How Forex Started

In This Chapter

- Back in Babylon
- Agreeing at Bretton Woods
- Smithsonian settlements
- Monetary system in Europe
- Forex today

The foreign exchange market as we know it today is relatively new. It was started just over 35 years ago, in 1973. But, of course, money has been around a lot longer than that. In this chapter, we review how money got started and how the current foreign exchange market developed.

Beginnings in Babylon

You must travel all the way back to the ancient kingdom of Hammurabi (third century B.C.E.) in Babylon to find the origins of banking. In those days, the royal palaces and temples served as secure places for the safe-keeping of grains and other commodities. People who deposited their commodities in the palaces and temples were given receipts that they could use to claim their commodities at a later date or give to others in payment for something else. These bills became the first known form of money.

Egypt also started a similar system of banking, providing state warehouses for the centralization of harvests. The written orders that depositors received were used to pay debts to others, including tax gatherers, priests, and traders.

Prior to these systems of deposits and receipts, the barter of goods was the primary way a person paid for goods and services. Egypt moved from these paper notes to introduce the first coins. The earliest countable metallic money was made of bronze or copper from China. Other objects used for coins were spades, hoes, and knives, also known as tool currencies. The ancient Greeks during the time of Julius Caesar used iron nails as coins.

When people engaged in foreign exchange, which was primarily in connection with military activities, the primary currencies used in trade were precious metals. Initially, precious metals were traded by weight, but a gradual transition was made from weight to quantity.

During the Middle Ages, the need arose for a currency other than coins or precious metals. Middle Eastern moneychangers were the first to use paper currency rather than coins for trade. These paper bills represented transferable, third-party payments of funds. They gradually became more accepted in foreign currency exchange trading, which made life much easier for merchants and traders. Regional currencies began to flourish.

From the Middle Ages to World War I, the foreign exchange markets were relatively stable. Not much speculative activity occurred. After WWI, however, the world of money changed. The foreign exchange markets became volatile, and speculative activity increased tenfold. Speculation in the foreign exchange market was not looked on as favorable by most institutions or the general public. The Great Depression of 1929 slowed the speculative fever considerably.

The dominant world currency before WWII was the British pound. In fact, the British pound got the nickname "cable" because the U.S. dollar was originally compared against it, and the U.S. dollar and the British pound were the first currencies traded by telegraphic cable. The British pound lost its seat at the top of the currency world during WWII because Germany launched a massive counterfeiting campaign to destroy the power of the pound. All confidence in the pound was lost during WWII.

The U.S. dollar, which was in disgrace since the market crash of 1929, emerged from WWII as the currency of choice, which it still is today. The U.S. dollar remains the favored currency for most foreign exchanges. The U.S. economy boomed after WWII, and the United States emerged as a world economic power. The other big advantage of the United States was that it was one of few countries that hadn't felt the ravages of war on its own shores, so its massive infrastructure was still intact.

The Bretton Woods Accord

After the war, the world's economy was in tatters. Something needed to be done to design a new global economic order and put all the pieces of the global economy back together. The United Nations Monetary Fund convened a global monetary and financial conference in Bretton Woods, New Hampshire, with representatives from the United States, Great Britain, and France, as well as 730 delegates from all 44 allied nations, to design a new global economic order.

The allies decided to hold the conference in the United States because it was the only suitable place that wasn't destroyed by the war. The conference ended with the Bretton Woods Accord, which established a system of international monetary management with rules for commercial and financial relations among the world's major industrial nations. The delegates hammered out the accord during the first three weeks of July 1944.

As part of the system of rules and procedures to regulate the international monetary system, the Bretton Woods Accord also established two key institutions: the *International Bank for Reconstruction and Development (IBRD)* and the *International Monetary Fund (IMF)*, which became operational in 1946 after a sufficient number of countries ratified the agreement.

The U.S. dollar emerged from Bretton Woods as the world's benchmark currency. It became the currency against which all other nations would measure their own currencies as they struggled to rebuild their economies.

DEFINITION

The **International Bank for Reconstruction and Development (IBRD)** initially served as a vehicle for the reconstruction of Europe and Japan after World War II. Today it fosters economic growth in developing countries in Africa, Asia, and Latin America, as well as the post-Socialist states of Eastern Europe and the former Soviet Union. The **International Monetary Fund (IMF)** oversees the global financial system. It monitors exchange rates and balance of payments for foreign exchange transactions, and provides technical and financial assistance when requested by individual member countries.

The Gold Standard

One of the chief features of the new Bretton Woods system of foreign exchange was an obligation for each country to adopt a monetary policy that pegged the value of their currency to the U.S. dollar. The price of the U.S. dollar was pegged to gold at $35 per ounce, which became known as the gold standard.

Each country had to maintain its currency within a fixed value—plus or minus 1 percent—in terms of its peg to the U.S. dollar. This is known as a *fixed exchange rate*. The IMF was given the ability to bridge temporary imbalances of payments. The central bank of each country was required to intervene in the foreign exchange market if its country's exchange rate fluctuated more than 1 percent in either direction. The agreement initially served to bring stability to other countries and the global foreign exchange market. It succeeded in reestablishing stability in Europe and Japan. Until the 1970s, the Bretton Woods system helped to control economic conflict and achieve the goals set by the leading countries involved, especially the United States.

DEFINITION

A **fixed exchange rate** is a type of exchange rate regime in which a currency's value is matched to the value of an individual country's currency or a basket of other countries' currencies.

Initially this system worked well and helped to fuel the world's economic growth, but the system eventually fell under its own weight. As more and more countries converted their dollars to gold, the U.S. gold reserves dwindled. Pressures started to build on the gold peg, and an attempt to ease the problem started in 1968 when a new system called special drawing rights (SDR) was established. Dollar exchange between banks was done using SDRs and was managed by the International Monetary Fund. Countries were encouraged to hold dollars rather than convert those dollars to gold.

By 1971, the United States had enough gold to cover only about 22 percent of its reserve obligations. There was no way the United States could cover the paper dollars at the exchange rate of $35 per ounce of gold as set by the Bretton Woods Accord.

On August 15, 1971, President Nixon single-handedly closed the gold window and made the dollar inconvertible to gold directly, except on the open market—removing the United States' need to balance the value of the dollar to the value of the gold held in its reserves. He made this decision without consulting with other members of the international monetary system and even without talking with the State Department.

CURRENCY COIN

Today the gold held by the United States is held at the U.S. Mint in Fort Knox, Kentucky. The gold depository opened in 1937, and the first gold was deposited there in January of that year. The highest gold holdings for the United States were in December 1941, when 649.6 million ounces were on deposit. Today, only 147.4 million troy ounces are left. Gold is held as an asset of the United States at a book value of $42.22 per ounce, or $6.2 billion total, but the market price of gold in December 2010 was $1,384.50 per ounce.

Nixon's shocking move killed the Bretton Woods Accord and threw the entire world's monetary system into shock. After the shock wore off, the United States led the efforts to develop a new system of international monetary management. During the next several months, the United States held a series of multilateral and bilateral negotiations with other countries known as the Group of Ten to try to develop the new system. Participating countries were Belgium, Canada, France, Germany, Italy, the Netherlands, Sweden, Switzerland, the United Kingdom, and the United States. Today the Group of Ten still exists, but Japan has joined its ranks, bringing the total to 11 countries, although it is still called the Group of Ten.

The Smithsonian Agreement

In December 1971, the Group of Ten met at the Smithsonian Institution in Washington, D.C., and created the Smithsonian Agreement, which devalued the dollar to $38 per ounce with trading allowed up to 2.25 percent above or below that value. Dollars could not be used to convert directly to gold. Instead, the Group of Ten officially adopted the SDR system, and the IMF held the responsibility of keeping the system in balance.

The United States continued its deficit spending, and the value of the U.S. dollar continued to fall. Gold's value began floating on the international markets, and its value gradually edged up to $44.20 per ounce in 1971 and $70.30 per ounce in 1972. Countries abandoned any peg to the U.S. dollar and let their currencies float. By 1976, all the developed countries' currencies were *floating*, and exchange rates were no longer the primary way governments administered monetary policy.

> **DEFINITION**
>
> A **floating** exchange rate is an exchange rate regime in which the value of a currency fluctuates according to the foreign exchange market, instead of being pegged to a specific commodity (such as gold) or a specific currency (such as under the Bretton Woods system where currencies were pegged to the U.S. dollar).

Today the currencies of developed countries float, but many of the emerging countries still peg the value of their currency to the U.S. dollar or to a basket of currencies from a number of countries. In Chapter 6, we discuss the key emerging countries, many of which use some type of fixed-rate regime.

The European Monetary System

At about the same time as the Smithsonian Agreement, European countries established a European Joint Float. The nations that joined this system included West Germany, France, Italy, the Netherlands, Belgium, and Luxembourg. The basic system was close to the exchange rate regime established at Bretton Woods.

The European Joint Float failed at about the same time as the Smithsonian Agreement, but the decision among the Europeans to work together economically remained in place. The European countries began working together officially in 1957, long before the European Joint Float, under a treaty that formed the European Economic Community.

When the European Joint Float failed, the European nations worked together to form the European Monetary System (EMS) in 1979, which included most of the nations of today's European Union. The goal of the EMS was to stabilize foreign exchange and counter inflation among the members of the EMS.

Periodic adjustments raised the values of the currencies whose economies were strong and lowered the values of the weaker ones. By 1986, a simpler system based on national interest rates was used to manage the currency values.

By the early 1990s, the EMS started to show strains, especially after Germany was reunited. Many European countries had very different economic policies, and faced varied economic conditions. Great Britain permanently withdrew from the EMS in 1991.

The EMS began efforts in the 1990s to establish a common currency in Europe. Its first step was to create the European Central Bank in 1994. By 1998, the bank was responsible for setting a single monetary policy and interest rate for the nations that chose to participate.

At the same time as the European countries moved to coordinate currency exchange, they also worked toward political and defense cooperation. The European Union (EU) was formed in 1992 with the Treaty of Maastricht.

By 1998, the first members of the European Central Bank were Austria, Belgium, Finland, France, Germany, Ireland, Luxembourg, the Netherlands, Portugal, and Spain. All cut their interest rates to a nearly uniform low level with the hope that this would promote growth and prepare for the unified currency. In 1999, the unified currency, the euro, was adopted by these countries.

Euro coins and notes did not begin to circulate until January 2002. Within two months, local currencies were no longer accepted as legal tender within the countries that had adopted the euro.

Great Britain is not the only European nation that has decided not to adopt the euro. Denmark and Sweden also decided to maintain their currencies. Citizens of all three countries oppose the adoption of the euro.

Of the countries that joined the EU since the fall of the Soviet Union, only Slovakia and Slovenia have adopted the euro, but several others are working to meet the economic requirements to do so. Countries must meet strict economic guidelines before becoming part of the EMS and adopting the euro. These requirements set limits on allowable government deficits and interest rates.

Today's Foreign Exchange Markets

Today's system of floating exchange rates was not carefully planned; it was one born by default as the Smithsonian Agreement and the European Joint Float failed to gain momentum. Yet the foreign exchange market is by far the largest and most liquid market in the world today.

The floating system allows the values of currencies to rise and fall based on the basic laws of supply and demand. When the supply of a particular currency is high, the price (the relative exchange rate) of the currency begins to drop because there is more supply than demand. The opposite is true when the supply of a currency is tight. When less money is available for trade, the relative exchange rate of the currency goes up, because people want more of the currency than is available for purchase. You learn more about the principles of supply and demand in Chapter 4.

Major currencies today move independently from other currencies. They can now be traded by anyone from individual retail investors to large central banks. Central banks do intervene occasionally to influence the exchange rate for their country's currency.

What are the key developments that made the foreign exchange market so vibrant and liquid? These developments include the following:

- The flexibility countries have today to choose either a floating exchange rate or a fixed exchange rate.

- Financial deregulation moves throughout the world that included elimination of government controls and restrictions on foreign exchange in nearly all countries. This permits greater freedom for national and international financial transactions, and greatly increases global competition among financial institutions.

- Internationalization of savings and investments provides fund managers and institutions around the globe with large sums available for investing and diversifying across country borders to maximize returns.

- Broader trends toward international trade liberalization within a framework of multilateral trade agreements encourage the globalization of business.

- Major technological advances have led to rapid and reliable execution of financial transactions, to reduced costs, and to instantaneous real-time transmission of vast amounts of market information worldwide.

The Least You Need to Know

- There are two types of currency exchange regimes: fixed rate and floating. The developed countries all use a floating exchange rate. Many emerging countries use a fixed exchange rate, most often pegged to the U.S. dollar or a basket of currencies.

- Although the Bretton Woods Accord and its fixed exchange rate regime helped to rebuild the world economy after WWII, it ultimately failed.

- The euro, the unified currency of Europe, was first adopted in 1999 and is rapidly becoming a key currency in the forex marketplace.

- Today the foreign exchange market is by far the largest and most liquid financial market in the world.

Understanding Money Jargon

In This Chapter

* Reading the spots
* Going forward
* Finding swaps
* Checking out options
* Looking for futures

Trading in the world of money means you must learn an entirely new language to understand what the traders are talking about. You'll hear traders talk about spot and forward transactions, swaps, options, and futures. This chapter introduces you to these terms and explains how you use them to trade foreign currency.

Spot Transactions

A spot transaction is the simplest type of transaction in the world of foreign exchange. It is simply the exchange of one currency for another. The spot rate is the current market price, also known as the benchmark price.

The actual transaction does not require immediate settlement or payment "on the spot." The settlement of a spot transaction happens within two business days after the trade is made, which is also known as the "trade day." The trade day is the day the two traders agree to the terms of the spot transaction.

This two-day period gives the traders time to confirm the agreement and arrange for the clearing of the funds through a financial institution, such as an international bank. Remember, many times these transactions are taking place between traders in two different countries and two different time zones, so it does take time for the clearing of funds.

The only spot transaction in the United States with a settlement period of one day is the U.S. dollar to Canadian dollar exchange.

Pricing Spot Transactions

Every currency being traded has two prices: a buying price and a selling price. The selling price is the price at which the sellers want to sell, and the buying price is the price at which the buyers want to buy. These are also known as the bid and offer prices, where the bid is the price at which a *market maker* will buy a specified currency pair, and the offer is the price at which the market maker will sell the pair. The market maker provides a quote with the bid and ask prices for customers. The difference between these two prices is called the spread.

DEFINITION

In the foreign exchange world, a **market maker** is a bank or forex dealer that provides tradable prices for specific currency pairs. Market makers add liquidity and provide a two-sided market. International banks serve as market makers for more than 70 percent of the foreign exchange market. Retail, or individual, customers typically go through licensed forex dealing firms that act as market makers because these firms can access the prices and liquidity of the international banks while providing individuals with market access.

Quoting Spot Exchange Rates

Spot exchange rates can be quoted in two ways: as a "direct" quotation or as an "indirect" quotation. A direct quote is one in which the amount of the domestic currency (i.e., dollars and cents if you are in the United States) is given per unit of the foreign currency. An indirect quotation is quoted in the amount of the foreign currency per unit of domestic currency. For example, in the United States, a direct quote for the euro would be 1.25 USD = 1 EUR. An indirect quote would be 0.80 EUR = 1 USD.

You may also hear the phrase "American terms." The phrase is used in the United States and refers to a direct quotation for U.S. dollars per one unit of the foreign currency. In Europe, you might hear the phrase "European terms," referring to a direct quotation for someone in Europe from their currency per one unit of

U.S. dollar. If you're in the United States and hear the phrase "European terms," that means you are being given the quote from the perspective of the foreign currency per one U.S. dollar.

In 1978, in an attempt to integrate the foreign exchange market into a single global market, the U.S. market changed its practices to conform to the European market. So today most quotes are given in European terms, as the foreign currency per one U.S. dollar.

Another set of terms you will likely hear when talking about foreign currency trading on the spot market is "base" and "terms" currency. The base currency is the underlying or fixed currency. For example, in European terms, the U.S. dollar is the base currency because it is the currency in the transaction that is fixed to one unit. The terms currency in the transaction is the foreign currency being quoted (priced) to one U.S. dollar. When you hear a quote, the base currency is stated first.

When a market maker quotes a currency for a trade in the spot market, he or she quotes it at the price at which he or she will buy or sell the currency per one unit of the base currency. For example, suppose you request a quote on a USD/CHF spot transaction. (USD is the ISO [standardized] code for the United States dollar, and CHF is the ISO code for the Swiss franc.) The spot transaction may also be called the "dollar-swissie." The market maker could respond with a quote of 0.9617/27, which means that the market maker is willing to buy CHF at a price of 0.9617 per one U.S. dollar and sell CHF at a price of 0.9627 per one U.S. dollar.

When you get a quote on a currency pair, it is most often presented to the fourth decimal place. This is called a "pip." A pip is the smallest amount that a currency pair can move in price. This is similar to a "tick" on the stock market.

If a dollar is not part of the transaction, the exchange is done at what is called "cross-rate trading." The base currency is always the currency listed first in the trade, and the pricing currency is listed second.

Forward Transactions

If you don't want to settle a transaction within two business days, you can also trade using an outright forward transaction. In this transaction, you trade one currency for another on a pre-agreed date at some time in the future, but it must be three or more days after the deal date. The forward transaction is a straightforward single purchase or sale of one currency for another.

The exchange rate for a forward transaction usually differs from the rate for a spot transaction because the buyer and seller making the deal know the rates will fluctuate in the future and try to make their best estimate of what the future rate will be. When the forward transaction is executed, the buy and sell price is fixed, but often no money changes hands. Sometimes foreign currency dealers ask customers to provide collateral in advance.

Who Uses Forward Transactions

Companies use outright forward transactions for many different purposes, including future expenditures, hedging, speculating, and investing. One of the most common uses is to plan for a future expenditure.

For example, a U.S. company that knows it will need to pay for parts from a factory in Japan will execute an outright forward transaction to be able to plan for the exact cost of the parts based on the forward transaction price. That way, even if the foreign exchange price changes dramatically, the company can still depend on the agreed price for the parts.

Outright forwards in major currencies are available from dealers for standard contract periods, also known as "straight dates." These periods can be 1, 2, 3, 6, or 12 months into the future. You can make arrangements for "odd-date" or "broken-date" for contract periods in between the standard dates, but these types of trades can be much more expensive.

Setting Rates for Forward Transactions

When setting the rate for a forward, two factors impact the price: the spot rate of the currency and the interest rate differential between the currencies. In setting the price, the market maker neutralizes the impact of the interest rate difference between the two currencies named in the forward transaction.

Although spot transactions are quoted in absolute terms, say x francs per dollar, forward transactions are quoted in differentials, which are premiums or discounts from the spot rate based on the interest rate differential. The differential is calculated in basis points to neutralize the difference in interest rates. For example, if interest rates are higher for the Swiss franc than the U.S. dollar, the number of basis points calculated is subtracted from the base spot price for the Swiss franc to offset the differential.

Foreign exchange traders know that for any currency pair, if the base currency earns a higher interest rate than the terms currency, the base currency will trade at a forward discount. If the base currency earns a lower interest rate, the base currency will trade at a forward premium, at or above the spot rate.

Swaps

If you don't want to buy another currency, but just want to borrow it for a certain period of time, you can use a foreign exchange swap (FX swap). An FX swap allows you to exchange one currency for another and then re-exchange back to the currency you first held.

Banks and others in the dealer market use FX swaps to shift temporarily into or out of one currency for a second currency without having to incur the risk of a change in the exchange rate, which could happen if they were to hold an open position.

The use of FX swaps is similar to borrowing and lending currencies on a collateral basis. FX swaps provide traders with a way to use the foreign exchange markets as a funding instrument. They are used by traders and other FX market participants in managing liquidity, shifting delivery dates, hedging speculation, and taking interest rate positions.

There are two legs to an FX swap that settle on two different value dates, but it is counted as one transaction. The two parties involved in the swap agree to exchange the two currencies at a particular rate on one date (the "near date") and to reverse the payments, usually at a different rate, on a specific date in the future (the "far date"). If both dates are less than one month from the deal date, it is called a "short-dated" swap. If one or both dates are one month or more from the deal date, it is known as a "forward swap."

Although an FX swap can be attached to any pair of value dates, in reality a limited number of standard maturities (length between the near date and far date) account for most swap transactions. The first leg (near date) of the FX swap usually occurs on the spot value date, and for about two thirds of all FX swaps the second leg (far date) occurs within a week. Longer FX swaps are available for one month, three months, or six months. Many foreign dealers arrange odd or broken dates for their traders, but the costs for those are higher than the standard maturities.

Buying or Selling?

FX swaps can be either a buy/sell swap, which means that you buy the base currency on the near date and sell it on the far date, or a sell/buy swap, which means you sell the base currency on the near date and buy it on the far date. For example, if you buy a fixed amount of pound sterling spot for U.S. dollars (exchange) and sell those pounds sterling six months forward for U.S. dollars (re-exchange), that is called a buy/sell sterling swap.

Pricing FX Swaps

The cost of the FX swap is set by the interest rate differential between the two currencies being swapped. The amount of interest that could be earned during the period of the swap is used by the dealer to calculate the price of the swap.

In calculating the cost for the swap, the dealer uses the spot rate and adjusts it for the interest rate differential between the base currency and the terms currency for the number of days of the swap. This calculates the borrowing and lending rates for the currencies involved. The rates are then used in a second calculation to determine the swap points that will be added or subtracted to determine the price.

Currency and Interest Rate Swaps

In addition to FX swaps, there are also interest rate swaps, which involve an exchange of a stream of interest payments without an exchange of principal; and currency swaps, which include an exchange and re-exchange of currency plus a stream of fixed or floating interest payments.

The currency swap gives companies a way to shift a loan from one currency to another or shift the underlying currency for an asset. A company can borrow funds in a currency different from the currency needed for its operations. The currency swap provides protection from exchange rate changes related to the loan.

Companies sometimes use currency swaps to gain access to a particular capital market otherwise unavailable to them because of currency restrictions in that particular market. They can also be used to avoid foreign exchange controls or taxes.

Currency swaps are not as popular as interest rate swaps because interest rate swaps do not involve the exchange of principal, so the cash requirements and the amount of risk are lower. The two parties involved in an interest rate swap agree to make periodic payments to each other for a set period of time. The principal amount on which the interest is based is called the "notional amount of principal," but the amount of principal does not change hands.

The most common form of interest rate swap is one in which the payments are calculated by setting a fixed rate of interest to the notional principal amount, which is then exchanged for a stream of payments calculated by using a floating rate of interest. This is called a fixed-for-floating interest rate swap. If both sides of the cash flows are to be exchanged using a calculation based on floating interest rates, it's called a money market swap.

Interest rate swaps are used by commercial banks, investment banks, insurance companies, mortgage companies, investors, trust companies, and government agencies for many different reasons; these are the most popular:

- To obtain lower-cost funding
- To hedge interest rate exposure
- To buy higher-yielding investment assets
- To obtain types of investment assets that might not otherwise be available
- To implement asset or liability management strategies
- To speculate on the future movement of interest rates

Foreign Currency Options

You don't have to actually buy any currency to speculate in the foreign currency market. You can buy a foreign exchange or currency option contract. This contract gives you the right but not the obligation to buy or sell a specified amount of one currency for another at a specified price on (or in some cases, depending on the contract, before) a specified date.

Options don't have to be exercised (meaning to actually buy or sell the currency). The holder can decide not to exercise his or her option. If the holder decides not to exercise the option on the specified date, the option expires. The holder doesn't have to come up with any funds on the specified date, but does lose any money spent to buy the option.

There are two types of options. A call option is the right, but not the obligation, to buy the underlying currency on a specified date. A put option is the right, but not the obligation, to sell the underlying currency on a specified date.

The person who purchases the option is the holder or buyer. The person who creates the option is the seller or writer. The price of the option is set by the seller and includes a premium that the buyer pays the seller in exchange for the right to buy or sell the underlying currency at some future date. The price at which the option is bought is called the strike price or exercise price.

The buyer of the option only risks losing the amount of money he or she paid in premium to buy the option. The writer of the option's risk is unbounded because he or she must come up with the underlying currency if the option's buyer decides to exercise his or her right on the specified date in the contract—even if the cost of buying or selling that underlying currency is considerably higher than when the option was originally written.

Options have been around for a long time, but only started to flourish in the foreign exchange market in the 1980s. Their popularity was aided by an international environment of floating exchange rates, deregulation, and financial innovation. Currency options started on the U.S. commodity exchanges, but are available in the over-the-counter market, too. Options are very popular, yet they make up a very small share of foreign exchange trading.

WEALTH BUILDERS

If you want to trade in options, your best place to start is through one of the U.S. exchanges. In the United States, options on foreign currencies are traded on the NASDAQ OMX PHLX (www.nasdaqtrader.com/Micro.aspx?id=phlx) and the Chicago Mercantile Exchange (www.cme.com). You can also trade options on the U.S. dollar index and on the euro index at Intercontinental Exchange, known as ICE (www.theice.com). Forex dealers also offer forex options.

Exchange-Traded Currency Futures

Another way you can get involved in the foreign currency exchange market without actually exchanging foreign currency is through exchange-traded currency futures. These are contracts between two parties to buy or sell a particular non–U.S. dollar currency at a particular price on a particular future date.

When you actually enter into the contract, no one is buying or selling any currency; it's just a contract with a promise to purchase a foreign currency at some future date. In reality, most futures contracts are canceled before maturity, and only about 2 percent result in delivery. Futures contracts are primarily used as a tool to hedge other financial positions or to speculate in the foreign exchange market.

You may think that futures seem to be the same as outright forwards, but they are not. Futures are traded on organized, centralized exchanges that are regulated in the United States by the *Commodity Futures Trading Commission*. Forward contracts are traded over the counter and are largely self-regulated, so they can be a much more risky transaction.

DEFINITION

The **Commodity Futures Trading Commission** (www.cftc.gov) is a U.S. government entity that protects market users and the public from fraud, manipulation, and abusive practices related to the sale of commodity and financial futures and options. The commission's mission also includes fostering open, competitive, and financially sound futures and options markets.

The fact that futures contracts are channeled through a clearinghouse with the guarantee of performance on both sides of the contract makes them a much safer bet than forward contracts. It's much easier to liquidate a futures contract, too, because there is an established futures market. Also, the high degree of standardization for the futures contracts means that traders only need to discuss contracts one wants to buy and the price for the contract. Transactions can be arranged quickly and efficiently.

Forward contracts do provide more flexibility in setting delivery dates. They tend to be for higher amounts, sometimes for millions of dollars. Futures contracts are much smaller and are usually set at about $100,000 or less. A trader who wants to buy more than that buys the number of contracts needed to hedge or speculate in the dollar amount desired. You can trade futures on the same exchanges mentioned in the "Foreign Currency Options" section of this chapter.

Comparing Forex

You are probably asking, "Is trading forex worth the risk?" and "How does it compare to other trading opportunities, such as futures and stocks?" or "Should I stick to a less-risky investment alternative?" The sections that follow discuss all these thoughts.

Forex vs. Futures

Forex gives the trader many advantages over trading futures. The biggest advantage forex has is that you can trade the market 24 hours a day, and trading only briefly closes on the weekends. It is rare for you to face a period of illiquidity (not being able to trade) in the forex market, whereas you are limited to the times the exchanges are open in the futures market.

If you hear news that could affect your positions at almost any time of day or night, you can trade on the forex market, but you'll have to wait until the exchanges open on the futures market. This gives the forex trader more flexibility and continuous market access, which just isn't available to the futures trader.

Forex traders have the advantage of three main economic zones that are linked throughout the world to give them trading opportunities throughout the day and night. For example, when the Pacific Rim markets, which include Japan and Singapore, begin to slow, the European markets of England, Switzerland, and Germany are just getting started. When the European markets are in full swing, the North American markets open, which includes the United States, Canada, and Mexico. When the United States markets begin to slow down in the evening, the Pacific Rim markets are just reopening.

Foreign exchange is the principal market of the world. The monetary volume (US$3.98 trillion a day) and participation in the forex market far exceeds any other financial market, including futures or stocks. Because the market is so large and available 24 hours a day, it is not affected by trading programs that can easily manipulate the stock or futures market.

The forex market offers a 24-hour daily trading opportunity, making it a haven for traders who don't want to worry about gaps (differences between when the futures market closes and reopens) or price movements, erratic spikes, and other choppy market conditions that can be seen in the futures market. However, slippage can occur when a dealer's office is closed, during times of extreme market volatility, or during major fundamental announcements. Slippage is when orders are filled at a price worse than the stop price requested by the trader.

If you study any market trading throughout the civilized world, you can quickly see that money is the root of all pricing. Global finance is distributed and redistributed using money through many different channels and different financial *derivatives*.

DEFINITION

Derivatives are a type of financial instrument whose value is dependent upon another instrument, such as a commodity, bond, stock, or currency. Futures and options are two types of financial derivatives.

Trading spot currencies can be done with many different methods, and you will find many different types of traders. You will find fundamental traders who speculate using mid- to long-term positions based on worldwide cash-flow analysis and fixed-income formulas, as well as economic indicators. We talk more about fundamental analysis in Chapter 8. You will also find technical traders who watch for patterns and indicators in consolidating markets. We talk more about technical analysis in Chapter 7.

Forex is where the "big boys" trade—that's all the major banking institutions in the world—but forex can also provide the small speculator with the opportunity for large profit potential, although the trader also has to be prepared for the corresponding large risk of trading foreign currency.

Another big advantage for forex traders is that the fees are typically less than those found in the futures market. All traders, whether in futures or forex, will find that financial instruments have a spread, which is the difference between the bid (the price at which a buyer will buy) and ask (the price at which a seller will sell) price. In the forex market, you only have to worry about the spread; in the futures market, however, you often have to pay commission charges, as well as clearing and exchange fees, on top of the spread.

Many currency dealers don't charge any additional fees to their customers for trading forex. Instead, they make their money through revenues as a currency dealer, including proceeds from buying, converting, and holding currencies. They also earn interest on deposited funds and rollover fees. So as a currency trader, you will be able to find commission-free trading at the best trading prices.

A good currency dealer should be able to offer you a way to make quick decisions on your forex trades without having to worry about how fees will impact your profit or loss. You also should not have to worry about any slippage between the price you see on your screen and the price at which your order will be filled. However, forex dealers cannot guarantee that slippage won't occur when a dealer's office is closed, during times of extreme market volatility, or during major fundamental announcements.

Better leverage is another advantage you can find when trading foreign currencies rather than futures. Trading using leverage is also called trading on *margin*. Spot currency traders have one low-margin requirement for trades conducted 24 hours a day. Futures traders can have one margin requirement for "day" trades and a different margin requirement for "overnight" positions. This can decrease the overall tradability of the currency futures markets.

Margin rates in spot currency trading vary from .25 to 5 percent, depending on the size of the transaction. You can find currency dealers who give their customers one rate all the time, with no hassles and no *margin calls*.

DEFINITION

Margin is the amount of money deposited by a customer that is required to be deposited to the broker or dealer. Margin is a percentage of the forex or futures position value. A **margin call** is a broker's or dealer's demand on a customer to deposit additional funds into his or her account. Margin calls are made to bring a customer's account up to a minimum level.

Forex vs. Stocks

When trading forex, you can primarily focus your attention on four major currency pairs (euro/U.S. dollar, U.S. dollar/yen, British pound/U.S. dollar, and U.S. dollar/ Swiss franc), with the potential to make a decent profit. These currency pairs are the most commonly traded, and the most liquid. You can add about 34 second-tier currencies for variation, but only if you commit yourself to the extra research time. With the majors, you can spend a lot less time on your computer researching potential trades and more time on other things you enjoy doing.

When you consider stocks, you have to choose among 8,000 stocks: 4,500 on the New York Stock Exchange and 3,500 on the NASDAQ. How do you pick the stocks you want to trade, and how do you make the time to continually research the companies you do pick?

Stocks are favored by many as an investment vehicle, but in the past 10 years stocks have taken on a much more speculative role. Securities face more and more volatility every day, especially with the forces of day trading and other factors you can't predict.

How many times have you heard that a large mutual fund was buying a particular stock or basket of stocks and those trades created unexpected movement in a stock you held? Mutual funds can also influence the market at the end of the fiscal year, just to make the numbers look better on a financial report.

No matter what some firms may claim, the stock market can be moved by large fund buying and selling, and the movement can take place before you have time to react. It is not uncommon for a mutual fund to sell or buy a particular stock for a few days in a row.

You won't find these types of problems in spot currency trading. The liquidity of the market makes the likelihood of any one fund or bank controlling a particular currency very slim. Banks, hedge funds, governmental agencies, retail currency conversion houses, and individuals are just some of the participants in the spot currency markets, which are the most liquid markets in the world.

Another big advantage spot currency trading offers to traders is that there is no middleman, so it costs less to trade. If you work directly with a dealer, who is a primary market maker, you do not deal through a middleman. However, brokers operate through a bank or an FCM, so they may charge additional fees to cover the added costs.

In the stock market, you have centralized exchanges, which means you have middlemen who run those exchanges, and they need to be paid, too. The cost of these middlemen can be in both time to do the trade and money. Spot currency trading doesn't have any middlemen. Traders can interact directly with the market maker for a particular currency who is responsible for pricing the currency pair. Forex traders get quicker access and cheaper costs than stock trading.

Analysts and brokerage firms are less likely to influence the forex market than the stock market. Too many scandals have been exposed since 2000 that show how analysts told clients to buy a stock while calling it garbage (and worse) in e-mails behind the scenes. These analyst cheerleaders kept the Internet and technology moving upward, whereas stock investors unknowingly bought into companies that ultimately proved to be worthless.

 CURRENCY COIN

Wall Street's big brokerage houses paid $1.4 billion in fines to settle charges from regulators that they tricked investors into buying stocks during the boom years of the 1990s. The brokerage houses did not admit guilt, but they did agree to cut ties between their analysts and investment banking activities, which shared research. Two star analysts, Jack Grubman (telecom stocks) and Henry Blodget (Internet stocks) were banned from the securities business for life. Civil cases related to these charges are still winding their way through the courts.

The difference in trading foreign currency is that the primary market for the currency is driven by the world's largest banks and foreign governments. Analysts don't drive the flow of deals in the foreign currency market. All they can do is analyze the flow that is occurring.

If you trade in the stock market, you've probably found that there are different costs depending upon how you trade. You pay more fees if you call in your order or ask for specific types of orders, such as a stop or limit order to minimize your risk. You should not find additional costs when placing an order for trading in foreign currency. We explain how brokers make money on forex sales in Chapter 15.

Margins and leverage opportunities are much better in the forex market, too. In spot trading, you can use your profits on open positions to add to those positions. That's something you might wish you could do when you own a hot stock and want to capitalize on the profits you've made by buying more of that stock. Although it's not possible in stock trading, you can do it when trading spot currency.

Forex vs. Other Less-Risky Investments

If you are concerned about the risks of forex trading and prefer less-risky investments, such as bonds and mutual funds, forex trading is probably not for you. If avoidance of risk is your primary investment concern, you probably won't be comfortable trading in the spot currency market.

Whether you are trading forex, stock, or futures, you must be willing to take on risk and must understand that the money you use for trading could be lost. There is no insurance to protect your money (except occasionally offered on stock accounts), and you should only trade with money that you can afford to lose.

We'll take a look at why currencies change value in Chapter 4.

The Least You Need to Know

- Most developed-country currencies are sold at floating exchange rates on the spot market.
- You can arrange to buy foreign currencies at some future date using a forward transaction.

- You can swap foreign currency or an interest stream from foreign currency using one of three types of swaps: forex swaps, currency swaps, or interest rate swaps.

- You can get involved in the foreign exchange market without actually buying and selling foreign currency by using options and futures contracts.

- Foreign exchange trading is not for you if you want to avoid risk entirely, but it can be a better trading opportunity if you want to assume risk in order to improve your profit potential. Foreign currency trading offers you 24-hour-a-day access to the most liquid market in the world.

Deciphering Money Differences

Part

2

Many things impact the value of currency. Economics, political developments, changing interest rates, stock news, inflation expectations, investment patterns, and government policies can all impact the value of money. We talk about *how* currency's value is impacted in this part.

Then we introduce you to the currencies of the developed countries. We review their fundamentals and then give you details on the key times to trade, the most liquid currency pairs, and the key economic releases that move these markets.

If you want to explore even riskier forex options, we introduce you to the currencies of emerging market countries. Don't even think about trading emerging-country currencies until you have considerable experience trading the more liquid currencies of developed countries.

Why Currency Changes Value

Chapter 4

In This Chapter

- Money and basic economics
- How politics impact currency
- Currency and interest rates
- Inflation and its money pressures
- International investors can move money values

Money makes the world go 'round, and lots of things can impact the value of that money. You can't control any of these factors, but you definitely need to understand what they are so you can make tactical decisions about when to buy or sell a particular currency.

This chapter reviews the key factors that can impact the value of currencies, including basic economics, political change, interest rate changes, international investment patterns, inflation predictions, and money or tax policies adopted by governments and central banks.

Economics and Business Cycles

Currency, just like any other item that is bought or sold, can be impacted by the basics of economics and the business cycle. The *laws of supply and demand* are just as valid when talking about the value of currency as they are when talking about the value of any commodity.

When the supply of a particular currency is high, the price for that currency goes down, as holders of the currency try to find ways to get rid of it. For example, if everyone decides that they don't want to hold U.S. dollars anymore and tries to sell them, they would likely have to lower their price to find a buyer. In this case, there is more supply than demand.

DEFINITION

The **law of supply** states that as price rises, the quantity supplied rises; as price falls, the quantity supplied falls. The **law of demand** states that as price falls, the quantity demanded rises; as price rises, the quantity of demand falls. When supply and demand are in balance, that means at a certain price and quantity, the amount the buyer wants to buy is equal to what the seller wants to sell.

You can compare this to the sale of real estate in your neighborhood. When there are a lot of houses on the market, they may sit unsold for many months or even years, as we've seen since the housing bubble burst in 2008. If someone has to move because of a job change or some other reason, that person will likely price his or her home to sell (price it below what all other homes are listed for) to get it sold more quickly.

Conversely, when the supply of the currency is low and there are more people who want to buy it than there is currency available, the price of the currency goes up as buyers compete for the currency. In this case, there is more demand than there is supply. Using the same comparison, when there are few homes available, buyers will offer the full asking price and sometimes bid even higher to be sure to get the home.

You may be wondering how a market could suddenly be flooded with a currency to increase supply and ultimately drive the price of the currency down. Well, that's one role governments and central banks, such as the Federal Reserve, take when they want to impact the value of a currency. We talk more about how the policies of governments and central banks impact the value of currency later in this chapter.

Governments can also decide they want the value of their currency to increase, and they have the buying power to buy their currency and make it scarce, making the price of the currency rise.

WEALTH BUILDERS

As a currency trader, if you do see a rapid increase or decrease in the price of a currency you trade, be sure you understand why that movement is happening before jumping in yourself. One website that does an excellent job of covering the forces that impact currency values is FXstreet (www.fxstreet.com). London's *Financial Times* (www.news.ft.com/markets/currencies) also provides excellent coverage in its "Currencies" section.

Government manipulation is not the only thing that can impact the value of a currency. The action of businesses and consumers as a whole can drive currency values up and down. However, because the forex market has so much volume—more than US$3.98 trillion traded daily—it is highly unlikely that one single entity could impact the value of a currency for a significant period of time.

The good news for currency traders is that they have the potential to make money no matter what direction the market moves. Whether the business world is prospering and we're in the middle of a bull market (in which prices are rising and business is expanding), or we are experiencing a slowdown in the middle of a bear market (in which prices are dropping and business is contracting), it is still possible to make money by trading currencies.

The key is to know which kind of market each country is facing and how that market is impacting the value of the currency. Remember that each currency trade involves at least two countries: the country of the currency you are selling and the country of the currency you are buying.

Political Developments

Political changes can have the most dramatic effects on the value of a currency. They also can happen very quickly (such as a coup by the military). So when you choose the currencies you want to trade, be sure you understand the politics of the country for each currency you follow.

You may hear about some incredible opportunity for trading the currency of a developing country, but be very cautious with such rumors. The more unstable the country's politics, the greater the chance you will be burned in currency trading. Be very careful about trading on rumors, especially in developing markets.

 CAPITAL CAUTIONS

As a beginning currency trader, stick to the major currencies, at least at first. Political changes can happen much more quickly and dramatically in the developing countries, which can significantly impact the value of that country's currency. Chapter 5 reviews the basics of trading in key currencies from developed countries and Chapter 6 reviews the risks of emerging countries.

Even in the most stable countries, after an election in which the party in power changes, the impact on the currency can be significant. For example, in the United

States, if the current president and his or her party in power believe a strong dollar is good for the economy, the U.S. government can reduce the supply of its currency by buying up dollars and thus force the price to rise.

Conversely, if the party in power changes with the next election and the new president believes a weaker dollar will increase U.S. exports and decrease imports, the government could take moves to weaken the dollar (lower its price) by increasing its supply on the open market. So even in a very stable country, you may find that political change can impact the future value of a currency.

How the party in power manages the country's domestic economy can also be critical. When the economy is in a period of growth with relative price stability, the currency of that country will be in demand. If a country is facing political turmoil, high inflation, or has few marketable exports, its currency will be less attractive.

For example, policies of the Obama, Bush, and Clinton administrations that created larger and larger imbalances, both in trade deficit and budget deficit, fueled the U.S. currency declines over the past few years against stronger currencies, such as the yen. As the U.S. government builds up trillions of dollars in new federal debt, financial markets will drive down the value of government bonds as these bonds create a future glut. Ultimately, the value of the dollar could suffer even more as investors move away from the dollar and U.S. government bonds to currencies and bonds they view as stronger or better investments.

Changes in Interest Rates

When interest rates go up or down, the value of a currency can fluctuate. When interest rates go up, the currency is more attractive to currency investors because they'll make more money holding it. So when interest rates rise, more traders and investors buy that currency, the supply of the currency becomes scarce, and the price of the currency rises.

The opposite happens when interest rates go down. Fewer investors want to hold on to the currency, especially if they can find a better deal someplace else. Many traders and investors start to sell the currency, and its supply goes up. As supply increases and demand decreases, the value of the currency goes down.

Be sure to watch the interest rate fluctuations in each of the countries whose currency you trade. Follow the pronouncements of the central banks and governments about their plans to raise or lower interest rates. Markets move rapidly on this type of news, and you can quickly get caught on the losing side if you hold a currency whose price is dropping because interest rates have just been lowered.

International Stock News

News about the stock market can also drive currency values up or down. Although the major stock markets (such as NASDAQ, New York Stock Exchange, American Stock Exchange, London Stock Exchange, and Tokyo Stock Exchange) get the most coverage, you'll find stock exchanges and stock news in most developed countries and many developing countries.

When trading foreign currency, keep your eye on the international stock market news, not only news from the U.S. exchanges. Keep an eye on stock index movements in any of the countries whose currency you trade. Stock market moves can impact the value of a currency.

Inflationary Expectations

Inflation and its impact on the economy can significantly impact the value of the currency, too, so keep your eyes and ears open for news about any inflationary expectations within the countries you monitor.

Of course, one of the first things to be changed if the central bank or government believes inflation may be on the rise is the interest rates. Remember that interest rate fluctuations can have a major impact on the supply and demand for the currency and ultimately the price at which the currency will sell.

Currencies of countries that are not raising their interest rates during an inflationary period will likely decrease in price, whereas the price of currencies in countries that are increasing the interest rates will likely increase.

Inflation can also impact where imports and exports are bought and sold as prices rise or fall. This will change a country's *balance of payments* and ultimately impact the value of the country's currency.

DEFINITION

The **balance of payments** measures the flow of money into and out of a particular country to other countries. Pieces of this calculation include a country's exports and imports of goods and services, as well as the transfer of financial capital. Basically, the balance of payments is the summary of all economic transactions between a country and all other countries during a particular period, usually a quarter (three months) or a year.

The payments and liabilities (debt) owed to foreign countries are listed as debits. The payments and obligations due from other countries are listed as credits. When that balance of payments is out of whack, especially if the country owes more than it receives, the value of the currency can drop.

Trade imbalance can lead to the loss of jobs, as we have seen in the United States, where millions of U.S. jobs moved to China or other developing nations between 1989 and 2010. Servicing of debt can also increase as the country that owes more to other countries must make its debt issues (bonds) more attractive to buyers by raising interest rates.

The United States does have one huge advantage that enables it to run large trade deficits: the U.S. dollar is the primary currency for all oil trades with OPEC. Every country that wants to buy oil from an OPEC country must use U.S. dollars. Some call these dollars petrodollars. That helps to prop up the value of the U.S. dollar.

Inflation occurs when too much money is available. The value of the money will decline and prices in the country will rise as exports become more expensive. When too little money is available, the economy will become sluggish and unemployment will rise.

International Investment Patterns

Money (and currency buyers) flows to the currency where traders or investors can get the highest return with the least amount of risk. Investors flock to a country when stocks and bonds command a high rate of return with relatively low risk.

For buyers to buy those stocks and bonds, they first must buy the currency. That increases the demand for the currency, and the currency's price increases.

WEALTH BUILDERS

When you see investments in a country rise and the economy booming, you'll likely also see the value of that currency rise. If investors are taking flight and getting out of a country, selling off their holdings, the value of the currency will likely fall. Traders should watch investment patterns to find currency trading opportunities.

When you're trading foreign currency, don't look at just the charts of the currency moving up and down. You should also follow news of what investors in other types of financial markets are doing.

You can get many clues by watching the flow of international investments. Read the key financial news sites, such as *The Wall Street Journal* (www.wsj.com), Bloomberg (www.bloomberg.com), *Business Week* (www.businessweek.com), and *CNN Money* (www.money.cnn.com) to find information about investment waves to locate your next trading opportunity.

Policies Adopted by Governments and Central Banks

Governments and central banks can impact a currency's value using two key tools: foreign exchange rates and tax policy. Government officials closely monitor economic activity to keep the money supply at a level appropriate to achieve their economic goals. Money supply can be increased or decreased, which is usually done by changing the interest rate or manipulating the supply of money on the market.

In the United States, the government agency responsible for setting foreign exchange rates is the U.S. Treasury Department. The entity responsible for carrying out those decisions is the Federal Reserve Bank of New York under the direction of the *Federal Open Market Committee (FOMC)* of the Federal Reserve.

DEFINITION

The **Federal Open Market Committee (FOMC)** is a group of 19 people plus about 40 staffers. The 7 members of the Federal Reserve Board and 12 presidents of the Federal Reserve Banks make up the committee. When the committee takes a vote, only 12 people can vote: the 7 Federal Reserve Board members, the president of the New York Fed, and 4 of the other 11 Federal Reserve Bank presidents. Voting rights rotate among the bank presidents.

The U.S. Treasury can impact exchange rates. If the U.S. government believes the exchange rate does not reflect fundamental economic conditions, it can instruct the New York Fed to buy or sell currency in the foreign exchange market to impact the value of the U.S. dollar. Sometimes the United States works diplomatically with other countries to get them to intervene, too, by buying or selling U.S. dollars.

The Federal Reserve Bank of New York also acts as an agent on behalf of other countries' central banks and international organizations. When the New York Fed acts as an agent for another country or organization, these transactions do not necessarily reflect the policy of the U.S. government. These actions can be done openly through the forex market, or they can be done discreetly through a confidential dealer in the brokers' market. We talk more about who the brokers are in Chapter 1.

Tax policy can also significantly affect the value of a country's currency. Tax policies can encourage or discourage investment by domestic businesses as well as by foreign investors.

How Traders Can Take Advantage of These Changes

Savvy traders learn to keep their eyes on all these factors as they look for opportunities to make money by trading currency. Key events to watch for include the following:

- News of political instability around the world drives up the value of currency from stable countries, such as the U.S. dollar, Japanese yen, Swiss franc, British pound, or the euro, as people seek safe havens in stable countries.

- A country's currency value can increase as foreign investors seek better interest rates in countries with more attractive interest rates than they can find in their own country. Watch interest rates move as you look for trading opportunities.

- The currency of a developing country that is making successful economic moves usually experiences an increase in value as foreign investors seek new investment opportunities. As you become a more experienced forex trader, watch for an increase of investment dollars into a developing country; the currency may also increase in value.

Currency traders try to predict the behavior of other market participants. If they correctly anticipate the strategies of others, they can act first and beat the crowd. You basically have two possible currency strategies: buy currency at a low price hoping to sell it later at a higher price, or sell currency at a high price hoping to buy it back later at a lower price.

In trying to predict their best moves, currency traders who use fundamentals try to determine whether the current price of a currency reflects the true economic conditions in the country. They look at inflation, interest rates, and the relative strength of the economy to make a determination about the future value of the country's currency. If they believe the currency is undervalued, they buy it with the expectations that the currency's value will increase. If they believe the currency is overvalued and they own some of it, they dump it.

The Least You Need to Know

- Keep your eyes on the economic conditions in each country whose currency you trade.
- When interest rates rise, purchases of that currency will likely increase, supply will become scarce, and the price of the currency will rise. The opposite happens when interest rates fall.
- Political change can greatly impact the value of a country's currency.
- Governments can impact the value of their currency through monetary and tax policy. They can intervene in the currency's value by changing the supply of the money on the market.

Looking for Safety—
Developed Country
Currencies

In This Chapter

- Exploring developed countries
- Determining key economic factors
- Reviewing political factors
- Eyeing characteristics and trends

When you trade foreign currency, you should know the key economic and political forces that drive that currency's value. You also need to explore the characteristics and trends that will likely impact the future value of that currency.

This chapter reviews the key information you need to know about the generally less volatile currencies from the developed countries: Australia, Canada, the European Union, Great Britain, Japan, New Zealand, Switzerland, and the United States. We listed these countries alphabetically, not by popularity or by their potential for foreign currency trades.

Australia (Australian Dollar—AUD)

Although Australia is small compared to the other developed countries discussed in this chapter, its per capita *GDP* of US$47,400 compares in size to major Western European economies. The AUD/USD is the fourth most actively traded currency pair by turnover, according to the Bank of International Settlement's 2010 FX Report.

DEFINITION

GDP or **gross domestic product** is the market value of all final goods and services produced within a country during a specified period of time. GDP is calculated as follows: GDP = consumption + investment + government spending + (exports – imports).

Services make up the lion's share of Australia's economy—70 percent. These components include finance, property, and business services. Major exports include coal, gold, aluminum, iron ore, and wheat; but Australia imports more than it exports. Its imports include machinery and transport equipment, computers and office machines, and telecommunication equipment and parts.

Australia's economic policy maker is the Reserve Bank of Australia (RBA), which emphasizes economic reforms and low inflation (1 to 3 percent target) in its management of monetary policy. The RBA meets 11 times per year on the first Tuesday of every month except January. The bank's board members discuss economic developments in the country and determine whether there will be any change in the interest rate, as well as other key economic decisions. Any changes in monetary policy are announced the next day.

WEALTH BUILDERS

You can quickly get information about RBA's decisions regarding Australia's monetary policy on its website at www.rba.gov.au. You can also find news briefs about Australia's economy on the website.

Key characteristics and trends to watch if you are considering trading the Australian dollar (AUD) include the following:

- Australia is the third-largest producer of gold in the world. The AUD appreciates when gold prices increase and depreciates when gold prices decrease.

- Australia's export economy is primarily based on commodities, which can be sensitive to severe weather conditions that can affect its agriculture and related industries and negatively impact its GDP.

- Australia's high interest rate makes it a very popular currency to buy for carry trades. An example of a currency *carry trade* is to borrow $1,000 AUD from an Australian bank, exchange the funds into U.S. dollars, and buy a bond for an equivalent amount. As long as the bond pays more than the amount owed to the bank for borrowing the funds, and the exchange rate does not move adversely, you can make a profit on this trade.

DEFINITION

A **carry trade** is a foreign exchange strategy where a trader sells a certain currency with a relatively low interest rate and uses the funds to purchase a different currency yielding a higher interest rate. The trader attempts to benefit from the difference in the two rates.

You can find a good summary about the political conditions and economy of countries by reading the Background Notes prepared by the U.S. State Department on its website at www.state.gov/r/pa/ei/bgn.

The three key currency cross pairs that don't involve the U.S. dollar include:

- AUD/JPY—Australian dollar/Japanese yen
- AUD/NZD—Australian dollar/New Zealand dollar
- AUD/CAD—Australian dollar/Canadian dollar

The most active trading hours for the Australian dollar include:

- 7:00 p.m. ET/23:00 GMT, Tokyo open
- 7:30 p.m. ET/23:30 GMT, Australian economic releases
- 8:30 a.m. ET/12:30 GMT, U.S. economic releases

Market-moving economic releases:

- Consumer and producer prices
- Employment change
- GDP (gross domestic product)
- RBA rate decision
- Retail sales
- Trade balance

Canada (Canadian Dollar—CAD)

Canada boasts the tenth-largest economy in the world. It's also a major trading partner with the United States. In fact, more than 85 percent of its exports go to the United States, so the fate of its economy and dollar are very sensitive to the state of the U.S. economy. The USD/CAD is the sixth most actively traded currency pair by turnover, according to the Bank of International Settlement's 2010 FX Report.

Prior to the mid-twentieth century, Canada was primarily a rural economy, but since then it has grown into an industrial-based economy with the growth of manufacturing, mining, and service industries. Nearly 75 percent of its workforce is employed in a service-oriented occupation.

Canada manages its fiscal policy well and has a long-term budget surplus, which reduces its approximately US$805 billion national debt annually; but rising medical costs and their impact on the publicly funded health-care system does raise political and economic debates among its politicians.

As of October 2010, Canada maintains a substantial trade surplus of US$22 billion with its main trading partner, the United States. Its major exports include motor vehicles and parts, industrial machinery, chemicals, plastics, wood pulp, timber, petroleum, and natural gas. With 178.9 billion barrels of proven oil reserves (the amount of recoverable petroleum from known reserves), Canada is second in the world behind Saudi Arabia.

The Bank of Canada sets Canadian monetary policy. It influences the economy primarily by ensuring price stability by adhering to an inflation target set by the Department of Finance. It achieves its inflationary targets by influencing short-term interest rates through its overnight lending rate to banks. Any changes in the interest rate are announced on eight scheduled dates during the year. You can find the schedule on its website at www.bankofcanada.ca/en/monetary/target.html.

The Bank of Canada periodically conducts foreign exchange market intervention by using the government's supply of foreign currencies in its exchange fund account. For example, if the Bank of Canada wants to offset a decline in the Canadian dollar (CAD), it buys CADs in foreign exchange markets with other countries' currencies, most often the U.S. dollar (USD). This creates a demand for CADs and helps support their strength or value. To be sure that this foreign exchange activity does not impact the local economy, the bank deposits the amount of dollars purchased into Canada's financial system. The bank does the exact opposite if it wants to weaken or lower the CAD on the foreign exchange market.

WEALTH BUILDERS

You can follow the Bank of Canada's interest rate and other economic policy decisions through updates on its website at www.bankofcanada.ca/en/index.html.

You can read about the bank's policies and strategies in a quarterly Monetary Policy Report and Update on its website on the same page as its interest rate schedule mentioned previously. Simply select "Monetary Policy" and look for the report on the scrolldown menu. Also published on that page weekly on Friday afternoons are key banking and money market statistics.

Key characteristics and trends to remember about Canadian currency include the following:

* The Canadian economy is highly dependent on commodities, so the CAD tends to increase when commodity prices increase and decrease when commodity prices decrease.

* Because Canada exports 85 percent of its products to the United States, its economy is highly sensitive to changes in the U.S. economy.

* Mergers and acquisitions between U.S. and Canadian companies occur regularly and can affect the value of both currencies.

* If Canada's interest rate is higher than the United States', the USD/CAD carry trade can become a popular way to make money.

Key currency cross pairs that don't involve the U.S. dollar include:

* CAD/GBP—Canadian dollar/British pound
* AUD/CAD—Australian dollar/Canadian dollar
* EUR/CAD—euro/Canadian dollar

Most active trading hours:

* 7:00 A.M. ET/11:00 GMT, Canadian economic releases
* 8:30 A.M. ET/12:30 GMT, U.S. economic releases

Market-moving economic releases:

* Bank of Canada rate decision
* Consumer prices

- Employment change

- GDP

- IVEY PMI (Purchasing Manager's Index)

- Retail sales

European Union (Euro)

The European Union (EU) includes 27 member countries in Europe. Sixteen of those countries have joined the European Monetary Union (EMU) and use the euro (EUR) as their currency. These include Austria, Belgium, Cyprus, Finland, France, Germany, Greece, Ireland, Italy, Luxembourg, Malta, the Netherlands, Portugal, Slovakia, Slovenia, and Spain. European Union members that have not yet adopted the euro include Bulgaria, the Czech Republic, Denmark, Estonia, Hungary, Latvia, Lithuania, Poland, Romania, Sweden, and the United Kingdom. The USD/euro is the most actively traded currency pair in the FX market, according to the Bank of International Settlements FX report 2010.

In creating the EU, one of the primary goals was to adopt a common currency to strengthen European trade, as well as international political and economic positions. Income disparities and disagreements among the nations regarding certain EU policies have delayed adoption of the currency among all member nations, as well as the adoption of an EU constitution.

The EU's overall economy is the largest in the world, with a GDP valued at US$16.4 trillion in 2009, which makes up 20 percent of the world's total gross product. The EU also has the third-largest workforce in the world, which is about a quarter of the size of China's labor force. Approximately 67 percent of the economy is based on service; but as one of the world's most technologically advanced industrial economies, its industries make up 27 percent of its GDP.

The EU is the largest exporter of goods and services, with US$1.525 trillion in annual exports from its member countries, including machinery, motor vehicles, aircraft, plastics, and pharmaceuticals. The United States imports 24 percent of the EU's products, which makes it the EU's most important trade partner. The formation of the EU and its significant clout on the world markets increases the bargaining power of its member nations.

The value of the euro is under great pressure as many of the Eurozone countries face significant financial problems. Ireland needed a bailout. Greece is also insolvent. Portugal has a liquidity problem and countries like Belgium and France have serious budget issues.

The euro is gradually developing as a key reserve currency, and there has been a shift in the global money markets toward the euro and away from the U.S. dollar. The trend likely will increase the EU's leveraging power.

The European Central Bank maintains the purchasing power of the euro and seeks to maintain price stability within the member countries of the EMU. The six-member governing council of the bank meets twice monthly to discuss monetary policy. Monetary policy decisions are made during the first meeting of the month. The bank uses various open-market operations to influence interest rates and manage market liquidity, including monetary transactions, issuance of debt certificates, foreign exchange swaps, and long-term deposits.

WEALTH BUILDERS

You can follow the economic and monetary policy decisions of the European Central Bank at its website: www.ecb.int/home/html/index.en.html. Two key reports to watch are its Monthly Bulletin and its Statistics Pocket Book. The Statistics Pocket Book contains selected macroeconomic indicators for the individual member states of the EU, as well as comparisons between the EU, the United States, and Japan.

Key euro characteristics and trends to watch include the following:

- EUR/USD is usually the most liquid currency pair, which makes this a popular currency trade. The movements of this pair are used as the primary gauge of European and U.S. strength and weaknesses.

- Because the euro is the common currency for 16 countries, it's highly sensitive to the political/economic instabilities in any of its member countries.

- Follow the differential in rates between the U.S. 10-year bond and the 10-year German bond. This is a good indicator of euro movement.

Key currency cross pairs for the euro are:

- EUR/GBP—euro/British pound.
- EUR/JPY—euro/Japanese yen
- EUR/CHF—euro/Swiss franc

Most active trading hours:

- 2:00 A.M. ET/6:00 GMT, London open
- 4:00 A.M. ET/8:00 GMT, EU economic releases
- 8:30 A.M. ET/12:30 GMT, U.S. economic releases

Market-moving economic releases:

- ECB rate decision
- German consumer prices
- German GDP
- German IFO (business confidence)
- German unemployment
- Manufacturing and service sector PMI

Great Britain (British pound—GBP)

Will it or won't it? If you ask that question about whether Great Britain will or won't join the EMU and give up its British pound (GBP), you can quickly send the money markets into a spin. Anytime the lead politicians in Britain mention that they favor adopting the euro, the British pound starts to drop in value. Politicians can just as quickly raise the value of the pound when they speak in opposition to the EMU and adopting its euro.

The British pound is probably the most widely held reserve currency next to the U.S. dollar and the euro. London is also the biggest hub for forex trading, with over a third of the global turnover based in London.

Why does Great Britain matter so much? It's the sixth-largest economy in the world, with a 2009 GDP of US$2.178 trillion. It's also the world's fifth-largest importer and eighth-largest exporter. The United States, Germany, and France are Britain's best trading partners. Britain's agricultural industry produces 60 percent of the country's food, a much more efficient industry than that seen in other European countries.

Britain also has significant coal, natural gas, and oil reserves. Its energy production makes up 10 percent of the country's GDP, one of the highest of any industrial nation.

Britain's workforce, however, is driven by service-oriented occupations, which employ 79.5 percent of its workforce. To strengthen its economic position and reduce its debt, the UK government greatly reduced public ownership and limited growth of social welfare programs. It has also raised taxes to support education, transportation, and health services.

The Bank of England (BOE) directs the UK's monetary policy. Its monetary policy committee sets interest rates to meet the inflation target set annually by the chancellor of the Exchequer. The Committee holds monthly meetings followed by announcements of state changes in monetary policy and interest rates. The BOE publishes two quarterly reports: the Inflation Report and the Quarterly Bulletin.

WEALTH BUILDERS

You can follow Bank of England announcements, as well as access its two key financial reports, the Inflation Report and the Quarterly Bulletin, by clicking on "Publications" on its website: www.bankofengland.co.uk.

Key characteristics and trends for the British pound that you should watch include the following:

- GBP/USD is one of the most liquid currency pairs in the world.

- Watch interest rates between *UK gilts*/U.S. treasuries and UK gilts/German bonds for potential currency-movement indicators. These matches indicate the differentials in premium yield in fixed-income assets.

- Energy production makes up 10 percent of the UK's GDP. When energy prices increase, so does the value of the GBP.

DEFINITION

The **UK gilt** is a government bond similar to U.S. Treasury bonds.

Key currency cross pairs that do not involve the U.S. dollar include:

- EUR/GBP—euro/British pound
- GBP/CHF—British pound and Swiss franc
- GBP/JPY—British pound and Japanese yen

Most active trading hours:

- 2:00 A.M. ET/6:00 GMT, London open
- 4:30 A.M. ET/8:30 GMT, UK economic releases
- 8:30 A.M. ET/12:30 GMT, U.S. economic releases

Market-moving economic releases:

- Bank of England rate decision
- Claimant count (unemployment claims)
- Consumer prices
- GDP
- Industrial production
- Retail sales

Japan (Japanese yen—JPY)

Japan boasts the world's third-largest economy and is the fourth-largest exporter in the world. China overtook Japan as the world's number two economy in 2010. Japan's most successful company, Toyota, recalled more than 10 million vehicles because of safety issues and sales tumbled. Four prime ministers resigned in three years. It's facing its decade of stagnation. The bad news that weighs down Japan's economy is that it also manages a fairly large national debt of 192.1 percent of its GDP. The earthquake and Tsunami of 2011 will slow Japan's recovery even more.

Yet even with this uncertainly, the USD/JPY is the second most heavily traded currency pair in the forex market, according to the Bank of International Settlements 2010 Triennial FX report. It's second only to the USD/EUR.

Japan's primary trade partners are the United States and China. Japan manages one of the world's largest and most technologically advanced industrial machines. Its industries produce motor vehicles, electronic equipment, machine tools, steel and nonferrous metals, ships, chemicals, textiles, and processed foods. Japan also owns more than half of the world's "working robots."

All is not good news for Japan. As a highly industrialized nation, it's heavily dependent on the import of raw materials and fuels. Its agricultural sector is small and highly subsidized.

Through the 1990s, Japan's economy suffered a major economic setback. Dramatic asset value drops, including a burst of the real estate bubble, left many of its developers and banks with bad debt and worthless collateral. Japan is still recovering from this economic downturn.

The Bank of Japan (BOJ), which directs the country's monetary policy, is working with the Japanese Ministry of Finance to fix the problems. The bank has poured funds into the ailing banks of Japan to prevent bankruptcies and attempt to grow the banks back to a healthier balance sheet. Therefore, the banking sector is very dependent on the government and its political whims. This makes the yen very sensitive to political developments, including pronouncements by government officials that indicate changes in monetary and fiscal policy.

The Bank of Japan seeks to maintain price stability as well as stability of the financial system. The BOJ's monetary policy board determines monetary policy at monthly policy meetings. The results of these meetings are announced in the Monthly Report of Recent Economic and Financial Developments. The bank also prepares a quarterly report called the Tankan Survey, an economic review of Japanese businesses.

WEALTH BUILDERS

You can access the Bank of Japan's key financial reports, the Monthly Report of Recent Economic and Financial Developments and the quarterly Tankan Survey, at the BOJ's website: www.boj.or.jp/en.

Japan intervenes regularly to manage the value of its currency. The minister of finance instructs the BOJ when to buy or sell the yen to either raise or lower its value. The BOJ uses government funds to carry out the minister's orders.

Japan's currency frequently faces rapid appreciation because of its strong trade surplus. The minister asks for foreign exchange interventions when the yen (JPY) appreciates or depreciates rapidly in value, to maintain a steady USD/JPY rate, or to direct speculative current positions.

Here are some key characteristics and trends for the Japanese yen you should watch for:

- Economic and political problems in other Asian economies can have a dramatic impact on the Japanese economy and JPY movements.

- Trades involving the JPY can become very active toward the end of the Japanese fiscal year (March 31), as exporters move their dollar-dominated assets.

- The JPY tends to be more volatile during the U.S. trading hours (7:20 A.M. to 2:00 P.M. EST) and during the Japanese lunch hour, which happens between 10 P.M. to 11 P.M. EST.

- Because the banking crisis is still a critical aspect of Japan's economic health, watch Japanese bank stock movements closely to find clues about JPY movements.

- The JPY has the lowest interest rate of all industrialized countries, so it is the primary currency sold in carry trades.

Key currency cross pairs that do not involve the U.S. dollar include:

- EUR/JPY—euro/Japanese yen

- NZD/JPY—New Zealand dollar/Japanese yen

- GBP/JPY—British pound/Japanese yen

Most active trading hours:

- 7:00 P.M. ET/23:00 GMT, Tokyo open

- 7:30 P.M. ET/23:30 GMT, JPY economic releases

- 8:30 A.M. ET/12:30 GMT, U.S. economic releases

Market-moving economic releases:

- Bank of Japan rate decision

- Consumer prices

- Corporate goods price index

- GDP

- Retail sales

- Tankan Survey (business sentiment)

New Zealand (New Zealand dollar—NZD)

New Zealand manages a small economy compared to the other industrialized nations, with its 2009 GDP valued at just US$117.794 billion. Its population is equivalent to just half the population of New York City, yet the population inhabits more than 300 times the area. Although the NZD has the highest interest rate of the eight major currencies, it has lower turnover than the Swedish krona, Hong Kong dollar, and Norwegian krone, according to the Bank of International Settlement's 2010 Triennial FX survey.

New Zealand worked hard over the past 25 years to transform the country into an industrialized, free-market economy that competes globally. This resulted in a boost to incomes, technological advances, and controlled inflation.

Trade of its agricultural products drives New Zealand's growth. Exports of goods and services make up 20 percent of the country's GDP. These factors make New Zealand's economic success heavily dependent on global performance. Its key trading partners include Australia, the United States, Japan, and China. Its national debt as a percentage of GDP is just 29.3 percent.

New Zealand's agricultural base for its economy makes it highly sensitive to severe weather conditions that can damage its farming activities. Its economy can also be sensitive to weather conditions in Australia.

The Reserve Bank of New Zealand (RBNZ) manages the country's currency, the New Zealand dollar (NZD). Its monetary policy seeks to maintain stability and efficiency of the financial system, as well as meet the currency needs of the public. Working with the New Zealand minister of finance, the RBNZ outlines monetary policy in the Policy Targets Agreements (PTA). The most recent PTA requires RBNZ to keep inflation between 1 to 3 percent.

 WEALTH BUILDERS

You can learn more about the Reserve Bank of New Zealand and its open-market operations at www.rbnz.govt.nz. Just click on "Monetary Policy" from the home page .

The bank does this by borrowing from or lending cash to New Zealand's financial institutions in open-market operations. In fact, New Zealand has one of the most open-market operations in the world. Each banking day at 9:30 A.M. in New Zealand, the bank announces details of its operations. For the next 15 minutes, bidders submit bids with their interest rate demands. Based on these bids, the bank announces a minimum rate at which it will lend and a maximum rate at which it will borrow. If there aren't enough bids to fully offset the government's cash-flow needs, the bank then uses overnight operations to make up any shortages.

Key characteristics and trends you should watch in regard to the New Zealand dollar include the following:

- New Zealand's economy benefits from a strong Australian economy.
- Follow interest rate differentials between New Zealand and Australia, as well as interest rate yields of other industrial countries.
- The NZD is a commodity-linked currency, so as commodity prices increase, the NZD tends to appreciate.
- New Zealand's high interest rates tend to make the NZD a popular currency for carry trades.

Key currency pairs that do not include the U.S. dollar include:

- NZD/JPY—New Zealand dollar/Japanese yen
- AUD/NZD—Australian dollar/New Zealand dollar
- EUR/NZD—euro/New Zealand dollar

Most active trading hours:

- 7:00 P.M. ET/23:00 GMT, Tokyo open

- 7:30 P.M. ET/23:30 GMT, NZD economic releases

- 8:30 A.M. ET/12:30 GMT, U.S. economic releases

Market-moving economic releases:

- Consumer prices

- Employment change

- GDP

- Reserve Bank of New Zealand rate decision

- Retail sales

- Trade balance

Switzerland (Swiss franc—CHF)

Switzerland, known as a safe haven for money, is the place investors flock to when there is any uncertainty in the global marketplace. It gained its reputation as a safe haven because of the confidentiality its banks can offer depositors. The USD/CHF is the fifth most actively traded currency pair by turnover, according to the Bank of International Settlement's 2010 FX report.

Switzerland boasts a low unemployment rate that is half that of the European Union. About 70 percent of its workforce is employed by banking and insurance firms catering to investors taking advantage of Switzerland's safe and confidential banking haven.

Germany is Switzerland's key trading partner. Other key partners include the United States, France, and Italy. Its major exports include machinery, chemicals, consumer products, and agricultural products. Its national debt is 43.5 percent of its GDP.

The Swiss National Bank (SNB) manages the Swiss franc (CHF) and Switzerland's monetary policy, which strives to maintain price stability. The bank seeks to maintain no more than a 2 percent increase in the national consumer price index.

The bank monitors exchange rates very closely because excessive strength in the exchange rate for the Swiss franc can cause inflation. The franc's exchange rate can rise rapidly when investors flock to the currency during times of global uncertainty. For this reason, the SNB favors a weak franc and doesn't hesitate to intervene in the foreign exchange market. It also conducts open-market operations to influence its monetary policy.

WEALTH BUILDERS

You can find out more about the Swiss National Bank's monetary policies at its website: www.snb.ch. Click on "Publications" to find links to its quarterly and annual reports.

The SNB publishes a quarterly bulletin that includes a monetary policy report of the policy decisions made by its governing board. In its June annual report, it provides a three-year inflation forecast.

To implement its monetary policy, SNB sets an interest rate target range for the London Interbank Offered Rate (*Libor*) for three-month CHF deposits. The bank supplies more or less funds through *repos* to ensure the Libor rate stays in the target range.

DEFINITION

Repos are repurchase agreements. The SNB uses a type of repo where a financial institution sells securities to the SNB with the promise to repurchase the securities in a set period of time. The **Libor** is a trademark of the British Bank Association and is the most widely used benchmark for short-term interest rates worldwide.

Key characteristics and trends for the Swiss franc include the following:

- Funds move into the country during times of international economic instability, so the value of the CHF will appreciate during those periods.

- News about Swiss banking changes can negatively affect the Swiss economy and the CHF.

- Switzerland is the seventh-largest holder of gold, which is viewed as the ultimate safe haven, and the CHF has an almost 80 percent positive correlation with gold—when gold appreciates, the CHF appreciates.

- The CHF is one of the most popular currencies to sell for carry trades because of its low interest rates.

- Watch the interest rate differentials between the euro and the CHF for clues about money flows.

- Mergers and acquisitions are common in the Swiss banking and insurance industries and can affect CHF spot prices.

Key currency cross pairs that to do not involve the U.S. dollar:

- EUR/CHF—euro/Swiss franc

- CHF/JPY—Swiss franc/Japanese yen

- GBP/CHF—British pound/Swiss franc

Most active trading hours:

- 2:00 A.M. ET/6:00 GMT, London open

- 1:45 A.M. ET/4:45 GMT, Swiss economic releases

- 8:30 A.M. ET/12:30 GMT, U.S. economic releases

Market-moving economic releases:

- Consumer prices

- GDP

- Swiss Institute for Business Cycle Research (KOF) leading indicators

- Retail sales

- Swiss National Bank rate decision

- UBS consumption index

United States (U.S. dollar—USD)

The U.S. economy is the second largest in the world, with a GDP of US$14.1 trillion, which makes up more than 20 percent of the world's total gross product. The United

States has the world's fourth-largest labor force. Its market-based economy is largely service-oriented, with approximately 79 percent of its firms in the service sector, 20 percent in industry, and 1 percent in agriculture.

About 85 percent of all currency transactions involve the U.S. dollar. It's not only the world's primary reserve currency, but the currencies of more than 25 countries are pegged to the U.S. dollar, according to the Bank of International Settlements 2010 Triennial FX Report.

The United States imports significantly more than any other country and is the third-largest exporter of goods. Canada is its most important trade partner. Long-term financial risks for the country include insufficient investment in the country's economic infrastructure, rapidly rising medical and pension costs for the aging population, skyrocketing energy costs, the large trade and budget deficits, and the widening gap in family income between the lower- and upper-economic classes.

The central bank for the United States is the Federal Reserve (the Fed), which seeks to promote maximum employment, stability in the purchasing power of the dollar, and moderate long-term interest rates. It is an independent entity within the government that does not need presidential approval for its actions, but is under the regulatory supervision of the Congress.

The Fed's Federal Open Market Committee (FOMC) oversees market operations. The FOMC holds eight annual meetings at which interest rate changes and economic expectations are announced. The FOMC forecasts GDP growth, inflation, and unemployment rates. The Fed releases a biannual Monetary Policy Report in February and July.

One way the Fed manages monetary policy is through open-market operations, which include selling government securities based on projections of the supply and demand of Federal Reserve balances. When the Fed purchases securities, interest rates decrease; when it sells securities, interest rates increase.

The Fed also sets the federal funds rate target, which is the interest rate for funds that the Fed loans to other banks. This interest rate impacts all other types of interest rates, including rates for mortgages and consumer loans. The Fed has maintained a nearly zero target interest rate since December 2008 as the country tried to pull out of its most devastating recession since the Great Depression.

The U.S. Treasury gives instructions regarding whether the Fed should intervene in the foreign exchange markets. The U.S. Treasury may request that the Fed buy or sell the USD, depending upon whether it believes the dollar is over- or undervalued. The Federal Reserve Bank of New York carries out all foreign exchange interventions.

WEALTH BUILDERS

You can find out more about the New York Fed and its foreign exchange activities at www.newyorkfed.org/markets/foreignex.html. You can find out more about the Federal Reserve and its monetary policies at www.federalreserve.gov.

Key characteristics and trends for the United States dollar include the following:

- The USD is the currency used most often in international transactions and constitutes more than half of other countries' official reserves.

- Many emerging-market countries peg their local currency rates to the USD.

- Gold is measured in USD, so gold and the USD tend to have inverse relationships.

- There is a strong positive correlation between the U.S. stock and bond markets and the USD.

- U.S. economic policymakers favor a strong dollar.

- Interest rate differentiation between U.S. Treasury bonds and foreign bonds are a strong indicator of potential currency movements.

Most actively traded currency pairs based on the 2010 Bank of International Settlements Triennial FX Report:

- USD/EUR—28% of all FX turnovers

- USD/JPY—14% of all FX turnovers

- USD/GBP—9% of all FX turnovers

- USD/AUD—6% of all FX turnovers

- USD/CAD—5% of all FX turnovers

- USD/CHF—4% of all FX turnovers

Most active trading hours:

- 2:00 A.M. ET/6:00 GMT, London open
- 8:30 A.M. ET/12:30 GMT, U.S. economic releases

Market-moving economic releases:

- Consumer producer prices
- Consumer confidence
- Federal Reserve interest rate decision
- GDP
- Nonfarm payrolls
- Retail sales
- Service and manufacturing (Institute for Supply Management)
- Trade balance
- Treasury international capital flow report

The Least You Need to Know

- Learn as much as you can about the economic and monetary policies of any country whose currency you want to trade. Be sure you know how to find out more information about the monetary policies and follow any announcements or reports from the entity managing that country's currency.
- Strong central banks manage the currencies of all the industrial countries considered to have less risk for foreign currency exchange transactions.
- Be sure you know which currency pairs are the most liquid when trading currencies.
- Get to know the politics of the countries whose currencies you trade, as well as who sets monetary policy for those countries.

Taking More Risks—
Emerging Country
Currencies

Chapter

6

In This Chapter

- Understanding emerging markets
- Reviewing riskier country currencies
- Exploring liquidity concerns
- Discovering emerging markets with potential

After you've been trading for a while, you may want to try taking on more risk for the possibility of greater financial rewards. You can do that with more volatile emerging country currencies, but beware. Be certain the money you risk is money you can afford to lose.

Emerging country currencies are not only more risky and volatile, they can also be less liquid—meaning you may not be able to buy or sell them at the price you want because there may not be buyers or sellers for that currency pair. Some of these currencies are sold on the spot market, but many are not. We detail this as we discuss each country's currency.

This chapter briefly discusses what we consider to be the best potential emerging country currencies (at the time this was written) that you may want to consider. Before getting started, be sure you conduct your own intensive research about the countries and their currencies before you trade.

WEALTH BUILDERS

If you want to trade the currencies from emerging countries, you need to know about the political conditions and economy of the countries. One good source is the Background Notes prepared by the U.S. State Department on its website at www.state.gov/r/pa/ei/bgn. Another good source for country information is *The World Factbook* (www.cia.gov/library/publications/the-world-factbook).

China (Chinese renminbi—CNY)

China is by far the largest emerging country; and its currency, the Chinese renminbi (CNY), commonly known as yuan, may grow into a more dominant player in years to come. Before jumping on the CNY bandwagon, be sure you understand that China is a Communist Party–led state, which means the state is still very much in control even though it is dabbling in economic reform and opening its markets. The Communist Party leadership could change, and new Chinese Communist Party leaders could reverse all gains that were made in the past 10 to 20 years. The Chinese Communist Party has 76 million members. China does have eight minor parties, but they are all under Communist supervision.

China's 2009 GDP was US$4.814 trillion, which sounds large, but its per-capita GDP is only US$3,678 compared to US$47,123 in the developed industrial countries. China's GDP is growing rapidly. The growth rate in 2009 was 8.7 percent. China started to cool this growth rate by raising interest rates twice in 2010 and is expected to continue that tightening in 2011.

China has many exports. Its natural resources include coal, iron ore, crude oil, mercury, tin, tungsten, antimony, manganese, molybdenum, vanadium, magnetite, aluminum, lead, zinc, and uranium. China also has the world's largest potential for hydropower. Its farmers are among the world's largest producers of rice, wheat, potatoes, corn, peanuts, tea, millet, and barley. Their commercial crops include cotton, fibers, apples, oilseeds, pork, and fish. China also produces a variety of livestock products.

Chinese industry is growing rapidly, too, and includes mining and ore processing, iron, steel, aluminum, coal, machinery, textiles, apparel, armaments, petroleum, cement, chemicals, fertilizers, consumer products (such as footwear, toys, and electronics), automobiles and other transportation equipment (such as railcars, locomotives, ships, and aircraft), and telecommunications products.

China is firmly committed to economic reform and opening to the outside world. Reform of state industries and the establishment of a social safety network are the two top government priorities named by China's leaders. The government has privatized unprofitable state-owned enterprises and developed a pension system for workers. China's leadership has also downsized the government bureaucracy.

For investors and firms, China represents a vast market that has yet to be fully tapped and a low-cost base for export-oriented production. The rapid growth of new businesses outpaced the government's ability to regulate them. China has been faced with sorting out mounting competition and poor oversight. Drastic measures have led to increased profit margins, but at the expense of consumer safety. In 2007, the United States placed a number of restrictions on problematic Chinese exports. The Chinese government recognizes the severity of the problem, concluding in 2007 that nearly 20 percent of the country's products are substandard or tainted, and is undertaking efforts in coordination with the United States and others to better regulate the problem. The U.S. trade deficit with China fell 15.4 percent in 2009 to $227 billion, primarily because Chinese imports were down 12 percent, to $296 billion. The China portion of the global U.S. trade deficit rose to 43.9 percent in 2009, from 31.9 percent one year earlier. U.S. imports from China accounted for 19 percent of overall U.S. imports in 2009.

Exports of U.S. goods to China fell slightly in 2009, down 0.2 percent (to $69.5 billion), but were up as an overall percentage of U.S. exports from 5.5 percent in 2008 to 6.6 percent in 2009, a record high share, indicating that China was a more significant and robust trading partner than it had been before. The top three U.S. exports to China in 2008 were electrical machinery ($9.5 billion), oil seeds and related products ($9.3 billion), and nuclear reactors and related machinery ($8.4 billion). Chinese exports totaled US$1.194 trillion in 2009, including trade in electronics; machinery; apparel; optical, photographic, and medical equipment; and furniture. Its main export trading partners include the United States, Hong Kong, Japan, Germany, and South Korea. China imported US$921.5 billion worth of products in 2009 in electronics, machinery, petroleum products, chemicals, and steel. China's main import trading partners are Japan, Germany, Taiwan, South Korea, and the United States.

Cooperation between U.S. and Chinese companies continues to blossom. U.S. companies established more than 20,000 equity joint ventures, contractual joint ventures, and wholly foreign-owned enterprises in China. More than 100 U.S.–based multinationals have projects in China, some with multiple investments. Investments by U.S. companies totaled an estimated $60 billion through the end of 2008. This makes the United States the fourth-largest foreign investor in China.

Two-way trade continues to grow between China and the United States. In 1992 it was just $33 billion and in 2007 it had grown to $386 billion. U.S. exports to China have grown more rapidly than to any other market. The USD/CNY is the most liquid currency pair involving the CNY, but the average trading volume is very small; so if you buy USD/CNY, you may not be able to sell the pair quickly. From 1994 until mid-2005, the CNY was pegged to the U.S. dollar. In mid-2005, China removed the USD peg and it is now pegged to a basket of currencies. The PRC has stated that the basket is dominated by the U.S. dollar, Euro, Japanese yen, and South Korean won, with a smaller proportion made up of the British pound, Thai baht, Russian ruble, Australian dollar, Canadian dollar, and Singapore dollar.

Hong Kong (Hong Kong dollar—HKD)

Hong Kong became a Special Administrative Region of the People's Republic of China in 1997 after 150 years of British rule, yet it does enjoy a high degree of autonomy in all matters except foreign and defense affairs.

The Sino-British Joint Declaration (1984) guarantees that Hong Kong will retain its political, economic, and judicial systems, as well as its unique way of life, for 50 years. During 2010, the Hong Kong Monetary Authority announced that the total amount of Chinese renminbi deposits in Hong Kong reached $42 billion as of the end of November, which is a 246 percent jump from a year earlier. Hong Kong plans to expand its role as an offshore center for renminbi trade settlement, as well as build its role as a trading middleman for a significant portion of the labor-intensive exports from mainland China. Hong Kong also plays this role for exports from Singapore, Malaysia, South Korea, and Japan.

Hong Kong is one of the world's most open and dynamic economies. Its per-capita GDP is comparable to other developed countries. Real GDP was $209.3 billion in 2009 and its per-capita GDP was $29,879.

Hong Kong enjoys a number of economic strengths, including accumulated public and private wealth from decades of unprecedented growth, a sound banking system, virtually no public debt, a strong legal system, and an able and rigorously enforced anticorruption regime.

Hong Kong exports totaled $316.5 billion in 2009 including clothing, electronics, textiles, watches and clocks, office machinery, electrical machinery, and telecommunications equipment. Its major trading partners include China, the United States, the EU, Japan, Singapore, and Taiwan.

The Hong Kong dollar (HKD) is pegged to the U.S. dollar. A bank can only issue the HKD if it has the same amount of USD on deposit. In 2005, the upper and lower interest rates were adjusted to narrow the interest rate gap between Hong Kong and the United States. Decisions about Hong Kong's currency are managed by a currency board system run by the Hong Kong Monetary Authority. Some push for Hong Kong to abolish the HDK and adopt the Chinese renminbi (CNY).

WEALTH BUILDERS

You can get the latest news about Hong Kong monetary policy at the Hong Kong Monetary Authority website: www.info.gov.hk/hkma/eng/currency/link_ex/index.htm. You can also read more about how a currency board system works.

There is no distinction between local and offshore trading. There are no spot or forward trading restrictions, but documentation is required. There is a liquid government bond market (Exchange Fund Notes) with maturities of up to 10 years. Interest rate swaps and options are liquid up to 10 years.

The most liquid currency pair involving the HKD is USD/HKD.

India (Indian rupee—INR)

Many expect India's currency, the Indian rupee (INR), to become the first of the emerging markets to become *spot* eligible without restrictions and documentation, but for now the currency is still a *managed float*, with the U.S. dollar being its *de facto* controlled exchange rate. Still, rates such as the EUR/INR and INR/JPY have volatilities that are typical of floating exchange rates. Similar to the United States, India has a federal form of government, but the central government in India has greater power in relation to its states. It has also adopted the British-style parliamentary system.

DEFINITION

A **spot** forex market is one in which the currency is bought and sold for cash and delivered immediately.

A **managed float** regime, also known as a "dirty float," is one in which the exchange rates fluctuate from day to day, but a central bank attempts to influence the country's exchange rates by buying and selling currencies.

The government exercises its broad administrative powers in the name of the president, but the real national executive power is centered in the Council of Ministers (its cabinet), led by the prime minister. The president appoints the prime minister, who is designated by legislators of the political party or coalition that holds the largest parliamentary majority in its lower house *(Lok Sabha)*. The president then appoints subordinate ministers on the advice of the prime minister.

India's 2009 GDP was US$1.095 trillion, with a growth rate of 6.5 percent, which translates into a per-capita GDP of US$3,100. Its exports in 2009 totaled US$164.3 billion, including engineering goods, petroleum products, precious stones, cotton apparel and fabrics, gems and jewelry, handicrafts, and tea. India's major trade partners include the United States, China, the EU, U.A.E., Russia, and Japan.

The Indian rupee is managed by the Reserve Bank of India and is classified as a managed float regime. Documentation is needed for offshore trading.

India does have a very liquid bond market with maturities of up to 25 years available because the government does need to fund a substantial budget deficit.

Korea (South Korean won—KRW)

The Republic of Korea (South Korea) has experienced phenomenal growth over the past 45 years. Its per-capita GNP climbed from just US$100 in 1963 to US$17,074 in 2009. South Korea is the United States' seventh-largest trading partner and commands the twelfth-largest economy in the world. On June 30, 2007, the United States and Korea signed a comprehensive trade agreement to eliminate virtually all barriers to trade and investment between the two countries. Tariffs on 95 percent of trade between the two countries were to be eliminated by 2010, with virtually all the remaining tariffs to be removed within 10 years of implementation.

South Korea is a republic with powers shared between the presidency, the legislature, and the judiciary. The president is chief of state and is elected for a single term of five years. The prime minister is the head of the government.

In the past few years, South Korea's economic growth potential fell due to structural problems as well as a rapidly aging population. One of the biggest concerns is South Korea's rigid labor regulations and the need for more constructive relations between management and workers. Korea also has experienced one of the largest rates of emigration, with ethnic Koreans residing primarily in China (2.4 million), the United States (2.1 million), Japan (600,000), and the countries of the former Soviet Union (532,000).

Korea's GDP in 2009 was US$1.364 trillion. Its exports totaled US$363.5 billion, including electronic products (semiconductors, cellular phones, and computers), automobiles, machinery and equipment, steel, ships, and textiles. Its major trading partners include China, the United States, Japan, Hong Kong, Saudi Arabia, and Singapore.

The Korean won (KRW) is a floating currency, but local and offshore markets are treated separately. Documentation is required for delivery at maturity. The most liquid currency pair involving the KRW is the USD/KRW.

Mexico (Mexican peso—MXN)

Mexico's economy is highly dependent on exports to the United States, which account for almost a quarter of the country's GDP, so its economy is strongly linked to the ups and downs of the U.S. business cycle. The United States buys about 80 percent of Mexico's exports, including petroleum, cars, and electronic equipment. Mexico's trade policy is among the most open in the world, which includes free-trade agreements with the United States, Canada, the EU, and many other countries. Because of this connection, Mexico experienced its deepest recession since the 1930s as it waits for the United States to climb out of its recession.

Mexico's trade regime is built upon free trade agreements with the United States, Canada, the European Union, and many other countries (44 total). Since the 1994 devaluation of the peso, successive Mexican governments have worked toward improving its economy. Inflation and public-sector deficits are under control. Mexico's debt remains investment-grade, with a stable outlook.

One of Mexico's biggest assets is its oil industry. Mexico is the world's fifth-largest producer of oil and the tenth-largest oil exporter. It is also the United States' second-largest supplier of oil. Oil and gas revenues provide about one third of all Mexican government revenues. The state owns the oil company Pemex, which holds a constitutionally established monopoly for the exploration, production, transportation, and marketing of the nation's oil.

The Mexican government is a republic with a president as a chief of state, as well as a legislative and judicial branch.

Mexico's foreign exchange and local debt markets are very liquid. The government on a weekly basis issues bills with terms ranging from one month up to one year. It also issues longer-term debt with terms of up to five years, but the shorter-term bills are more liquid.

The most commonly traded currency pairs are the USD/MXN and the EUR/MXN.

Poland (Polish zloty—PLN)

Reforms since 1989 have brought success and new challenges for Poland. Since joining the EU in 2004, Poland's per-capita economic growth rate has outpaced those of the United States and its EU partners.

Polish incomes have risen to 37 percent of U.S. incomes (up from 29 percent in 1997), while inflation and unemployment have dropped to historic lows. A lot of hard work is still needed to restructure Poland's economy if it is to reach full parity in terms of income with the historically wealthy countries of Western Europe.

Opportunities for trade and investment in virtually all sectors continue to attract investors from around the world. The American Chamber of Commerce in Poland grew from seven members in 1991 to 300 members in 2009. Strong economic growth potential, a large domestic market, tariff-free access to the EU, and political stability are the top reasons U.S. and other foreign companies do business in Poland.

The Polish government is a republic with a president as head of state, a legislative branch, and a judicial branch. Poland's GDP in 2009 was US$430 billion. Its exports totaled US$133.6 billion, including furniture, cars, ships, coal, and apparel. Its imports totaled US$145.8 billion, including crude oil, passenger cars, pharmaceuticals, car parts, and computers.

The United States and other Western countries helped to support Poland's growth of a free-enterprise economy by reducing Poland's foreign debt burden in the 1990s, and by providing economic aid and lowering trade barriers. Poland officially joined the EU in 2004. It had planned to convert its currency, the Polish zloty (PLN), to the euro in 2008, but the government extended that deadline to at least 2014 because economic conditions do not yet meet requirements.

The Polish zloty has been a floating currency since 2000. Most money market transactions are conducted through foreign exchange swaps for offshore investors. The most liquid currency pairs for the PLN are the USD/PLN and the EUR/PLN.

Singapore (Singapore dollar—SGD)

Singapore's strategic location on major sea lanes and its industrious population give the country an economic importance in Southeast Asia disproportionate to its small size. In 2009, the economy expanded by 8.6 percent.

Singapore's government is largely corruption-free. It also boasts a skilled workforce and an advanced and efficient infrastructure, which has attracted investors from more than 7,000 multinational corporations based in the United States, Japan, and Europe. There are also 1,500 companies from China and another 1,500 from India. Foreign firms are found in almost all sectors of the economy. Multinational corporations account for more than two thirds of manufacturing output and direct export sales, although certain services sectors remain dominated by government-linked companies.

Manufacturing (including construction) and services drive the Singapore economy and in 2009 accounted for 26.3 percent and 69.1 percent, respectively, of Singapore's gross domestic product. The electronics and biomedical manufacturing industries lead Singapore's manufacturing sector, accounting for 30.6 percent and 20.8 percent, respectively, of Singapore's manufacturing output in 2009.

Singapore is also trying to grow its tourism sector; in April 2005 the government approved the development of two casinos that resulted in investments of more than US$5 billion. Las Vegas Sands' Marina Bay Sands Resort opened for business in April 2010, while Genting International's Resort World Sentosa opened its doors in February 2010.

Singapore's rising wages are a threat to its competitive position, so the government promotes higher value-added activities in the manufacturing and services sectors. It opened its financial services, telecommunications, and power-generation and retailing sectors to foreign service providers and greater competition.

The government is actively negotiating eight free trade agreements (FTAs) with emerging economic partners and has already concluded 18 FTAs with many of its key trade partners, including one with the United States that came into force January 1, 2004. As a member of the Association of Southeast Asian Nations (ASEAN), Singapore is part of the ASEAN Free Trade Area (AFTA), and is signatory to ASEAN FTAs with China, Korea, Japan, India, and a joint agreement with New Zealand and Australia. Singapore is also a party to the Transpacific Strategic Economic Partnership Agreement, which includes Brunei, Chile, and New Zealand.

The United States leads in foreign investment, accounting for 11.2 percent of new commitments to the manufacturing sector in 2008. As of 2009, the stock of investment by U.S. companies in the manufacturing and services sectors in Singapore reached about US$76.86 billion. The bulk of U.S. investment is in electronics manufacturing, oil refining and storage, and the chemical industry. About 1,500 U.S. firms operate in Singapore.

Singapore's total trade in 2009 was $513.9 billion, which is 19.4 percent lower than 2008. In 2009, Singapore's imports totaled $245 billion, and exports totaled $269 billion. Malaysia, which buys 11.5 percent of Singapore's exports, was its main importer, as well as its second-largest export market. Hong Kong is its largest export market at 11.5. Other major export markets include the United States, China, and Indonesia. Singapore was the 13th-largest trading partner of the United States in 2009.

Singapore's principal exports are petroleum products, food and beverages, chemicals, pharmaceuticals, electronic components, telecommunication hardware, and transport equipment. Singapore's main imports are aircraft, crude oil and petroleum products, electronic components, consumer electronics, industrial machinery and equipment, motor vehicles, chemicals, food and beverages, electricity generators, and iron and steel.

Singapore has a parliamentary republic with a president as chief of state and a prime minister as head of the government. It also has legislative and judicial branches.

The Monetary Authority of Singapore, a government agency, manages the Singapore dollar (SGD) using a managed float regime. The Monetary Authority seeks to reduce import inflation and to balance demand. There are no local or offshore restrictions, so documentation is not required to trade the currency. There is a liquid spot market and a limited forward foreign exchange market. Both the government and the corporate bond markets have grown in popularity in recent years. The most liquid currency pair involving the SGD is the USD/SGD.

South Africa (South African rand—ZAR)

South Africa has a two-tiered economy: one that rivals other developed countries and the other with only the most basic infrastructure. This results in uneven distribution of wealth and income, which was primarily caused by apartheid. The country's transition to a democratic, nonracial government began in early 1990.

Because of this two-tiered economy, South Africa is a productive and industrialized economy that exhibits many characteristics associated with developing countries, including a division of labor between formal and informal sectors, and uneven distribution of wealth and income. The formal sector, based on mining, manufacturing, services, and agriculture, is well developed.

The debate on the direction of economic policies to both achieve sustained economic growth and deal with the socioeconomic disparities created by apartheid continue to dominate the political climate.

The government of South Africa demonstrated its commitment to open markets, privatization, and a favorable investment climate, but its wealth remains very unequally distributed along racial lines. However, South Africa's budgetary reforms that aim at better reporting, auditing, and increased accountability, and the structural changes to its monetary policy framework, including inflation targeting, have created transparency and predictability and are widely acclaimed. Trade liberalization has been a primary goal since the early 1990s. South Africa has reduced its import-weighted average tariff rate from more than 20 percent in 1994 to 7 percent in 2002. South Africa is moving toward the acceptance of free-market principles.

WEALTH BUILDERS

You can find out more about the South African Reserve Bank at www.resbank. co.za/pages/default.aspx. Click on "Monetary Policy" to find economic news and more about South Africa's monetary policy.

South Africa's sophisticated financial structure with a large and active stock exchange ranks seventeenth in the world in terms of total market capitalization. The South African Reserve Bank (SARB) performs all central banking functions. The SARB is independent and operates similarly to Western central banks, influencing interest rates and controlling liquidity of its currency, the South African rand (ZAR), through its interest rates on funds provided to private sector banks.

The South African government has taken steps to gradually reduce remaining foreign exchange controls, which apply only to South African residents. Private citizens are now allowed a one-time investment of up to 2 million ZAR in offshore accounts. During 2007, the shareholding threshold (the percentage of shareholding that must be South African) for foreign direct investment outside Africa was lowered from

50 percent to 25 percent to enable South African companies to engage in strategic international partnerships.

South African companies involved in international trade can operate a single Customer Foreign Currency (CFC) account for all international transactions. Permission was also granted to the Johannesburg Securities Exchange (JSE) to establish a rand currency futures market, in order to deepen South Africa's financial markets and increase liquidity in the local foreign exchange market.

South Africa has rich mineral resources. It is the world's largest producer and exporter of platinum and also produces a significant amount of gold, manganese, chrome, vanadium, and titanium, as well as exporting coal.

Its GDP was US$287 billion in 2009. Trade exports totaled US$71.9 billion, including minerals and metals, agricultural products, and motor vehicles and parts. Imports totaled US$75.7 billion, including machinery, transport equipment, chemicals, petroleum products, textiles, and scientific instruments. Its trading partners include China, the United Kingdom, the United States, Germany, Italy, Japan, Saudi Arabia, Sub-Saharan Africa, and eastern Asia.

South Africa's foreign exchange and money markets are liquid, with active participation from onshore and offshore investors. The bond market also is well developed with a term structure of 30 years. There are restrictions for offshore investors, but these are rarely enforced.

Thailand (Thai baht—THB)

The Thai economy is export-dependent, with exports accounting for 60 percent of GDP in 2009, which was US$264 billion in 2009. Its government is a constitutional monarchy with a king as head of state and a prime minister as head of the government, which does include legislative and judicial branches.

Political uncertainty and the global financial crisis in 2008 weakened Thailand's economic growth by reducing domestic and international demand for both its goods and services (including tourism). But Thai banks had little exposure to toxic assets, so they experienced limited direct impact from the global financial crisis.

Even so, Thai economic growth slowed to 2.5 percent in 2008, with fourth-quarter growth dropping below zero. In 2009, the contraction continued. Over the first three quarters, GDP contracted by 5 percent year-on-year on average and hit bottom in the first quarter. To offset weak external demand and to shore up confidence, the Thai administration introduced two nonbudgetary stimulus packages worth $43.4 billion, focusing on key sectors such as mass transit and transportation, irrigation, education, public health, and energy. The Thai economy reversed to positive growth in the fourth quarter (5.9 percent year-on-year), improving the 2009 full-year average to minus 2.2 percent year-on-year.

In the first quarter of 2010, the Thai economy surged by 12 percent year-on-year, the highest quarterly growth since 1995. The uptick was mostly due to strong exports (up 32 percent) from continued global growth; however, growth continued through the second quarter of the year despite the political protests in Bangkok. The government projected that the Thai economy in 2010 would grow between 5 percent and 7 percent year-on-year.

The Royal Thai government welcomes foreign investment. Investors who are willing to meet certain requirements can apply for special investment privileges through the Board of Investment. U.S. investors may qualify for additional privileges under the Treaty of Amity and Economic Relations. To attract additional foreign investment, the government of Prime Minister Abhisit has promised to look for ways to expand investment opportunities, focusing more on green technology and manufacturers.

Roughly 40 percent of Thailand's labor force is employed in agriculture. Rice is the country's most important crop. Other agricultural commodities produced in significant amounts include fish and fishery products, tapioca, rubber, corn, and sugar. Thailand also exports processed foods such as canned tuna, pineapples, and frozen shrimp.

Thailand's diversified manufacturing sector contributed the greatest share of the country's growth in the past 15 years. Industries with rapid increases in production include computers and electronics, furniture, wood products, canned food, toys, plastic products, and vehicles and vehicle parts. High-technology products such as integrated circuits and parts, hard disk drives, electrical appliances, and vehicles are now leading Thailand's strong growth in exports. Thailand's relative shortage of engineers and skilled technical personnel may limit its future technological creativity and productivity. The government is pushing for an increase in the proportion that creative industries contribute to GDP from 12 percent to 20 percent by 2015.

The United States is Thailand's largest export market and third-largest supplier, after Japan and China. Thailand's major markets are North America, Japan, Europe, Singapore, Malaysia, Indonesia, the Philippines, and Vietnam. Growing export markets include China, Hong Kong, Australia, the Middle East, South Africa, and India.

Thailand's currency, the Thai baht (THB), is a freely floating currency with segregated domestic and offshore markets. Official documentation is required to trade the baht in the spot and forward markets. The most liquid currency pair including the THB is the USD/THB.

Taiwan (Taiwan dollar—TWD)

Taiwan transformed itself from an underdeveloped, agricultural island to an economic power that has been a leading producer of high-technology goods over the past 50 years. The transformation began in the 1960s, when foreign investment helped to introduce modern, labor-intensive technology to the island. Taiwan became a major exporter of labor-intensive products.

The focus shifted in the 1980s, when sophisticated, capital- and technology-intensive products for export began to dominate new investment, as well as a shift toward developing the service sector. These moves resulted in the appreciation of the Taiwan dollar (TWD) and rising labor costs. Movement toward high tech continued as increasing environmental consciousness in Taiwan caused many labor-intensive industries, such as shoe manufacturing, to move to China and Southeast Asia.

Taiwan, which was a recipient of U.S. aid in the 1950s and early 1960s, is now an aid donor and major foreign investor, especially in Asia. Taiwan holds the world's fourth-largest stock of foreign exchange reserves ($380.5 billion as of September 2010).

In 2001, Taiwan joined other regional economies in its first recession since 1949. From 2002 to 2007, Taiwan's economic growth ranged from 3.5 percent to 6.2 percent per year. With the global economic downturn, Taiwan's economy slumped into recession in the second half of 2008. Its real GDP, following growth of 5.7 percent in 2007, rose 0.73 percent in 2008 and contracted 1.91 percent in 2009. The economy began to recover in 2010 and the official forecast anticipated GDP to grow by 8.24 percent in 2010.

Foreign trade is the engine of Taiwan's rapid growth during the past 50 years, so its economy remains export-oriented. That means it's dependent on an open world trade regime and remains vulnerable to fluctuations in the world economy. Export composition changed from predominantly agricultural commodities to industrial goods (now 98 percent). The electronics sector is Taiwan's most important industrial export sector and is the largest recipient of U.S. investment.

Taiwan firms are the world's largest suppliers of computer monitors and leaders in PC manufacturing, although now much of the final assembly of these products occurs overseas, typically in China. Imports are dominated by raw materials and capital goods, which account for more than 90 percent of the total.

Taiwan imports coal, crude oil, and gas to meet most of its energy needs. In 2009, China (including Hong Kong) accounted for over 28.9 percent of Taiwan's total trade and 41.1 percent of Taiwan's exports. Japan was Taiwan's second-largest trading partner with 13.4 percent of total trade, including 20.8 percent of Taiwan's imports. The United States is now Taiwan's third-largest trade partner, taking 11.6 percent of Taiwan's exports and supplying 10.4 percent of its imports.

Taiwan's two-way trade with the United States amounted to $46.8 billion in 2009. Imports from the United States consist mostly of agricultural and industrial raw materials as well as machinery and equipment. Exports to the United States are mainly electronics and consumer goods.

Taiwan maintains trade offices in nearly 100 countries. It's a member of the Asian Development Bank, the WTO, and the Asia-Pacific Economic Cooperation (APEC) forum. Taiwan is also an observer at the Organization for Economic Cooperation and Development (OECD). In 2009, Taiwan acceded to the WTO Government Procurement Agreement. Taiwan continues to increase its economic importance in world trade and shows its desire to become further integrated into the global economy.

The Taiwan dollar was originally issued by the Bank of Taiwan, but since 2000 it has been issued by the Central Bank of the Republic of China. The exchange rate as compared to the United States dollar (USD) has varied from less than 10 TWD per 1 USD in the mid-1950s to more than 40 TWD per 1 USD in the 1960s and about 25 TWD per 1 USD around 1992. The exchange rate as of December 1, 2010 sits around 30.36 TWD per 1 USD.

The Least You Need to Know

- Be sure you understand the emerging country's political structure as well as its economic structure before trading the currency.

- Not all emerging country currencies are currently available to trade in spot forex. Some are available only as currency swaps or futures.

- Do your research to find out who in the emerging country manages its foreign exchange and how openly that foreign exchange is managed.
- Many emerging market currencies are not allowed to float, but instead are managed more carefully by government intervention, known as a managed float.

Trading Basics

Trading foreign exchange requires learning some new basic tools, as well as using some other basic tools in different ways. We discuss how you can use technical and fundamental analysis to improve your trading potential.

Then we give you the information you need to consider your overall investment plan and how forex fits into that plan. Once you've explored your investing goals, we talk about how to identify the trends and pick your trades.

And, of course, we can't forget the risks. We explore all the types of risks you must understand when you trade foreign currency.

Finally we explore your trading habits and the mindset you need to develop to make sure those habits improve your trading success. You want to avoid developing bad habits that can put your trading at greater risk.

Using Technical Analysis

In This Chapter

- Interpreting charts
- Noticing trends
- Finding support
- Recognizing patterns

Technical analysis looks at the historical price movements of a currency. Technical analysts believe all that needs to be known about a currency can be seen by tracking its historical price, and from that historical data you can spot trends and predict future price movements.

That's very different from fundamental analysts, who look at economic data and other key changes that impact a currency's value to try to predict future price movements. We explore the basics of fundamental analysis in Chapter 8.

In this chapter, we introduce you to the basic types of charts and price patterns, as well as how to recognize trends. You'll need to do a lot of practice and some more study to really be able to master technical analysis. In Chapter 10, you'll see how you can use the charts to spot key trends. In Appendix B, we recommend books that focus solely on how to use technical analysis in currency trading.

Understanding and Reading Charts

Charts used for technical analysis in forex trading are like a road map to the historical price movement of a currency. If you took statistics when you were in college, these charts would be known as times series plots.

The price scale is located on the *y*-axis (vertical axis), and the time scale is located on the *x*-axis (horizontal axis). Historical prices for the currency are plotted from left to right across the *x*-axis, with the most recent price shown on the point farthest to the right.

The following is a chart for the U.S. dollar from the charting package included with GFT's DealBook® 360. You can try out this package when you download the software at www.gftforex.com/idiotsguide.

You can pick the time periods you want shown on the chart. This chart was set up in one-hour price points, which means each point on the chart represents one hour of trading. Your charting software, which is included with most trading packages, can be set with many different time intervals.

When you set the time periods, it compresses the data. A *tick* chart would be the least compressed and a monthly chart would be the most compressed. For example, you may want to see the data intraday, daily, weekly, or monthly. The less compressed the data, the more detail you will see.

DEFINITION

A **tick** chart changes whenever the price changes, which often occurs in less than a minute.

When you pick an interval, the points shown on the table represent price points during that trading interval. Intervals included on most currency charting software include tick, 1-minute, 5-minute, 10-minute, 15-minute, 20-minute, 25-minute, 30-minute, 35-minute, 40-minute, 45-minute, 50-minute, 55-minute, 1-hour, 2-hour, 4-hour, daily, weekly, and monthly.

Currency traders usually concentrate on charts that show intraday data to forecast short-term price movements. Remember the shorter the time frame, the less compressed the data will be. That's when you can see the most detail.

But short-term charts can be volatile and contain a lot of noise, such as sudden price movements and wide high-low ranges, which can distort the overall picture. Try out different time periods using the practice software you downloaded from GFT to see how different the picture will be, depending on the time frame you choose. One-hour time periods like in the following figure are the most commonly used by forex traders to pick up intraday trends.

On this basic line chart, you can see the time points along the x-axis and the prices along the y-axis. Price points are plotted from left to right, with the last point on the right being the most recent price.

Line Chart

The previous figure shows the simplest type of chart called a line chart. This chart is created by plotting one price point of a currency over a specified period of time. The line is made by connecting the dots of each of these plotted points.

Bar Chart

The most popular charting method used by traders is the bar chart (see the following figure). This shows the highs and lows for the currency during the time period selected. Each bar on the chart represents one time period.

Bar charts display a large amount of data. The addition of the high-low range for each time period helps you to recognize the movement between the time periods and more easily pick up the trends. The little lines inside the high-low bar show the opening and closing price for the time period.

This is a one-hour bar chart for the U.S. dollar. Each bar on the chart shows the high and low trading price for each hour of trading on the chart. This chart was made using GFT's DealBook® 360 software.

Candlestick Chart

Candlestick charts, which originated in Japan over 300 years ago, are regaining popularity among traders. In these charts, instead of just bar lines representing the time periods, you'll see a little box form. The top of the box is the opening price for the period and the bottom of the box is the closing price on a down candle. The opposite is true for an up candle (see the following figure).

On most candlesticks, you'll also see a line above and below the box. The line above the box shows you the high during the period and the line below the box shows you the low.

Many traders find the candlestick charts easier to read, especially when you're trying to judge the relationship between the open and close price. Note that a lighter-colored box indicates when the close is higher than the open and a darker-colored box illustrates when the close is lower than the open. Officially, the box formed to show the open and close is called the *body*. The lines to show the high and low above and below the body are called *shadows*.

Candlestick charts show more detail using small boxes to indicate the open and close price for the period. The line above the box shows the high price for the period and the line below the box shows the low price. This chart of the U.S. dollar in one-hour intervals was made using GFT's DealBook® 360 software.

Spotting Trends

You're probably wondering what exactly you're trying to find in all these squiggly lines. You're looking for a trend or a specific pattern for the price movement to attempt to figure out where the price is going and pick good buy and sell points for the currency.

Basically, what you can see in these charts is a picture of the psychology of buyers and sellers by looking at the historical price movements. When prices are moving upward, buyers are more interested in buying and sellers are less interested in selling. Conversely, when prices are falling, sellers are more interested in selling to get out before they lose their gains, while buyers are more interested in buying with the hope they can get in at the right price to make a profit on the next upward movement.

Drawing Trend Lines

The first thing you must do is draw a trend line. All you need to do to draw the line is connect two high swings (or peaks) and two low swings (or troughs). We show you the connections in the trend lines that we've drawn in the figure that follows.

As you can see, when you draw a trend line, it's like connecting the dots. You find two points and draw a line between them. On the following chart, you can see an upward trend on the left and a downward trend on the right.

We then expand the chart to a daily chart, which shows the price movement between April and July in the next figure. You can see that the dollar has been on an upward trend since mid-May after seeing a major drop in value from its high on this chart in mid-April.

As a trader, what you want to do is predict which way the dollar is going based on the price history you see in the chart. You determine the trend, upward or downward, and develop a plan to figure out at what point you want to buy and at what point you want to sell the pair.

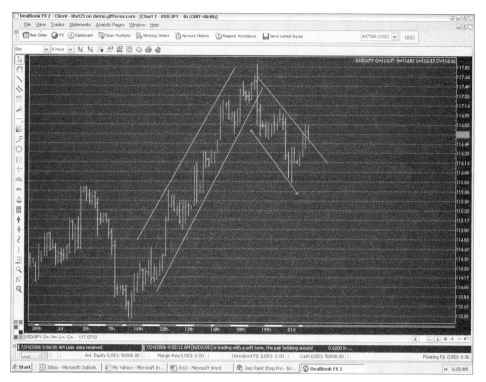

Trend lines drawn on a four-hour chart for the pair USD/JPY (U.S. dollar/ Japanese yen). The lines were drawn using the charting package included in the DealBook® 360 software, which can be downloaded when you open a free practice account at www.gftforex.com/idiotsguide.

Support and Resistance Levels

As you try to make the determination of when to buy or sell a currency, look for signs of support and resistance.

- Support is a price point below the current market price where buying occurs. It is always the lower trading range boundary. When the price drops to the support level, buyers start to buy because they think the price will rise from this level.

- Resistance is a price point above the current market price at which sellers decide to sell. It is always the upper trading range boundary. When a currency pair hits the resistance point, buyers are losing interest in buying because the price is too high and sellers must lower their price in order to find buyers.

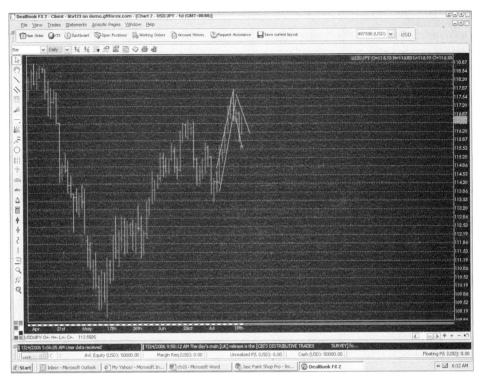

A daily chart of the USD/JPY pair showing the price trends between April and July 2006. Note the lines that were drawn using the four-hour chart to the right of the line appear tiny when you expand the chart for the longer time frame. The DealBook® 360 charting software was used to draw this chart.

When reading the chart shown in the previous figure, you can see a number of times when the resistance point was reached and the price for the pair started to head downward. The point to the farthest right shows that when the pair reached a high price of 117.86, it started to drop in value. At that point buyers resisted the price and sellers had to start dropping the price to sell.

You can see that, when the pair reached a low of 113.44 in early July, it proved to be a support point and buyers started buying to stop the price from falling any lower.

You determine these support and resistance points visually by reading your chart. But don't think of charting as an exact science. Although we talk about price points as specific numbers to help you learn to read these charts, it's better to think of zones of support and resistance, which translates into buying and selling ranges. Forex traders will see a lot of trading activity around these price points.

What you're trying to locate when you follow trend lines is a breakout point—that's the point when a currency pair drops out of the trading range and heads in the opposite direction. An easy breakout point to spot in the previous figure is in mid-May when the low hits 108.98 after a long drop from the high of 118.82 in mid-April. There you see how an upward trend breaks out and heads back up to 116.60 before it corrects and heads downward again.

Most forex traders use shorter-term charts to pick up intraday trading signals, but we used this longer-term chart because it is easier to discuss the trends on a less volatile chart. The ups and downs of the market are smoothed out when you look at a longer time frame, so it's easier to see the patterns when you have less detail. You get more detail and the most amount of noise from charts in the shorter time frames, such as 5- or 10-minute charts.

Types of Price Patterns

As you get more experienced working with charting, you'll see that markets follow certain patterns. These patterns become very well known to traders. We review the basics of some of the better-known patterns, but no pattern guarantees you a perfect reading of the future trend for the market.

A well-known phrase among traders is, "The trend is your friend until it ends." When you see a strong trend, try to research the fundamentals behind that trend (see Chapter 8) and you'll have an even better idea of what may be driving that trend and what the next moves for that currency pair might be.

Wedges

The wedge pattern forms when your trend lines look a lot like a symmetrical triangle. You'll see that the trend lines you draw have highs and lows that come together at an angle. Usually this angle points up or down. Then you'll see a trend, either up or down, form outside this pattern. An upward line would be a bullish trend indicating a good time to buy. A downward line would be a bearish trend indicating a good time to sell.

Channels

When you see your trend lines run almost flat with no indication of an upward or downward trend, then what you are seeing is called a channel. This type of pattern indicates that both buyers and sellers are undecided about the direction of the market. When you see this type of pattern, your best bet is to wait until you see signs of a breakout of the market in one direction or the other before picking your buy and sell points.

Gaps

A price gap usually forms when the opening price of the current bar is above or below the closing price of the bar for the previous period. You'll see gaps most often on daily charts, such as the one in the preceding figure. One noticeable gap falls between May 5 and May 8, when the close on May 5 is 112.56 and the open on May 8 is 112.02. Frequently a gap can be an indication of a more dramatic breakout. In this situation, the pair continued to fall in value.

Traders use many other types of patterns to determine their buying and selling strategies. We don't have the space in one brief chapter to teach you all the basics of technical trading, but we at least wanted to give you a taste of the possibilities.

The keys to successfully working with charts are dedication, focus, and consistency:

- **Dedication:** You must decide you want to take the time to learn the basics of chart analysis and then apply this knowledge on a regular basis so you can continue to develop your skills.

- **Focus:** Once you have a good idea of which types of charts and patterns you like to use, concentrate on learning how to use them very well. Use a demonstration account with your forex dealer to test out your charting skills for picking the best buy and sell points.

- **Consistency:** Be sure that you maintain your charts regularly. Preparing them daily even if you don't plan to trade that day will help you develop strong and consistent trading strategies. This daily routine will enable you to quickly recognize patterns and make good trading decisions.

The Least You Need to Know

- Learning to read and understand charts can give you a road map to the direction the currency market may be headed.
- Spotting trends helps you determine if the currency market is heading up or down.
- Recognizing patterns helps you spot possible breakouts and good trading opportunities.

Exploring Fundamental Analysis

In This Chapter

- Flows of currency
- Policies and rates
- Economic red flags

Fundamental analysts look at the underlying economic conditions and use that information to attempt to predict a currency's current and future valuation. This is very different from technical analysts, who believe all the information that is needed to predict the price of a currency and a directional trend is a database of historical prices.

It's important to understand both fundamental and technical analysis when making trading decisions. In this chapter, we focus on the key aspects of fundamental analysis that should be used by currency traders.

What Is Fundamental Analysis?

Fundamental analysts collect data about what is happening in the economy and try to understand how these economic conditions impact the current value of a particular currency, as well as predict what might happen to the currency's future value. Many things can impact the state of the economy, including monetary policy set by government agencies, capital and trade flows, production, and employment (or unemployment). Understanding these key economic indicators and how they impact the value of money is critical for currency traders.

Watching the Flows

Money flows in waves. Watching those flows can help you determine where your next best trading opportunity might occur. There are two types of money flows you need to watch—capital flows and trade flows. In Chapter 24, we discuss some key news sources for watching those flows.

Capital Flows

Capital flows gauge the amount of a currency that is bought or sold for the purpose of capital investment. When you read that a country has a positive capital flow balance, this means that foreign inflows of capital exceed the outflows of capital. The reverse is true if there is a negative flow balance.

There are two types of capital flows you need to watch—physical flows and portfolio flows. Physical flows involve investment activity that produces products and services, while portfolio flows involve the exchange of equities, such as stocks and bonds.

The physical flows currency traders want to watch include:

- **Foreign direct investment:** Whenever you read that a major corporation is building a plant in another country, it is considered a foreign direct investment. For example, if Coca-Cola builds a processing plant in China, that would be a foreign direct investment.

- **Joint ventures:** If you read about a U.S. corporation partnering with a corporation in another country, it is considered a joint venture. For example, if you read that Toyota and GM are working together to build a hybrid car, that would be a joint venture.

- **Third-party licensing agreements:** If you hear that a foreign company is buying the rights to patented products or business processes or the rights to use a brand name, this would fit in the category of third-party licensing agreements. For example, if you hear that Chinese computer makers have signed agreements to buy operating system software from Microsoft, that would be a third-party licensing agreement.

Any major deals affecting physical flows could move the currency market, because in order to carry out these agreements, currency would need to be bought and sold. Currently, most of the world's capital belongs to the United States, Europe, and

Japan, while most of the world's cheapest labor is found in China, India, and other emerging nations.

What we see today in the business world is many agreements that send capital to the emerging nations through various means of physical flows. By doing this, they take advantage of cheap labor markets. In fact, the *World Bank* found that net private capital flows to developing countries in 2009 was down to $462 billion from a record high of $643 billion in 2007, as the global economic downturn continued to be a drag on foreign investment.

DEFINITION

The **World Bank** provides financial and technical assistance to developing countries around the world. The bank is owned by 184 member countries and works to reduce global poverty and improve the living standards of people in developing countries. The bank provides low-interest loans, as well as interest-free credit and grants to developing countries for education, health, infrastructure, communications, and other purposes.

Growth in the developing nations is also much stronger than that of the developed nations. Afghanistan and China lead the pack. In 2009, Afghanistan's economy grew 22.5 percent and China's economy grew by 9.1 percent. Growth for the other emerging nations averaged 5.2 percent, while growth in the developed countries averaged 2.5 percent, down from 4.3 percent in 2005.

Money has been moving from developed to emerging nations for years, so why do we seem to feel the economic pain in the United States more than we have in past years? One major factor that explains this new pain is the speed at which capital can flow. Today, massive amounts of capital can move quickly around the world through electronic transmission many times in a matter of seconds. In addition, the costs of moving this capital from one country to another dropped dramatically over the past 20 years, as barriers to currency trading were lifted (see Chapter 2 for more information about this change).

Unfortunately for U.S. workers, all this means that the corporations that own all this capital have a wide variety of high-return investments for their money. As corporations find better investments outside the country, U.S. workers get downsized, yet U.S. corporations' profits continue to rise dramatically.

Currency traders can make up for some of these lost wages by taking advantage of the money to be made as capital moves around the world. For example, when a U.S.

corporation invests in a business in China, that company must sell dollars and buy Chinese yuan. The fact that many U.S. corporations are currently investing in China does not have a big impact on the value of the dollar because the Chinese yuan is pegged to the dollar, but that could change in the future if the yuan is allowed to flow freely. Generally, when large amounts of a currency are sold, the currency will drop in value.

In addition to physical flows, you should also watch portfolio flows. These involve the buying and selling of stocks (equity market) and bonds (fixed-income market).

When a stock market rallies in any part of the world, this becomes an investment opportunity for investors in any other part of the world, thanks to the speed at which capital can flow. Geographic location is no longer a barrier for stock investors. Why does this matter to currency traders? In order for investors to buy stocks in another country, they must first buy that country's currency. When a currency is in demand for stock investment, then the value of that currency will rise.

CURRENCY COIN

Capital has flowed around the world since the days of Marco Polo, if not before. If you watched it move in Polo's time, it would look like it was in slow motion. At first it moved very slowly as raw materials were traded, then it progressed to finished products. Next came financial capital, which moved slowly at first because barriers to trading currency were put in place by countries seeking to protect the value of their currency. Today those barriers are gone for the major currencies, allowing capital to flow much more quickly around the world, and increasing opportunities to make money in foreign currency trading.

If a stock market is headed into a free fall, people will want to get out of that market. That means that once they sell their stock in that country, they will also want to sell that country's currency, driving the value of the currency down as well. Major stock market moves can serve as either great opportunities to make money or as times of increased risk in foreign currency trading.

Some currency traders watch key global stock indexes to pick their trading opportunities, including:

- **Dow Jones Industrial Index (DOW):** The DOW is the most widely used indicator of the overall condition of the stock market, but it only tracks 30 actively traded blue-chip stocks. The stocks tracked are picked by the editors of *The Wall Street Journal.* The DOW index was founded in 1896 by Charles Dow.

- **S&P 500:** The S&P 500 provides a broader picture of the U.S. stock market. It tracks a basket of 500 stocks, which actually reflects over 70 percent of the movement of the U.S. stock market. Companies are picked for the index based on their market size, liquidity, and industrial sector. The index was first created in 1957 by Standard & Poor's, primarily known for its credit-rating services.

- **Nasdaq Composite:** The Nasdaq Composite Index tracks primarily technology stocks, so it is not a good indicator of the broader stock market, but is a good indicator of what is happening in growth stocks. The index dates back to 1971, when the Nasdaq stock exchange was first created.

- **Nikkei Index:** The Nikkei index is the most respected index of Japanese stocks. The index is calculated using Japan's top 225 blue-chip companies on the Tokyo Stock Exchange. Many think of the Nikkei as the equivalent of the DOW index in the United States. It was even named the Nikkei Dow Jones Stock Average from 1975 to 1985. The index was started in 1950 by Japan's leading business newspaper, *The Nikkei*.

- **DAX 100:** The DAX 100 is an index of the 100 most heavily traded stocks in the German stock market.

- **FTSE 100:** This stock index tracks the top 100 stocks on the London Stock Exchange and is similar to the S&P 500. The index is co-owned by the *Financial Times* daily newspaper of London and the London Stock Exchange.

As a currency trader, if you see major movement in a stock market index, look for trading opportunities for the currencies impacted by the moves.

Fixed-income investments or bonds can also be attractive to investors because they offer more safety and a constant flow of income from the interest paid on them. In order to buy bonds in a foreign country, one must first buy the currency; so bond purchases can also impact the value of a currency. Watch the yields on foreign bonds compared to U.S. bonds. When interest rates are higher outside the United States, you will see more investors buying foreign bonds, which means they likely are buying the currency with the most attractive bond interest rates and possibly selling U.S. dollars to do so.

Trade Flows

Trade flows are another key indicator of where money is going. The best indicator for watching trade flows is a country's net trade balance. Countries that are net trade exporters—meaning they export more goods and services than they import—will carry a net trade surplus. Countries with a net trade surplus are more likely to see their currencies rise in value.

Conversely, countries that have a trade deficit, meaning they import more goods and services than they export, could end up with a loss in the value of their currency. As the euro builds as an international currency, the value of the U.S. dollar could be more severely impacted by the United States' propensity to run huge trade deficits. When the U.S. government's rising debt levels are added to this, it could spell disaster for the value of the U.S. dollar.

CAPITAL CAUTIONS

What will these rising trade deficits and debt levels mean for those of us who live in the United States? It will cost more for us to buy foreign goods and services as the value of the dollar weakens.

Monetary Policy and Interest Rates

Countries can dramatically alter economic activity within their borders by making changes to monetary policy. Most governments can control two key economic policies: interest rates and tax rates.

In the United States, interest rate policy is set by the U.S. Federal Reserve Bank (the Fed), an independent entity under the aegis of the U.S. Congress. Although the president appoints the Federal Reserve chairman as well as the other members of the Fed's board of governors, he or she cannot control the decisions these appointees make. The Fed protects its independence fiercely, but it must report its activities periodically to Congress.

Through its reports to Congress and other key speeches, the Fed's chairman can quickly impact the global markets if he or she announces a major change in the Fed's monetary policy. For example, if the chairman announces an unexpected increase or decrease in interest rates, it will send shock waves through the stock market. Of course, that will in turn result in the buying and selling of currency, creating foreign currency trading opportunities.

A lowering of interest rates can initially stimulate a country's economic conditions, but if money flows too freely, inflation can set in. If a currency loses its value during an inflationary period, it will be punished in the currency markets.

An increase in interest rates tends to attract new capital flows and pushes up the value of a currency for at least the short term, but as other countries raise their interest rates, the benefit of the rate increase will be reduced.

Whenever a country's central bank changes interest rates, you can guarantee the markets will react. As you pick the currencies you plan to trade, don't forget to keep a close watch on any interest rate changes.

Major changes in tax policy can also impact the value of a country's currency. Generally, capitalists prefer tax cuts and reward a country that cuts taxes with an increase in its currency's value. But if those cuts create a major debt increase, it could result in a long-term loss of a currency's value as currency traders switch to safer countries where debt is not as high.

Economic Indicators

Economic indicators provide a snapshot of key parts of a country's economy. You can read stories almost every day about how well a country is doing based on some economic indicator. Popular indicators track employment, money supply, interest rates, housing starts, housing sales, production levels, purchasing statistics, consumer confidence, and many factors that impact the health of a country's economy.

All these indicators are important, but we're going to focus on just a few of the most critical ones. You could go crazy trying to keep your eye on all the indicators and what they mean. We've picked four key types of economic reports for you to watch: Gross Domestic Product (GDP), employment statistics, the Fed's Beige Book, and trade balance statistics.

Gross Domestic Product

The GDP is the total value of all final goods and services produced within a country's borders each year. This indicator measures the national income and output for a country.

Each quarter the government releases the percentage of growth in the GDP. Most industrial nations, such as the United States, Japan, and European countries, experience a GDP growth of between 3 and 5 percent in good economic times. If growth falls below this level, it's usually a sign of trouble and an indication that the country's economy may be stalling—or worse, heading into a recession. If growth climbs above that window, it could also be a sign of trouble: inflation. In extreme situations, the run-up could lead to a crash, like we saw during the late 1990s and early 2000s.

Developing countries can grow at a faster pace, but that can also lead to trouble. For example, China has been growing at a pace of 8 to 9 percent per year since 2003. However, too much growth and too much money can drive a country toward a severe economic downturn. When a country doesn't act quickly to stem its overheated growth, it can result in a crisis. Thailand experienced this with a major loss of its currency's value in the 1990s. Its crash led to currency speculation, failing banks, and falling stock prices. The Philippines, Indonesia, and Korea have faced similar problems.

If you want to find out if there are signs of trouble in a developing country, one good source of information is the World Bank, which regularly reports on economic indicators in the developing world. You can read its reports at www.worldbank.org.

Employment

Employment reports can be an important indicator of a country's economic health. When the economy is strong, jobs are created, but as the economy contracts, jobs are lost. If the economy is going too strongly and too many jobs are created, then wages begin to rise as companies compete for the best workers. Rising wages can lead to inflation, which will likely result in a country's central bank raising interest rates to cool the economy. People will then buy fewer goods as interest rates rise, which means less production is needed. When less production is needed, jobs get cut, leading to a weaker economy.

The country's central bank will stimulate the economy by lowering interest rates and starting the entire cycle yet again. Watching employment reports can help you determine where in this cycle a country's economy stands.

When the employment report is released, you should watch for three key factors:

- **Payroll:** This measures the change in the number of workers in a given month. In the United States, this report's estimates are based on a survey of larger businesses and government entities. It's important to compare this number to a monthly moving average for six or nine months to get a good idea of the trend for payrolls and employment. Expanding payrolls means the country's economy is growing. Contracting payrolls means the economy is heading for a slowdown.

- **Unemployment rate:** This measures the percentage of the civilian labor force actively looking for a job but not able to find one. This number can be skewed, especially during a weak economy—as workers get discouraged looking for work, they tend to drop off the unemployment lists. During particularly long periods of unemployment, the number of unemployed can be higher than shown in this rate.

- **Average hourly earnings growth:** This number shows the growth rate of average hourly wages each month. This can be a good way to keep your eye on the potential for inflation. As wages increase, the possibility of inflation also increases.

Conversely, a high unemployment number can be good news and stimulate the economy. That's because high unemployment usually results in a lowering of interest rates, which can increase spending. When unemployment numbers improve and jobs are created, stock markets will likely fall because they are expecting the Fed to raise interest rates to slow things down again.

Beige Book

One of the easiest ways to get a good overview of what is happening throughout the U.S. economy is to read the Fed's Beige Book, which is officially known as the Summary of Commentary on Current Economic Conditions. This book is published eight times a year by the Federal Reserve Bank and includes anecdotal information on economic and business conditions in each of the Fed's districts.

Information for the book is collected by bank staff through interviews with key business leaders, economists, market experts, and other sources from within each of the bank's 12 districts. This book is like the Bible to the Federal Reserve Board of Governors. If the Beige Book shows warning signs of inflation, recession, or high unemployment, you are more likely to see the Fed act and change interest rates.

WEALTH BUILDERS

You can read the Beige Book online at the Fed's website. You can find a calendar for release dates of the book and links to each book at www.federalreserve.gov/ FOMC/BeigeBook. From this page, you can also research economic conditions and access Fed Beige Books dating back as far as 1970. If you want to find all the key economic indicators in one place, the Fed's Fred (Federal Reserve Economic Data) database is an excellent resource. You can access this online at research. stlouisfed.org/fred2.

Trade Balance

The most critical data you need to find out about the current and potential future status of a country's currency is its trade balance. Nations that regularly run a trade deficit can expect to see the value of their currency fall. As a nation's currency flows overseas, it gets converted.

The two key indicators of trade balance to watch are balance of payments and balance of trade. Balance of payments measures the financial capital that flows from one nation to another. If more money flows in than out, a country has a positive balance of payments. Conversely, if more money flows out than in, a country has a negative balance of payments.

Balance of trade calculates the sum of money in a specific country's economy by the selling exports minus the cost of buying imports. Transactions involving foreign investment in a country are also figured into this equation. A positive trade balance is called a trade surplus. A negative trade balance is called a trade deficit.

The more a nation's currency is sold rather than bought, the greater the risk that the demand for that currency will fall. When demand falls, prices drop. The value of the U.S. dollar continues to drop as its trade deficits grow and debt levels increase. As the dollar loses its popularity, expect to see increases in the value of the euro and Japanese yen, which hit a 15-year high in 2010. At the time this edition was written, it was too soon after the major earthquake and tsunami to know the full impacts of these events on the trade balance.

As a trader, you should make use of both fundamental and technical analysis. Technical analysis provides a map for analyzing a currency's price action and helps you recognize trends in those prices. Fundamental analysis helps you to determine what is actually happening in the market to explain the trends you see in your technical analysis. Using both types of analysis will help you make better trading decisions.

The Least You Need to Know

- Capital flows help you determine where the money is going and which currencies may be impacted by that movement.
- Following changes in monetary policy and interest rates enables you to recognize potential shifts in a currency's value.
- Economic indicators help you recognize economic trends, as well as the potential for a change in monetary policy.

Forex and Your Overall Investing Plan

In This Chapter

- Trading levels
- Researching the market
- Gauging your time
- Testing your risk tolerance

When you decide to trade forex, you're trading with the big boys—central banks, international financial institutions, and major corporations. Your trades will comprise just a tiny portion of the trillions of dollars traded each year.

In this chapter, we'll look at the issues you must consider before deciding to risk your money on foreign currency trading. We'll also discuss how forex should fit into your long-term investment portfolio.

How Much Should You Trade?

You do have the potential to make a positive impact on your personal portfolio if you learn to trade forex successfully. But you must carefully determine how much money you can put at risk and what part of your portfolio you want to risk trading foreign currency.

Forex is a highly volatile market. You can lose all your money in a forex account in a matter of minutes if the market turns dramatically against you, so you should never put more than 5 percent of your portfolio at risk for forex trading at any one time.

CAPITAL CAUTIONS

Unexpected storms or earthquakes can also dramatically impact the money markets quickly. If you are trading currency in a region that was hit, be sure to carefully watch what happens to each of your currency pairs.

You need to ask yourself whether trading forex fits your plans for your long-term portfolio-management strategies. If you're not sure, think about your time horizon for needing the money. Also, remember that forex is very risky and should only be a small part of that long-term portfolio—no more than five percent. If you think you're going to need the money in the next five years, you're putting a lot at risk. What happens if you lose that money? Will you be able to replace the lost funds in time for when you need them?

Generally, when determining how you should allocate your funds in a long-term portfolio, think about how soon you will need the funds. If you'll definitely need them in the next one to two years, you should put them in a safe place, such as a savings bank, certificate of deposit, or money market.

You can place funds you'll need in three to five years in something a bit more risky like bonds. Bonds may sound safe, but when the housing bubble burst and the market crashed in 2008, even bonds lost principal value.

Currency markets were turbulent in 2008 as well. The U.S. dollar soured against the euro and more exotic currencies lost favor. Panicked traders jumped into the dollar. These gains receded as a recession in the U.S. economy put added pressure on the dollar. So if you were a trader betting against the dollar and in favor of the euro in 2008, you could have lost everything quickly. As the U.S. economy took a nosedive, the Japanese yen appreciated to a 13-year high against the dollar. The yen appreciated due to the poor economic conditions in the United States, along with a record low U.S. interest rate that was still in place at the beginning of 2011.

The market conditions that rocked the currency markets as well as the stock and bond markets happened over a matter of days, starting with the fall of Lehman Brothers. No one planning a long-term portfolio could have expected such a swift turn. That's why most financial planners recommend that money you'll need in the next two years be kept safely in a cash account such as a savings account or certificate of deposit.

Money invested in bonds or stocks can be left in those assets to gradually regain their value over a number of years. As long as you're not forced to sell them because you need the funds, you have time for the markets to recover. With forex you might not be so lucky when there is a crash involving a currency you're trading. All your funds could be lost in a matter of minutes. So the money you put into forex must be money you can afford to lose.

CAPITAL CAUTIONS

Think about how long it would take you to replace any funds lost that you want to trade with forex. If it will take you 10 years, then that's your time horizon. Don't trade any money with forex that you will need in the next 10 years.

You should carefully manage even the money you are trading in forex, so you know you'll have money to trade the next day. We'll talk more about money management strategies in Chapter 12.

Get to Know the Market

Once you determine that you do have money to risk trading forex, ask yourself: *Do I understand the foreign currency exchange market fully, as well as the risks I'll be taking?*

If the answer is no, take the time to learn more about the forex market. As you learn more, determine which countries interest you most and pick the currencies you may want to trade.

Remember, as a forex trader you'll need to watch the political, economic, and other news that can impact the currency for each country that you trade. In Chapter 7, we talk about the basics you need to learn to develop charts so you can perform technical analysis for your trades. Then in Chapter 10 we talk about how you can use these charts to identify trading trends and pick your trades.

But before you can even start using the technical analysis, you need to pick the currencies you want to trade. You also need to know what can impact those currencies. In Chapter 8, we introduced you to fundamental analysis, which helps you to understand the economic, political, and other factors that can drive a currency up or down.

As you do your research, you'll find that certain countries and certain currency pairs interest you the most. Learn as much as you can about the currency pairs you think you might want to trade before you try to put together trading strategies. Also use the research time to find the best sources of information for the countries and currencies you'll be trading, so you can keep up-to-date on critical political, economic, or other changes that could impact the volatility of your trades.

Don't even think about trading unless you know the economic calendar for the currency pairs you'll be trading. For example, you need to know when the key economic reports are issued, such as employment reports issued by the government or decisions about interest rate changes issued by the central bank. In Chapter 5, we discuss the key economic reports you should follow for each of the developed country currencies. Put these key dates on your calendar and be ready to manage your trades closely on the days before and after a key economic report.

WEALTH BUILDERS

If you decide to trade currency pairs that include the U.S. dollar, one great place to find all the key economic indicators is the Fed's Fred (Federal Reserve Economic Data) database. You can access this online at research.stlouisfed.org/fred2.

If you decide to consider trading the even riskier currencies of the developing countries in Chapter 6, you'll need to find and follow similar economic reports.

Are You a Fundamental or Technical Trader?

Forex traders can be fundamental traders, technical traders, or they can use both styles. As you learn more about forex, you'll need to decide what's important to help you make your trading decisions.

Fundamental traders prefer to trade based on news and other financial and political data. Technical traders instead look to technical analysis tools (discussed in Chapters 7 and 10) to identify trends. As you learn more about forex trading, you may find you prefer one or the other or decide you'd like to use a combination of the two.

No matter what you use to research your trades and develop your trading strategies, you should learn how to use both technical and fundamental tools to help you find your best trading options.

CAPITAL CAUTIONS

Always use all the tools you have at your disposal to check the financial, economic, and market conditions before you place a trade. Never trade blindly without doing your research, even if you hear game-changing news that makes you want to jump into a trade.

Develop your trading plan based on what you've learned from your research. If the news changes what you anticipated with your trading plan, then get out of the trade. Don't try to ride out the trade until the news goes the way you expected. We talk more about managing your trades in Chapter 15.

Do You Have the Time to Trade?

Even if you think forex trading is a good move for your long-term portfolio, ask yourself whether you have the time to research this market daily and make sound forex trading decisions.

Although trades can be set up in seconds, most forex traders spend hours each day researching the political, economic, and weather conditions and other factors that might impact the currencies for the countries they plan to trade or the currencies in which they still have an *open trade*. Forex is a 24-hour market, so news that could impact the currencies you're trading can quickly turn what looked like a good trade into a bad one.

DEFINITION

An **open trade** is a trade that you've entered and remains open, exposed to the potential gains or risks of the market. You can avoid or reduce risks of an open trade by always setting a proper stop-loss or trailing stop. We talk more about how to place orders in Chapter 15.

Expect to spend at least three to four hours a day researching and executing your trades. Then you'll need to keep an eye out for game-changing news that might impact any trades you still have open. If you hear news that changes the game plan you had in mind, for example a major storm wipes out manufacturing plants in one country pair that you are trading, be ready to make some quick changes to your forex trades.

If you're not ready to risk the funds, take the time to learn more about the countries and currencies you want to trade, or put in the time to manage your trades, then you are not ready for forex trading. But if all this sounds good to you, then think of forex money management as you would if you were managing any other business. We talk more about setting up your forex trading as a business in Chapter 23.

Again, forex trading is a 24-hour business. Dramatic moves can occur at any time, depending on world conditions. For example, when Egypt and Jordan faced revolutionary protests within their borders, the risks for turmoil in the Middle East changed overnight. No one expected the protests and many feared the protests could change the political make-up of the Middle East. Oil prices skyrocketed and the money markets became more volatile within hours of the start of the protests.

Your life can change quickly if you choose to become a forex trader. You have to start thinking about how any world news can impact the trades you have on the table. Even though you may not need the money you put in forex trading for 10 years or more, whether or not you'll even have that money tomorrow could depend upon what happens over the span of a few minutes or a few hours.

Can You Handle the Risk?

So the final question you must ask yourself before deciding to add forex as one part of your overall investing strategy is whether you can tolerate the risk. We talk more about the types of risks you'll face in Chapter 11.

Does putting money at risk for the potential of great reward excite you? Can you calmly handle the quick decision making that might be necessary? Or would that level of risk make you sick?

A good way to test that out before you put any of your money at risk is to try it with play money. Most of the forex dealers allow you to open practice accounts where you can try out your trading strategies and get a feel for what it's like to trade forex.

 WEALTH BUILDERS

You can practice trading forex to see if it's for you by getting a free practice account at GFT (www.gftforex.com/Practice-Account/Default.aspx). Even if you're certain forex is for you, it's good to use a practice account to hone your strategies before you put your own money at risk.

A practice account gives you the opportunity to trade in real market conditions, but it's risk-free. You may lose your practice money, but none of your real money is at risk. If you have a trading plan in mind, you can test it out by taking it for a test drive. If it fails, you can try again with a new plan. Continue to hone your skills with a practice account until you feel comfortable not only with the *trading platform* but also with the currency pairs you plan to use.

DEFINITION

Trading platforms are software programs through which investors and traders can open, close, and manage their forex trades. Forex brokers offer trading platforms for free or at a discount in exchange for maintaining a funded account or promising to make a specified number of trades per month.

Even when you use a practice account, you still won't get the full impact of what it's like to have your own money on the table. But if you find that you get nervous even trading with a practice account, you probably aren't ready for forex trading.

Keep It Small

If, after doing all the research, you decide that you do want to make forex a part of your long-term investment portfolio, start small and keep it small.

You may find that you've developed a great strategy for forex trading and you're doing well with your trades, but keep an eye on the proportion of forex to your overall portfolio. The general rule of thumb is that it should not be more than 5 percent of your overall portfolio, but if you do well you may find that forex trading creeps up to 10 percent or more.

Don't get overly confident: invest some of those gains in other types of investments, whether stocks, mutual funds, commodities, or whatever else you choose. Try to keep your forex exposure small so you will have the money when you need it in the future. Also by keeping just 5 percent in your portfolio in forex, you'll always have other money you can tap if you do take a major loss but want to continue to trade.

Just because you're doing well at one point, there are no guarantees and the market winds can shift quickly against you. So don't put too many eggs in the forex basket at one time.

The Least You Need to Know

- Before you start trading, determine what percentage of your investment portfolio you can afford to use for forex trading.
- Take the time to research the forex market. Get to know the countries and the currencies you plan to trade.

- Determine whether you will be a fundamental or technical trader or both. Learn the key skills of both even if you lean toward one type or the other.
- Keep the portion of your portfolio set aside for forex trading small. Even if you're successful, don't let it grow too large.

Identifying the Trends and Your Trades

Chapter 10

In This Chapter

- Testing the relative strength
- Finding double tops and double bottoms
- Anticipating market reversals
- Retracements by the numbers

Forex trading can be thrilling, surprising, and often frightening. If you get into the market without a solid plan and a sound foundation in technical and fundamental analysis, it's like getting on a roller coaster without a safety harness. Any major change in direction of the pair you're trading and you'll be tossed right out of the market (or off the roller coaster).

Luckily, with forex trading there are safety harnesses you can put on, because the forex market has clear trends that can be identified. Although the market does have periods of increased volatility and unpredictable activity, there are a number of tools and techniques that you can use to forecast potential outcomes and help manage risk in most market conditions.

In this chapter, we take a closer look at four top ways to identify the trends and plan your trades. You'll get the tools to spot potential forex market tops and bottoms, which can help you determine when to enter and exit the market.

RSI Roller Coaster Strategy

One of author Gary Tilkin's favorite trend spotters is the RSI Roller Coaster Strategy, which helps him to determine the potential change in a trend on a shorter time frame. RSI stands for *Relative Strength Index,* which compares the recent gains to recent losses and attempts to determine when the market for a particular pair may be overbought or oversold.

DEFINITION

The **Relative Strength Index** compares recent gains to recent losses. The Index can be used to determine when the market for a particular pair may be overbought or oversold.

You can calculate the RSI using this formula:

RSI = 100 − 100 ÷ (1 + RS)

In this formula, RS is calculated by dividing the average number of days the pair closed up by the average number of days the pair closed down. So suppose you looked at the market closes for 100 days, and on 80 days the market closed up and on 20 days the market closed down. To find the RS, divide 80 by 20 to get an RS of 4. Then you would plug the RS into the RSI formula:

RSI = 100 − 100 ÷ (1 = 4) = 100 − 100 ÷ 5 = 100 − 20 = 80.

An RSI of 80 would be a an indication that the market is overbought. Typically when the RSI rises above 70, the market is overbought. That indicates that you likely want to take a short (sell) position in your holdings. When you get an RSI below 30, that's an indication that the market is oversold and likely presents a buying opportunity.

Looking at this trend indicator, there are some key points to remember when you want to go long—buy a particular pair—and when you want to go short—sell a particular pair.

Going Long—Buy

When you are thinking of taking a long position in a forex pair:

- Be certain your RSI reading is less than 30.

- Look for an up-candle to form and close sending an RSI reading to greater than 30.

- Consider going long (buying) at the market price on the open of the next candle.

- Set profit targets and risk management levels based on your individual strategy and tolerance for risk. We talk more about managing risks in Chapter 11.

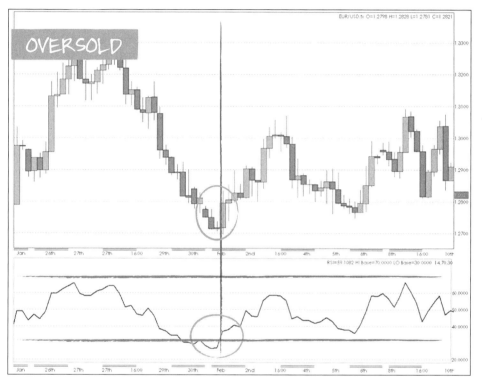

The EUR/USD four-hour chart above shows the RSI Roller Coaster in action.

The pair in the preceding figure ranges with no clear trend over the course of a couple of days. The RSI reading finally breaks below the 30 level after a temporary decline. The RSI Roller Coaster strategy then sets up as the candle sends the RSI back above 30 and triggers a potential buy signal.

Going Short—Sell

When you are thinking of taking a short position (sell) in a forex pair (for more information about reading candlestick charts review Chapter 7):

- Be certain the RSI reading is above 70.
- Look for a down-candle to form and close pushing an RSI reading to less than 70.

- Consider going short at the market price on the open of the next candle.

- Set profit targets and risk management levels based on your individual trading strategy and tolerance for risk.

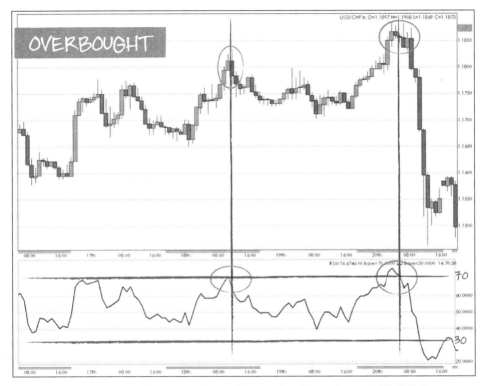

Shorter-term time frames tend to produce an abundance of potential RSI Roller Coaster formations.

On the one-hour chart shown here, the USD/CHF developed two setups within 24 hours. During the first formation, the RSI briefly spiked through an overbought region, breaking above 70. However, a down candle pushed it below 70, offering an opportunity to sell. Later a break to a fresh high took the RSI back into the overbought zone.

The RSI Roller Coaster strategy generally is a low-probability/high-reward setup. You might experience some mediocre or even negative rides, while you wait for a single great one. To find that great one, you will need to trade as often as your risk-management strategy will allow to catch that one potential big win.

Capital management is key when using the RSI Roller Coaster strategy. You must plan on small, highly defined risks while waiting patiently for that potential big-profit trade. Half the value of this strategy is in the rules themselves; the other half requires strict money management.

WEALTH BUILDERS

You don't have to calculate the RSI yourself on all trades. GFT's DealBook® 360 includes an RSI Indicator. You can take it for a test drive with a free practice account at www.gftforex.com/idiotsguide.

Locating Double Tops and Double Bottoms

You can also find trading opportunities by watching price trends. Two of the easiest purely chart-based ways to spot a potential trend reversal is looking for *double tops* and *double bottoms*.

DEFINITION

A **double top** is a sharp rise in price followed by a retracement (reversal in the movement of the stock's price) and another sharp rally to the previous levels, finally concluding the run with another drop. It looks like an *M* on the chart.

A **double bottom** is the opposite of a double top, with a drop and then a sharp rise. Then another sharp drop and rise. This will resemble a letter *W* on the chart.

The forex market is known for both its trending up and trending down, often in quick succession. So what comes down will probably go up and vice versa. Often this can be in a dramatic fashion, so be ready for quick turns.

After a prolonged decline to multiyear lows, the pair finally emerged to form the first bottom at around 87.00. A rapid retracement was followed quickly by a retest of previous lows, creating a second bottom. The pair then consolidated for a week before changing trend. Finally, the pattern and change in trend were confirmed after the pair breached the retracement level around 94.

Just like a roller coaster, forex markets can surprise you with unexpected twists, turns, or loops. Many market movements can look like a double top or double bottom formation. Just because a market tests the same high or low on two separate occasions does not automatically mean you are seeing a viable double top or double bottom pattern. These patterns are not complete until the market breaches the previous level of retracement.

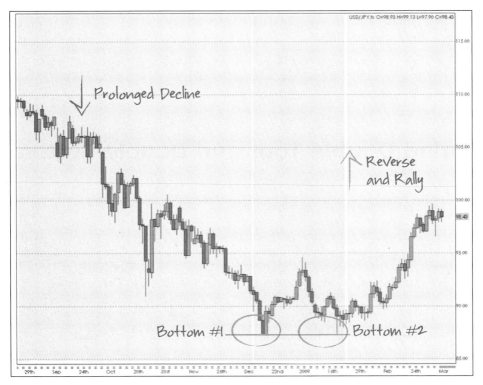

The chart above shows a double bottom formation for the pair USD/JPY.

For example, triple top and triple bottom formations can also be a sign of a strong potential reversal pattern. Just like a double top or double bottom, a triple top or triple bottom will test the support or resistance two times. However, when there is a double top or double bottom, you will then see a move through the previous retracement. A triple top or triple bottom tests the support or resistance line one more time.

One of the most common mistakes traders make when trying to spot double tops and double bottoms is to identify a potential double top or double bottom when in actuality a triple top or triple bottom will eventually form. If you make that mistake, you can enter the market too early. Use a practice account to learn how to identify the tops and bottoms. When you feel confident you can spot the trends, it's time to use your real money.

Spotting Market Reversals with Bollinger Bands

Another useful tool for identifying potential tops and bottoms are Bollinger Bands. This technical analysis tool consists of a center line enveloped by an upper and lower band. The distance between the upper and lower bands is determined by market volatility. Typically your bands will be wider as the market becomes more volatile. Most charting tools enable you to draw Bollinger Bands.

Generally, a move through either the upper or lower band indicates that the pair is either overbought or oversold. When this happens the probability of a turn increases.

In the USD/CAD example above, a clear puncture of the upper band occurs along with a triple top pattern. The technical pattern provides a confirmation, increasing the odds of a top. Following the spike, the pair falls nearly 1,200 pips. For more information on pips, see Chapter 11.

Depending on the Numbers: Fibonacci Retracements

You can't expect any of these indicators to be correct 100 percent of the time, so it's important to confirm or enhance your chart analysis with other types of analysis, such as Fibonacci retracements.

First let's take a step back in history to learn more about *Fibonacci numbers.* These sequences and ratios are the result of work done by a famous Italian mathematician named Leonardo Pisano (his nickname was Fibonacci, which is pronounced fee-bo-NOTCH-ee, taken from his father's name meaning "Son of (a) Bonacci").

 DEFINITION

Fibonacci numbers were developed by the Italian mathematician Leonardo Pisano. He showed there was a mathematical order for everything in nature. Traders use his ratios to spot entry and exit points for trades.

Basically, his work showed that a mathematical "order" is found again and again in nature, which describes everything from ocean waves to spider webs to snail shells. He determined the frequency of these mathematical relationships was observed too often to be considered random. Pisano determined there was some significance in these sequences and ratios and called them Fibonacci numbers.

You're probably asking yourself: *what does the mathematical relationship of a snail shell have to do with making money in the forex market?* It's a fair question and luckily you don't have to delve deeply into the study of Fibonacci numbers to understand the relationship.

Fibonacci numbers are actually useful to recognize retracements and extensions. Even if you feel these numbers can't possibly be relevant to forex traders, stay tuned. You will find that Fibonacci analysis actually works!

Forex traders only need to know two facts to understand the value of Fibonacci analysis:

1. Fibonacci determined there were certain ratios found everywhere in nature—and that these ratios were "significant."

2. Some forex traders know and consider Fibonacci ratios when planning their entry and exit points.

CURRENCY COIN

You don't need to study Fibonacci Numbers to learn how to use them as a forex trader, but if you want to learn about them you can do so at Math World (mathworld.wolfram.com/FibonacciNumber.html).

Some argue that Fibonacci ratios only appear to be significant in the forex market because everyone pays attention to them. They say that the collective attention given to the ratios becomes a self-fulfilling prophecy.

Does everyone look at Fibonacci ratios because they're significant? Or are Fibonacci ratios significant because everyone looks at them? Let philosophers try to answer that question. As a forex trader, don't worry about it. Just use the figures to further your research and ultimately get better analysis.

Fibonacci Ratios to Watch

Fibonacci analysis suggests there are ratios, or percentages, that are more significant than all other ratios. For forex the four key ratios are: 38.2 percent, 50 percent, 61.8 percent, and 75 percent. When you consider these significant ratios in conjunction with other trading methodologies, you can have more insight into profitable entry and exit points.

Buying on a Dip

So how do Fibonacci numbers help you buy on a dip? Assume you've noticed a strong upward trend in the EUR/USD, but don't want to buy at the highest point on the trend. Fibonacci analysis suggests the price could retrace a portion of the upward move—either by 38.2 percent, 50 percent, or 61.8 percent—before resuming the uptrend.

The trend trader looking to join the trend, but at a good price, could buy the EUR/USD when it pulls back to any of the Fibonacci retracement levels—38.2 percent, 50 percent, or 61.8 percent. All good charting programs will enable you to see these key Fibonacci retracement ratios.

For this method of trading, Fibonacci analysis suggests that if the uptrend retraces by 75 percent, the probability of the uptrend continuing is very low. Therefore, when buying into the trend at the 38.2 percent, 50 percent, and 61.8 percent levels, a logical level to place a stop-loss order is just below the 75 percent retracement price.

Taking Profits

Fibonacci retracements help you pick the best prices to exit a profitable trade. For example, suppose you determine a recent uptrend in the GBP/USD is ending and initiate a short position. You expect the GBP/USD to go lower—but how much lower? Using Fibonacci analysis, you could expect prices to fall to levels equal to 38.2 percent, 50 percent, or 61.8 percent retracements of the exhausted uptrend.

Yes, prices could fall even lower, but Fibonacci analysis and probability suggests it's more likely prices fall to one of these levels and then turn around and go up. Taking profits on one third of the total short position at each of these levels—38.2 percent, 50 percent, and 61.8 percent—can be a very interesting strategy.

Now it's time for you to take a ride on the roller coaster and practice these strategies to identify potential trades. Test your skills for spotting potential trends by using a practice account.

The Least You Need to Know

- The RSI Roller Coaster Strategy uses calculations to determine when the market is overbought or oversold to help you figure out whether it's time to buy or sell a forex pair.
- You can spot a potential reversal in price by using double tops and double bottoms to forecast market moves, but be sure you're not missing out on a triple top or triple bottom.
- Bollinger Bands are an alternative for spotting the potential tops or bottoms of the forex market.
- Fibonacci retracements help you identify good market entry and exit points.

Risk Management Strategies

In This Chapter

- Exploring the risks
- Borrowing money to trade
- Facing volatility
- Losing liquidity

Trading in foreign currency is risky business. Currency markets can be volatile, and it is highly speculative. You could lose the entire amount you deposited in your forex account in a matter of minutes if the market moves against you.

You must understand the risks before you start trading. Many of the risks are similar to those you face in the stock market, but others are unique to foreign currency trading. In this chapter, we introduce you to the risks you may face when trading currency.

Leverage Risk

All currency traders use leverage to attempt to make a profit trading currency. Leverage is the use of borrowed money in an attempt to increase the potential return of a trade. Leverage is used in the currency markets because profits are made at exchange rate differences that are only fractions of a cent, so you must trade with large sums of money in order to make a notable profit.

Banks or brokers set the amount of leverage they will offer you. This is called "buying on margin." You won't find the strict government regulations regarding margin rules that you find in margin accounts available when trading stocks or options. We talk more about the rules for margin accounts in Chapter 15.

When a forex dealer or broker approves your trading account, he or she sets the rules for how much you can borrow, which is your leverage allowance. Most forex dealers allow you to trade on a 2 percent margin. That means with just $2,000 you can control $100,000 worth of currency. There are not many markets in which you will find that level of leverage, but remember increased leverage means you also have the potential to lose more money.

CAPITAL CAUTIONS

Trading hundreds of thousands of dollars may sound very exciting, but remember that, when you trade at these high volumes, even a minor mistake can wipe out your account in a matter of minutes. Don't rush into trading your money. Read, take a course or two, and practice trading with a demonstration account before you start trading your hard-earned money. Never put more money at risk than you can afford to lose.

When you pick a pair of currencies you want to trade, the difference in the price at which you can buy and sell the currencies is just fractions of a cent. Each of these fractions is called a pip. For example, when you trade a standard lot in the currency pair EUR/USD (you can read more about currency pairs in Chapters 5), you can gain or lose $10 per pip. So if you buy five standard lots of 100,000 units (a total of 500,000), you could gain or lose $50 per pip.

When trading a lot size of 100,000 of any currency pair that is quoted out to 4 decimal places, the pip value will always be 10 units of the counter currency. If the counter currency is the same as the currency in which the account is funded, each pip will equal 10 units of the deposit currency. For example, for a trader with an account funded in U.S. dollars, one pip equals $10 on a 100,000 lot of EUR/USD. In cases where the counter currency is different than the currency the trader's account is funded in, each pip will still be worth 10 units, but it will have to be converted to the currency in which the account is funded to determine actual profit or loss amount.

If you are using 2 percent leverage and trade five lots, you would need to have $2,000 for each lot. Therefore, you would need $10,000 in your trading account.

Let's assume you bought five standard lots of this pair at the exchange rate of 1.2522 and it dropped by 100 pips to 1.2422 by the time you were able to sell it. Your loss would be $5,000—a complete wipeout.

Even a drop of just 10 pips, from 1.2522 to 1.2512, would be a loss of $500 or 5 percent of your money. Of course, using the same scenario, you stand to gain $5,000 if the currency moves in your direction with a 100 pip swing. We talk more about how to buy and sell currency in Chapter 15.

Market Risk

All traders, no matter what you are trading—currency, stock, options, or futures—face market risk. Market risk basically encompasses any price movement that impacts your trade unfavorably.

From the moment you first place your trade to the moment you successfully exit it, you are facing the risk that the price of the currency may move against your position. Of course, you're hoping that the market will move in your favor, but you can never be sure that it will.

When it comes to currency, there are two key factors that impact currency values—exchange rates and interest rates—so of course these both represent a type of risk for currency traders.

Exchange Rate Risk

Whenever you open a trade involving currency, whether you are trading through the forex spot or forward market or using options or futures transactions, you face exchange rate risk. You are immediately exposed to the possibility that the exchange rate for the currency pair you've chosen will move against your position.

Exchange rates change every few seconds, so a loss due to exchange rate risk can happen very quickly. In just a few seconds, a profitable transaction can turn into a loss. We talk more about how to manage this loss potential using various trading tools in Chapters 10, 12, and 15.

CURRENCY COIN

Major global corporations manage their exchange rate risks in many different ways. As they buy and sell items around the world, many companies manage their exchange rate risk through buying currency options. This hedges their bets against a change in exchange rates. About 5 percent of global corporations even speculate in currency trading. For example, Caterpillar turned losses in its core businesses into profits through its currency trading operations when the company was having a bad year in 1986. Its $100-million profit in foreign exchange trading turned its $24-million operating loss into a $76-million net profit.

Interest Rate Risk

The exchange rate is not the only thing that can impact the value of the currencies you hold. A change in interest rates by the central bank that manages the currency for the country can dramatically affect your currency positions involving the country whose rate was changed.

For example, every time the Federal Reserve decides to raise or lower interest rates, the value of the U.S. dollar will be affected. Read more about the impact of interest rate changes in Chapter 4.

WEALTH BUILDERS

If you want to learn more about how corporations manage risks related to foreign currency exchange, read Gregory Millman's book, *The Floating Battlefield: Corporate Strategies in the Currency Wars,* published by AMACOM in 1990.

Generally, when a central bank announces an interest rate increase, the announcement will drive up the value of a currency because the higher rates increase demand for the currency. Conversely, a decrease in interest rates likely will result in selling of that currency, so it will likely drop in value due to the lower interest rate.

Counterparty Risk

When trading currency, you'll always face counterparty risk. Whenever you enter into a currency transaction, there must be two parties involved; one party is selling and the other party is buying. The person or entity with which you are trading is called the counterparty. Whenever you trade with another party, you risk the possibility that the other party will not be able to meet his or her obligations. This is called counterparty risk.

You can avoid this risk by trading only with known entities with excellent credit ratings. You should investigate any entity that you intend to work with as a currency trader by researching whether any problems have been reported, such as insolvency or questions of ethical conduct. A good place to begin your research is the Commodity Futures Trading Commission (www.cftc.gov). We talk more about how to avoid currency fraud in Chapter 18.

Volatility Risk

Currency prices change every second, so you can see movement in a currency thousands of times per day. This makes currency trading a very volatile endeavor. Volatility is a key part of the currency trading experience, which can be an opportunity or a risk.

If volatility in a market scares you, you probably want to think about another way to make your money. There is absolutely no way to completely avoid volatility risk when you trade foreign currencies. The good news is that you can minimize your volatility risk by sticking to the major currency pairs involving the developed countries. We talk more about these pairs in Chapter 5.

CURRENCY COIN

Many global corporations hire currency traders to manage their foreign exchange operations. With the large amounts of money they trade each year, they can earn hefty profits for the company by speculating and taking advantage of the volatility of the markets. For example, in 1992 there were many stories about how computer company Dell was speculating in foreign currency. Dell refused to comment on it, so financial analysts scoured its financial statements to figure out whether or not this was true. No one succeeded in proving it one way or another until one of Dell's foreign exchange traders was looking for a job and the press found out he had indicated on his resumé that he had traded $1 billion in currency contracts.

Liquidity Risk

You won't likely face liquidity risk when trading any of the major currency pairs. Over $3.98 trillion are traded daily, so you're not likely to find it difficult to get rid of a currency when you want to.

But (of course there's a but), if you do decide to take on more risk by trading emerging countries' currencies, liquidity risk can be a factor. Liquidity risk means that you might not be able to sell a currency you hold when you want to sell it. Of course, that is not likely to happen with the U.S. dollar, the yen, or the euro (or any other major currency), but you could have a hard time finding a buyer if you hold the currency of an emerging country. Liquidity can be particularly tricky if the country whose currency you hold just experienced a major change in political leadership—whether a violent coup or an unexpected election result.

Country Risk

When trading currency, what is happening in a particular country could greatly impact the value of its currency. There are a number of different types of country risks—political risk, regulation risk, legal risk, and holiday risk.

CURRENCY COIN

Some companies must operate regularly in countries that face hyperinflation or during a period of war. Managing foreign exchange trading can be crucial to their ability to operate profitably in these difficult environments. For example, in the 1980s and 1990s, Union Carbide Corporation had a task force of 30 people who managed currency operations throughout the corporation. Operating units sold their foreign currency exposures to this currency risk management unit. Dow Chemical bought Union Carbide in 2001 and the currency risk management is done through the parent company.

Political Risk

Political risk involves the stability of the country's government. As long as you stick to trading currency from countries whose governments are relatively stable, you won't face severe problems with political risk. Even if a developed country faces a major change in political leaders, the currency isn't likely to face a dramatic shift in price, but you will likely see some price movement depending upon the new leader's economic policies and the expected impact of the new leader on the country's economy.

When emerging countries face major political turmoil, you will most likely see a drop in the value of that country's currency as people try to sell it in order to get out before an even bigger fall. If you are trading the currency of an emerging country that does not have a large volume of sales even before the change in political leadership, you likely will face not only the political risk, but also liquidity risk as you try to sell.

For example, Mexico's closely fought presidential race in 2006 could have driven the value of the peso down dramatically if the leftist party leader had won the race. Instead, Mexico's currency surged after Felipe Calderon won because he pledged to continue the economic policies of Vicente Fox, which the capital markets have supported.

CURRENCY COIN

Operating in a war zone can be particularly difficult for a company. Halliburton has been doing just that as it supports the U.S. military in its operations overseas. In its 2002 annual report, Halliburton stated that it does not trade currency for speculation, but does for operations. It also talks about the difficulty of working with nontraded currencies. When operating in a country where currency cannot be traded, Halliburton states that it prices its products and services in these countries to attempt to cover the cost of exchange rate devaluations. Halliburton reported that it historically incurred transaction losses in its nontraded currencies.

Regulation Risk

If a government changes regulations that impact a country's currency, you face the potential of a loss because of regulation risk. Sometimes, especially when you are trading currencies involving emerging countries, the central bank will change a regulation that makes it more difficult for you to trade that currency.

For example, if you are a foreigner who holds currency in a country that changes its regulations to make it more difficult for you to hold the currency of that country, you may be forced into a position of selling the currency no matter what the loss may be to you. If you do decide to trade currencies of emerging countries, be sure you carefully research its current and potential future regulations.

You are not likely to face regulation risk in currencies of major developed nations. These currencies have been trading unimpeded on the spot market for years and are not likely to be impacted by changes in regulations.

You can read more about emerging countries and their fixed-float systems that could face regulatory change in Chapter 6.

Legal Risk

You face legal risks whenever you do business outside the country in which you live. When currency trading is involved, you often trade with a counterparty that does not reside in the same country as you do. If the counterparty were to default on the deal, you could face a legal risk depending upon which country has jurisdiction over the contract. How the contract can be enforced will depend on that jurisdiction.

If the host country of the counterparty enforces contract law differently than your home country, you could find it difficult to resolve the question. In fact, the host country could even determine that your contract was invalid or illegal. You can lose your entire position in that host country's currency.

Be sure you know who you are buying from and under which country's law the contract will be mediated if there is a problem. If you find out that U.S. contract law will not be the prevailing law, be certain you understand the law of the country that will prevail if there are any problems before you get involved in the deal.

As long as you work with a retail broker or dealer who is registered and regulated by the National Futures Association or the Commodity Futures Trading Commission, you likely will never have to worry about legal risk. But if you decide to trade with a broker or dealer not based in the United States or not regulated by the NFA or CFTC, this risk could become a big problem if you have trouble enforcing a contract.

Holiday Risk

Each country celebrates different holidays on different days. Holiday risk involves the possibility that the currency you wish to trade cannot be traded because of a bank holiday in that country. Different religious, political, or government holidays can stop the trading in the currency if the banks are closed. That could mean you can't get your money when you want it, and you will have to wait for the banks to reopen after the holiday.

When trading foreign currency, be sure you know the key holiday celebrations when the banks will be closed and plan your trading around these holidays.

Avoid Risks by Trading Through Regulated Entities

There is no way to totally eliminate your exposure to risk, but you can avoid some of these risks by being certain that you trade solely through regulated entities.

If you do business with a nonbanking institution not regulated by a government entity, you are operating in unprotected waters. You will have no regulatory agency to turn to for help if you face a problem. If you work with unregulated firms, you will be operating under the rule of *caveat emptor*, which is Latin for "let the buyer beware."

CAPITAL CAUTIONS

If you do plan to work with a non–U.S. entity, be sure to research the organization through the Bank for International Settlement (www.bis.org) before depositing any money with the entity. The BIS has the responsibility of evaluating foreign exchange trading institutions on a global basis. Unfortunately, you can't look up the information online; you must call or write BIS to research a foreign entity.

Some clearinghouses have paved the way to help you avoid counterparty risk and other risk associated with foreign exchange trading. Be sure to use all resources available to you to minimize foreign exchange trading risks—it's risky enough without them.

In addition to understanding and managing these risks, you also can effectively manage risks by the way you actually place your trades. You'll find out more about precautions you can take when placing trades in Chapter 15.

The Least You Need to Know

- The greatest risk all traders face is leverage risk. No matter what currency you trade, you must borrow significantly in order to make money because profits are made on differences of fractions of a cent.
- Foreign exchange traders face numerous risks inherent to the process of trading money globally. Become familiar with these risks and how you can minimize your exposure.
- Trading currencies of emerging nations exposes you to a number of risks you are not likely to face if you stick to trading the major currencies of developed industrialized nations. These risks include liquidity risks, political risks, regulation risks, and legal risks.

Developing Your Trading Strategies

12

In This Chapter

- Disciplining yourself
- Controlling your emotions
- Minimizing your risks
- Tips for avoiding trading tragedies

We're sure you've heard stories of people making millions of dollars trading forex in a matter of hours or even minutes. While that may have happened for a lucky few, more often than not you won't be seeing that kind of win. You could even lose more than the total balance in your forex account in a matter of minutes if you're not careful.

In this chapter, we talk about how to develop a disciplined trading plan. We also discuss the importance of keeping your emotions in check, as well as exploring risk management strategies. We end the chapter with 10 tips to avoid a trading tragedy.

Taking Steps to Discipline Your Trades

Every forex trader needs to develop a sound trading strategy that they can follow regularly. We won't recommend a specific strategy. That's something you need to develop for yourself based on your own emotional tendencies, as well as your knowledge and understanding of the marketplace.

But no matter what strategies you develop, you should use the classic approach to trading forex—the inverted pyramid approach. This approach uses both fundamental (Chapter 8) and technical (Chapters 7 and 10) analysis to help you develop your trading plan.

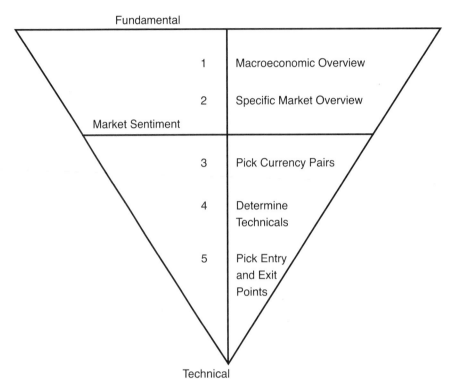

Classic trading model—the inverted pyramid.

There are several factors to consider when developing your overall trading plan. The following sections walk you through each of the five steps to developing your trading plan.

Step 1: Take a Macroeconomic View

Start your research by looking at the economic conditions around the world. What are the key pressures driving economic forces—including wars, oil prices, trade agreements among nations, storms, earthquakes, or holiday shopping? Look at whether the economy is being viewed globally in a generally pessimistic (most people expect things to get worse) or optimistic (most people expect things to get better) way. One of the easiest ways to judge this quickly is to watch one of the business cable news networks. We talk about good news sources in Chapter 24.

Step 2: Find News About Specific Money Market Conditions

Start focusing on what is happening in the money markets. If something could dramatically affect the money markets, all the business analysts will be talking about it. For example, if there is going to be a major rate meeting by one of the key central banks, such as the Federal Reserve in the United States or the Bank of England, we can guarantee there will be much speculation about what the central bank might do regarding a possible rate increase or decrease.

Once you've completed Steps 1 and 2, you should have a good idea of what the *market sentiment* is around the world, as well as in the countries on which you plan to focus your attention.

DEFINITION

Market sentiment reflects the general mood surrounding the currency market. Understanding this general mood will help you develop a plan based on the expected behavior of the market, which can be critical to developing a good trading plan.

Economic indicators include any variable that gives you an idea of where the market may be headed, such as new employment statistics or trading balances.

Step 3: Pick Your Currency Pairs

Once you have a good understanding of the currency market, you will be able to pick the currency pairs you wish to trade. You want to focus on pairs that may be volatile that day, week, or month—whatever your trading horizon might be. Decide which *economic indicators* will be the most important for market moves during the window of your trading plan.

Also look at the recent trends in prices for the currency pairs you're considering trading. Do you see a strong trend or do you see a lot of volatility (no clear direction)? Use this step to narrow down the potential currency pairs for which you expect to set up a trading plan.

Step 4: Determine Your Basic Technical Points

Start using your favorite chart types to look for signs of support (a point on your chart at which sellers won't let the price fall below as they start buying the currency pair) and resistance (a point on the chart at which buyers won't let the price go above as they stop buying the currency pair).

Use this information to pick currency pairs you want to trade based on the direction in which you expect the market to move. The fundamental information you gathered in Step 2 will help confirm the trends you are seeing in your charts.

Step 5: Pick Your Entry and Exit Points

Fine-tune your trading plan by actually picking your entry and exit points. If you look at the charts and still don't know how to do that, you need to spend more time learning how to apply technical analysis. As you become more comfortable with it, you'll pick the tools that best match your trading style and your knowledge or abilities. We discuss some key tools you can use in Chapter 10. You must know both your entry and exit points before you even try to make the trade. Determine your plan and stick to it!

As you are learning how to use the inverted pyramid method, test your successes or failures with the method by opening a demonstration account with a forex broker. We discuss how to choose a broker in Chapter 15. We also talk about trading platforms in Chapter 13. Practice trading with your plan and see if it works before using your hard-earned cash for a live account.

Keeping Your Emotions in Check

When trading, your emotions can jump up and down almost as quickly as the market. Although you can't deny your emotions, the key is to keep them under control so you can stick to your plan. But some people don't have the emotional stamina to even try to trade.

Ask yourself these questions:

- Does the idea of losing money keep you up at night?
- Can you not read the financial news without reacting emotionally?
- Do you make trading decisions quickly based on the latest tip you've heard?

If you answered yes to these questions, you probably don't have the emotional make-up to be a successful forex trader. Forex traders must remain calm and focused on their plans. They must research the currency pairs they trade regularly. It is best if you can set aside time to watch the market daily, even if you don't plan to trade daily. By paying close attention to moves in the markets on a daily, consistent basis, you will be able to understand when there is a long-term trend driving the market or when the market takes a different direction. One of the hardest things for some traders to do is to sell a position they are attached to. Don't get too attached. Remember that it is a business. You write a business plan (trading plan) and you follow that plan. Don't let your emotions take control and get you to alter your plans. We talk more about writing a business plan in Chapter 23.

We know that can be easier said than done. You spend days, weeks, or months researching the markets and finally develop a strategy and plan that work for you. If your plan works brilliantly, you have a sizeable profit. Now it's time to sell or buy according to your plan. But you just can't break away. You may want to ride the trade to the top, but don't. The fall can be quick and you could lose even more than your initial deposit. Don't let your emotions drive your trading decisions; let your plan be your guide.

Emotions can also make it hard for you to sell, even if the exit point you set to minimize a loss is approaching quickly. You can't figure out how you were so wrong and don't want to admit to a mistake. You still think it's a good trade and you want to hold on just a bit longer to try to prove yourself right. Don't do it. Letting go can be hard to do, but keep yourself focused on your plan and don't let your emotions take control.

Most forex brokers offer commission-free trades. It's not like trading stock, where you must worry about the commissions you must pay to get in and out of a position. But the trades aren't free. Your primary cost is determined by the spread between the bid (the price at which someone is willing to buy) and ask (the price at which someone is willing to sell), and that cost can be steep. We talk more about the bid and ask spread in Chapter 15. Then take a deep breath. Take another look at your plan and determine whether you still think it's a good one and if you might consider different points for entering and exiting a new trade that reflects the recent market moves. Do a calm, focused job of researching your position again. If a position moved much differently than you expected, do more research to see what might be different in both fundamental and technical analysis assumptions. It could be that a major economic shock you missed took control of the markets after you set your plan.

Try to find the reason for the difference from your expectations. Even if you aren't going to trade that pair again in the next day, week, or month, understand why you made a mistake so you don't repeat your mistake again in the future. Keeping a journal of your trades can help you avoid repeating mistakes and take advantage of successes. We talk more about how do to that in Chapter 17.

Risk-Management Strategies

The best way to manage your risk is by setting up orders to take your profits when you first open your position. That way you don't risk getting caught up emotionally in the winning moment and ride your profits to a loss.

Set up stop-loss orders when you first open your position. That way your logic will be in control rather than your greed or your disappointment if the trade doesn't go as planned.

We talk about how to place orders in Chapter 15, but in this chapter, we want to explore how you can use limit orders (take profit) and stop-loss orders (minimize loss) to help you manage your risk.

Limit Orders (Take Profit)

Use a limit order to protect your profits. This sets you up to exit the forex market as planned without letting your emotions get the better of you. Avoid being tempted to ride a gain that could turn into a loss by sticking with the trade for too long.

If you are shorting a currency pair (selling), your broker's system should allow you to place a limit order below the current market price. When selling a currency pair, the profit zone is below the current price. The opposite is true if you are going long (buying) on a currency pair.

The system will allow you to set up a limit order to secure your profits at a price above the current market price. When buying a currency pair, the profit zone is above the current price. The take-profit order helps you maintain a disciplined trading strategy.

Don't set it up or change your limit order after watching your order for a while without carefully reviewing and updating your fundamental and technical analysis. Set up the limit order at the same time you make your trade.

Because you don't pay commissions, you can always develop a new plan to buy or sell the same pair again, so it's better not to get into the practice of changing your limit or stop-loss orders. Instead, let them play out and develop a new plan for the next trade based on the information learned during your previous trades.

Stop-Loss Orders (Minimize Loss)

Use stop-loss orders to minimize your losses. Set up your stop-loss order at the time of your trade to protect yourself from being driven by your emotions. A stop-loss order sets up an exit point as you enter a trade that will get you out of your trade before your losses become too large.

If you short a currency pair, the stop-loss order should be set above the current price. Remember that when you are shorting a pair, the profit zone is below the price of the pair. If you go long on a currency pair, set up your stop-loss order below the current market price.

Obviously, you hope your stop-loss orders will never be needed, but don't forget to set them. When they are needed, you want the logic you used to set your entry and exit prices as you developed your plan to be in control, not your emotions.

Picking the Right Points

You're probably wondering how to determine where to set your limit and stop-loss orders. Many traders set their stop-loss orders closer to their opening price than their limit orders. For example, a guideline you can follow when you're getting started is to set your stop-loss point at 30 pips and your take-profit orders at 100 pips.

Where you set your stop-loss and limit orders is purely up to you. The tighter the point, the less risky your trade will be, but remember, if you set your order points too tight, normal market volatility could trigger your order long before you want it to. To make money you have to move outside the normal volatility range, so you do have to take some risk.

Another general rule most traders follow is to go long or neutral when you see a bull market. Go short or neutral if you believe the market conditions are ripe for a bear market. Don't trade against the bull or bear trend. You will suffer emotional distress and will most likely suffer losses as well.

Top Ten Tips to Remember to Avoid Trading Tragedies

We've talked about the importance of using both fundamental and technical trading, as well as key risk management steps you can take when placing trades. Let's quickly review the top 10 tips you should remember to avoid a trading tragedy:

1. **Learn the rules of the road.** Educate yourself about the markets. Be sure you take the time to study the markets and learn all the intricacies of trading before you risk your real capital.

2. **Pick a route and stick to it.** Always create a plan to guide your trading. This plan should include your profit goals, risk tolerance, methodology, and evaluation criteria. Write down your plan and make sure each trade you consider falls within your plan's parameters. You're most rational before you place a trade and most irrational once your trade is live.

3. **Practice.** Put your plan to work in real market conditions using a risk-free practice account at GFT (www.gftforex.com/idiotsguide) or a practice account from the broker you choose. You'll get a chance to see what it's like to trade in real market conditions and take your trading plan for a test drive without risking real capital.

4. **Check the conditions before placing a trade.** Fundamental traders prefer to trade on news and other financial and political data. Technical traders prefer to use technical analysis tools like the ones you'll find in Chapter 10. Some traders use both. No matter what style you prefer, use both to help you find higher-probability trades.

5. **Know how far you can afford to go.** Develop a risk-to-reward ratio that fits your financial situation. Know your limits and how much you are willing to risk on each trade. Never risk more than you can afford to lose. Always make sure you'll have enough capital left to trade another day.

6. **Know where to stop along the way.** Stop and limit orders can help manage risk and protect potential profits by helping you get in or out of the market at specified prices. You can use these tools to set up an entire trade including both entry and exit points and manage your risk with one quick step.

7. **Avoid road rage.** Stick to your plan and keep your emotions in check. "Revenge trading" always results in losses. When you have a losing trade, don't go all-in to try to make it all back in one shot. Stick with your initial strategy. It's smarter to make it back a little at a time than to be stuck with two (or more) crippling losses.

8. **Know what type of driver you are.** Become aware of your tendencies and personality traits so you can combat your weaknesses and maximize your strengths more effectively. We talk more about how to do this by evaluating your trades in Chapter 17.

9. **Remember, slow and steady wins the race.** The key to success is to be consistent. All great traders have lost money, but as long as they maintain a positive edge, they may still come out a winner. Educate yourself, stick to your trading plan, manage your risk, and practice discipline and patience.

10. **Never be afraid to explore a new path.** Although it's important to be consistent, don't be afraid to re-evaluate your trading plan if it's not working for you. As your experience grows, your needs may change.

You will find that as you get more experience in forex trading, your goals or financial situation may change. You'll need to regularly reassess your plan to be sure it meets your current goals and financial situation. Don't be afraid to reflect on your goals and revise your plan when the time is right.

In addition to putting together a good trading plan, you'll also need the right hardware and software to trade successfully. In the next chapter we look at those tools.

The Least You Need to Know

- Discipline your trading strategies by using the inverted pyramid method.
- Control your emotions. Let your trading plan rather than your emotions determine your entry and exit points for a trade.
- Use stop-loss and limit orders and stick by them to ensure that your logic rather than your emotions dictates your trades.
- Remember the 10 tips to avoid trading tragedies.

Tools for Trading

We start this part by introducing you to the key trading platforms and software. Then we introduce you to the new world of forex robots—a way to automate your trades.

Next we review the basics of how to actually place orders. You'll also get some tips on how to find the right forex broker.

Then we discuss how to manage your trades. You need to know when to get out once you get in.

Finally we help you develop a method of evaluating your results. If you don't take the time to evaluate both your successes and your failures, you miss an opportunity to improve your future results.

Trading Platforms, Hardware, and Software

In This Chapter

- Determining computer specs
- Getting connected
- Finding platforms

Forex trading used to be the province solely of banks, multinational corporations, and hedge funds. Just 10 years ago, most banks closely guarded forex information, making it difficult to determine exchange rates. This led to an inefficient market where the bid and ask spreads were wide and the costs of trading forex were high.

That is no longer the case today. Anyone, whether in small-town America or a major European financial center, can trade forex as long as he or she has a basic computer and high-speed Internet. A reputable forex firm can give you a retail platform that gives you the pricing and execution comparable to the interbank market. This chapter discusses your computer hardware and software needs and what to look for in trading platforms.

Computer Hardware and Software Needs

If you're planning to trade forex, you definitely need a high-performance computer that can run trading software, which consumes considerable system resources. Good trading platforms require the ability to test trading strategies and use multiple charts. You must use a multi-window environment and possibly more than one monitor.

Most trading platforms are designed to work on Windows, so a computer with a Windows XP or Windows 7 operating system is best. Although there are trading systems that can work on the Apple OS/2 operating system and Linux, you may have some difficulty finding them and finding up-to-date software.

Here are the basic components of the ideal computer workstation:

- **Central processing unit (CPU):** Your processor speed should be at a minimum 1 GHz. Ideally even faster is better. Trading programs do rely on the ability to make many mathematical calculations, so you should select a DualCore processor. Avoid using Intel Celeron or AMD Duron chips because they cannot handle these high-demand applications. Most modern computers have enough CPU horsepower to run the trading software you need, but some high-end software could require even specialty hardware, such as multi-CPU and hyperthreading configurations. When choosing a trading platform, read the CPU requirements and make sure you have the hardware to support it.

- **RAM memory:** You should have a minimum of 1 GB (gigabytes) of RAM, but it is best to have considerably more. You can't have too much RAM, and if you have too little the software will run very slowly. Extra memory is not an expensive upgrade, so don't be cheap about it.

- **Disk space:** Although 1 GB of free disk space should be enough to run most trading platforms, you'll probably want a lot more to store exchange-rate data. We recommend at least 5 GB of free space.

- **Operating system:** Your best bet is to pick a system with Windows 7 or Windows XP. Although you may find some trading applications that can run on older versions of Windows, the reliability and stability of Windows 7 or XP is critical for trading. You don't want your system to crash in the middle of a trade, and crashes happen much more frequently on the older Windows systems.

- **Video card:** Your best bet is to choose a computer system with a video card that uses its own video memory rather than one that shares its memory with your RAM. You can squeak by with a video card that has 128 MB of video memory, but it is better to get one with 256 MB or more. If you are going to run more than one monitor, at least 128 MB per monitor is suggested.

- **Monitor size:** You should have at least a 17-inch monitor. A 19-inch or larger is better because you will likely be running several windows at the same time.

- **Dual-monitor configurations:** Many traders prefer to have more than one monitor. They use one monitor for their charts and a second monitor for everything else. If you do decide to use a dual-monitor configuration, be sure your video cards support the configuration.

- **Network interface:** You need either a built-in Ethernet port or an extra Ethernet interface card to access a high-speed Internet connection. We do not recommend trading through a wireless network. Wireless networks are not as secure, and can be affected by cell phones, cordless phones, and a variety of other household items.

- **Power supply:** For safety, we do recommend that you get an uninterruptible power supply (UPS). In addition to giving the safety of 30 minutes to a couple of hours of power if your electric power goes out, many also come with protection against a lightning strike. You definitely don't want to lose power in the middle of a trade.

- **Security:** You must secure your computer and its data against viruses, worms, and other nasty bugs out there. You also want to be sure to have a firewall that defends against any attacks from the World Wide Web on your computer. Norton AntiVirus or McAfee's AntiVirus Plus are two good virus-protection alternatives. ZoneAlarm is a good firewall package that monitors your Internet activities and detects any Trojans or worms that are trying to call your computer home. Be sure you keep these security software packages up-to-date, because new bugs enter the Internet environment almost every day.

Internet Access

Don't think about trading forex using the Internet unless you have reliable high-speed access. A dial-up connection will not give you the type of access you need to be able to trade in the fast-paced world of forex, where exchange rates can change every three seconds.

Your access can be a digital subscriber line (DSL) through your telephone provider or a cable modem through your cable provider. Some active traders want even more reliability and opt for an expensive T1 line, but that isn't necessary.

Full-time traders need redundancy, and although a dial-up line is not recommended for trading, we do recommend having a dial-up or alternative Internet connection available and ready to go in case your primary connection fails. The Internet is an unpredictable network with many carriers trying to work together to provide global communication. There will be issues from time to time with your Internet connection, and you don't want to have an open trade and have your sole Internet connection go down.

For added protection, it's best that your backup connection not be provided by the same carrier as your primary connection. If you have high-speed access through your cable provider, then set up a dial-up account through some other company.

Trading Platforms

Finding the right platform for trading can be a much more difficult choice. You definitely want to find a forex trading platform that can offer the basics: the ability to buy, sell, and settle currency pairs. But all trading platforms are not created equal. Do your research!

Be sure to first check out the forex firm before even trying out their software. If you are using a firm based in the United States, one of the best places to research a forex firm is the *National Futures Association* (*NFA*) at www.nfa.futures.org, a self-regulatory body for the futures industry that was given its authority by the *Commodity Futures Trading Commission* (*CFTC*).

DEFINITION

The **National Futures Association (NFA)** is the industry-wide, self-regulatory organization for the United States futures industry that develops rules, programs, and services to safeguard market integrity, protect investors, and help its members meet regulatory responsibilities.

The **Commodity Futures Trading Commission (CFTC)** is an independent U.S. agency that regulates the commodity futures and options markets in the United States. It ensures the economic utility of the futures markets by encouraging competitiveness and efficiency; ensuring integrity; protecting market participants against manipulation, abusive trading practices, and fraud; and ensuring the financial integrity of the clearing process.

Remember, forex dealers are not regulated in the same way. Only regulated entities, such as banks, insurance companies, broker dealers, or futures commission merchants that are affiliates of regulated entities, can handle forex trades for retail customers.

The company you trade with should be a bank, a broker dealer (registered with the SEC), or an FCM (registered with the CFTC). You learn more about forex fraud in Chapter 18.

On the NFA site, review the basic broker/firm information section for member companies. You can find out information about the firm's registration status and research whether the broker or firm has been disciplined. You can check out the financial information about all registered forex dealers at the CFTC website (www.cftc.gov).

You can also check out information about forex brokers and dealers at forums online, but be careful out there. Not all posters are independent traders, so you need to read these forums regularly and get to know who is posting. Two forums with forex sections are MoneyTec Traders Community Forum (www.moneytec.com) and Elite Trader (www.elitetrader.com).

The MoneyTec Traders Community Forum is a discussion forum that serves as a resource to help forex traders become better traders. You can meet fellow traders from around the world and learn more about forex trading, as well as discuss trading ideas, techniques, and strategies. Elite Trader provides an online community for discussion of not only forex, but also stock, options, and futures trading. Remember to take the information found on these postings with a grain of salt, and be sure to conduct additional research.

After you narrow down your retail platform alternatives, take them out for a test drive before you decide which one is right for you. All reputable firms allow you to download a demonstration of their software so that you can try out the software on your own computer before you open an account.

After downloading the demo, make sure it's not too complicated to use. Sometimes you'll find the software so overloaded with features that it's not the best choice for you. When a software package is overloaded with options, you'll find that streaming quotes sometimes can be jumpy, updates to your account can be slow, and trying to execute orders can be confusing. All the bells and whistles and pretty colors may look great, but make sure that the extras don't impede your ability to trade efficiently. You certainly don't want a software package with these problems when you're trying to trade quickly in the forex market. The most important feature is the software's navigation. You want to be able to get to where you're going onscreen quickly and easily.

CURRENCY COIN

Co-author Gary Tilkin's company, GFT, designed one of the first forex trading platforms in 1999, and the platform is ranked as one of the best in the market today. Tilkin thought the old system of floor trading was slow and filled with confusion about prices. Customers quickly found that the trading platform GFT designed was far superior because it provided them with almost instantaneous trades. The current version of GFT's software, DealBook® 360, is now available at GFT (www.gftforex.com).

DealBook® 360 Opening Screen.

Key Parts of a Trading Platform

Here are the key pieces of information you want to find on a forex platform:

- **Dealing rates:** You want to locate all available currency pairs for which the dealer can make a market. You want information about how much you can sell a currency pair for and how much you can buy one for (a two-sided quote).

You also want to be able to see the highest and lowest prices during the trading period. You want to know the time and date the last quote was posted. Another good feature is to know the interest rates for the currency pair.

- **Account summary:** You want to have quick access to the status of your account. You need to know your balance (the total amount of capital in your account), the currency pairs you hold, the amount of margin you have used, the amount of margin you have available to use, and your total profit or loss.

- **Open orders:** You should be able to quickly see what type of order was executed, such as a market or limit order. You learn about order types in Chapter 15. You need to know the currency pair, the price at which the order will be executed, and the size of the trade (or amount of the order). You also want to see any predetermined stop-loss or limit orders you set, and the time you entered the order.

- **Open positions:** You need to know the specific currency pairs you have traded. You need to know the size of each position (amount). You need to know which side of the market you are on (either sell or buy). You need to know the price at which the position was opened. You need to know the current price of your position. You need to know the price at which you entered a stop order. You need to know the price at which you entered a limit order. You need to know the profit or loss of the specific trade. You need to know whether any commissions were charged. You need to know the interest gain or loss on the position.

You may find some additional features in the system you are considering:

- **Request for quote (RFQ):** This feature enables you to send an instant message within the trading platform to the market maker. You can ask for a quote on a specific currency pair based on the size of the trade you want to make. This process can favor market makers because they're the only ones who see the price. This is an older trading feature and not the preferred method.

- **ECN:** You will find companies offering an ECN model, which allows multicounterparty trading. Each participant in the network can post bids and offers and trade with each other. The trader can choose the counterparty with which he or she wants to trade. The name can be deceiving, as these systems don't replicate the ECN model that is known to stock traders. Retail customers must still conduct trades through an intermediary. Although brokers using this type of system boast about greater transparency and more competitive pricing, there are often hidden costs or commission fees. Also, sometimes many traders are on the same side of a currency pair and the liquidity is not there for the currency you wish to buy or sell.

- **Direct Deal:** This is the type of system that is the most common platform for retail forex traders. It's called click and deal because "what you click is what you get." In basic terms, you click on the trade you want based on the price quote you see. This does increase transparency regarding the deals available and limits the power of the market maker. The quotes you see are live and can be instantly traded upon. In most trading platforms, the prices are streamed, which means they're continuously updated in real time. This platform is transparent because the market maker must post a two-sided quote—both the buy and sell side. In an RFQ system, the market maker is in control because he can quote the price based on the pair and size the trader requests. Click and deal is well suited for most retail forex traders.

In the previous figure, you can see the first screen for GFT's DealBook® 360, which gives you a lot of information. On the left is the quote board, which shows major currency pairs and changes every second as the pricing changes. On the right is the charting feature, which also updates based on the time you set. At the bottom of the screen are details for open and working orders. You can see at the top of the screen that our account has almost $990,000 in working cash. (Just to set the record straight, this is not my real money. It's a demonstration account.)

In the following figure, you can see how easy it is to place an order using GFT's DealBook® Direct Deal feature. In the New Order box, a drop-down menu gives you all the possible currency pairs you can trade and another allows you to select your account. When you select a pair, the bid and ask price shows at the top of the Order box. You can get a history of price activity or get a quick chart by clicking on the buttons to the right of the quote box. You can then pick your order type and your order options, as well as the number of lots you want to sell. When ready, you click Submit to place the order.

- **News:** The news feature can be a useful addition, but it's not always the best source for information. In many platforms, the news feature lags the market. By the time you receive the news, it could already be known by other traders. Seconds can make a huge difference in forex trading, where prices can change by the second. GFT's DealBook® 360 offers real-time streaming news. This platform even has an RSS feature, allowing you to add whatever streaming news updates you'd like. If you don't have a real-time news feature, you'll want to supplement it with coverage on a TV news channel such as Bloomberg or CNBC.

Placing an order with DealBook® 360.

- **Charts:** You must have a good charting package. This is critical for successful trades and should be included with your forex software. Charts represent historical price data. You can then manipulate the data by timescale and period, by currency pairs, and by technical indicators to find your trading opportunity. You can read more about technical analysis and charting in Chapters 7 and 10.

- **Research:** The research about various currency and currency pairs that you get along with your trading platform is useful, but it's always wise to do your own research and not depend solely on the trading platform you choose for information.

Not every trade will go smoothly. Sometimes glitches will occur. Here are a couple of glitches you should watch out for:

- **Requotes:** A requote is when a dealer does not accept the price that you see on your screen and quotes you a new price. This happens most often when the market is particularly volatile; but if it starts to happen often, watch out. Your dealer could be cheating you and altering quotes in his favor to make more money. If you find your trading platform is resulting in frequent requotes, find a new platform.

- **Network connection:** As anyone who's worked on the Internet knows, you can have problems with connectivity. Be sure the trading platform you select has an indicator you can easily see that lets you know whether the data stream you are seeing is connected. Otherwise you could be making decisions on price quotes that are not the most current.

Retail Forex Trading Platforms

Although of course we are partial to DealBook® 360, which was developed by co-author Gary Tilkin's company, GFT, we do think you should do your own research to find the platform that's best for you based not only on the software but also on the currencies that you plan to trade.

DealBook® 360 is available in Arabic, Chinese (simplified and traditional), Dutch, English, French, German, Hebrew, Hungarian, Italian, Japanese, Korean, Polish, Portuguese, Romanian, Russian, Spanish, and Turkish.

You need US$200 to open an account. The minimum transaction is US$10,000. That minimum transaction amount is true for all companies listed here. Remember, you only need 2 percent of the transaction amount ($200 in this case) to trade on leverage.

In addition to GFT's DealBook® 360, here are some other trading platforms you can try out:

- **Capital Market Services** (www.cmsfx.com)—You can open an account with US$500. Languages available include Arabic, Bulgarian, Chinese, English, French, Italian, German, Japanese, Korean, Polish, Russian, Spanish, Slovakian, and Turkish.

- **Forex.com** (www.Forex.com)—You can open a mini account with US$500. Languages available include Chinese, English, Japanese, and Russian.

- **FX Solutions** (www.fxsolutions.com)—You can open an account with a minimum of US$250. Languages available include Arabic, Chinese, English, and Spanish.

All companies listed are regulated by the National Futures Association and the Commodity Futures Trading Commission.

The Least You Need to Know

- Be sure you have a computer with the right hardware and software that can handle your trading needs.
- Not all forex trading platforms are created equal. Try out whatever system you pick by downloading the demo onto your computer and trying it out.
- There are many firms out there. Be sure to choose one that is registered with the National Futures Association and regulated by the NFA and the Commodity Futures Trading Commission.

Putting Your Forex Trading on Autopilot

In This Chapter

- Meeting the "pilots"
- Automated trading strategies
- Getting started with automated trading
- Autotrading platforms

Forex is a 24-hour-a-day marketplace, but humans do need to sleep. Some traders solve that problem with new software developed to automatically execute trades for the trader. This automated trading software is known by several names such as trading robots, algo trading, and expert advisors, which are exclusive to the popular MetaTrader system. This software is almost always created by experienced traders who write strategies that will automatically execute forex trades for you.

Do these programs actually work? Sometimes. The forex market can change dramatically, and some programs work better than others, depending on market conditions.

Putting your trading on autopilot might sound great, but you definitely shouldn't try it until you are an experienced trader and can truly evaluate what the robot is doing. In this chapter, we explore what automated trading is, who's using it, and how you evaluate these automated trading strategies. We also take a quick look at other software available to enhance your forex trading.

What Is Automated Trading?

Automated trading is a concept by which a computer script is written to run automated trading strategies. These scripts can be written to just advise traders about which trades to make or they can be programmed to automatically execute trades on a live account.

Basically these scripts (strategies) use technical signals to enter trades automatically or send signals that alert you to potential trade opportunities. Once you give an automated strategy, such as an expert advisor or a trading robot, the right to enter and exit trades for you, the strategy will run continuously—as long as you leave your computer on—making those trades based on signals developed by mathematical algorithms based on past price history.

But here's the big question you must always ask yourself before you set an automated trading strategy in motion: Will that past performance be an indicator of future success given the current market conditions on the day you enable the strategy to trade for you? You can only find that answer with a lot of research into the type of markets the strategy has worked best on in the past.

Even then the automated trading strategy's success is not guaranteed. It's best if you watch the strategy in action and can be certain the trades it's making are winners. Chances are you will only know this answer if you are an experienced trader, so don't even think about using automated trading until you feel confident in your own trading abilities.

CAPITAL CAUTIONS

Remember, the forex market can be volatile. The price fluctuation of currency pairs are a constantly moving target with an infinite variation in what outside forces will cause them to move one of three ways—up, down, or sideways. Not all trading strategies are programmed for all types of trading environments, and most are not even programmed to recognize a trading environment.

As a trader, you must still be the decision maker regarding which automated strategy to use and when. You'll only be ready to do that after you've acquired substantial experience trading currency pairs the old-fashioned way—manually. You'll need time to learn how forex markets behave. Until you've learned that, you will not have the experience to determine whether an automated strategy is good or bad given the current market conditions.

After you've done some research, read reviews about different automated trading strategies, and picked ones that you think will work given your trading style, you'll still need to test them and possibly even tweak them to meet your trading preferences.

Some experienced traders prefer to use automated trading strategies as their sole trading system. Others use it to manage a portion of their portfolio. What you decide to do will be based on experience trading forex manually. Your choice will also depend on how much you enjoy making your own decisions. Robots are not a good option if you like to stay in control of your trades.

You can buy an automated forex trading strategy, such as a robot or an expert advisor, for as little as $20 or as high as $5,000 or more. There are many scammers out there, so be careful and do your research before shelling out any cash.

WEALTH BUILDERS

You can start your research about automated trading by looking at forex robots at ForexBot (www.forexrobottrading.com) or Forex Robot Nation (forexrobotnation.com) and expert advisors at ExpertAdvisorsForex.com (www.expertadvisorsforex.com).

Many different types of traders are starting to turn to automated trading strategies some of the time.

If you do decide to try a trading robot or expert advisor, be sure to backtest it yourself using a practice forex program before using your own cash. You can figure out how it works and even test it in several different market conditions before putting your own money at risk.

Researching Automated Trading Strategies

You may be wondering what features you should even look for when researching an automated trading strategy. The first thing to look for when considering one is information about the currencies for which the strategy is programmed to trade. If the robot or expert advisor isn't programmed to trade the currency pairs you trade, it won't be worth anything to you.

CAPITAL CAUTIONS

Remember, before purchasing an automated trading strategy, be sure it's programmed to trade the currency pairs that meet your trading preferences. Also be sure you know the strategy's preferred market conditions for trading.

You also want to find out what time frame is the most optimal for using the system. For example, the automated strategy named Forex Monster has a review indicating that it prefers short-term trading to take advantage of quick drops, so obviously you'd only want to use this strategy if you plan to trade short-term and expect a down market.

Another key thing to look for when reading reviews is who the reviewer thinks will benefit most from using the respective automated strategy. In one review about a robot called Push Bottom Pips, released in February 2011, Forex Review (www.forexreview.com) posted that those who would benefit from the robot would be:

- Someone who wants to spend less than $50 on forex robots. It costs $39.

- Someone who "wishes to spend minimum time trading and prefers an automated trading software."

- Someone who "dislikes studying manual technical analysis like Fibonacci points, trendlines, and support/resistance levels."

But the problem with this review is that it really doesn't tell you the preferred time frame, average profit targets, or average stop-loss targets. It's a relatively new automated strategy that hasn't really been tested, so your portfolio becomes one of the guinea pigs for testing if you choose to buy it. Are you ready to be a test subject? If not, you may want to look for automated strategies with a longer track record.

Compare that review to the one for Forex Monster to see how much more information is provided for an older robot:

- "Produces consistent yearly profits through 6 years of backtesting." The review does provide a link to backtest results, but history doesn't always repeat itself in the forex market. Even with six years of backtesting, there is no guarantee of future success.

- "The trading methodology allows quick bursts of profits like $800 in 2 days, $1,700 in 24 hours and $1,543 in 24 hours." Big promises like that may be true, but how often do they happen and when can you expect them? You won't find any promises with that level of detail.

- "Generates **an average $1,543/day** with the automated trading system." This is yet another promise that can probably be proven with backtesting, but remember, this is still no guarantee that you will experience this average with your own trading.

It is best to run the strategy with play money on a demo account first. This allows you to test it out into the future to see how it compares to the backtest results before committing real money.

Who Uses Automated Trading?

Automated trading strategies are not only used by people who want to put their entire forex portfolio on autopilot; there are other key forex traders trying out expert advisors and robots as well. Among them are:

- Short-term traders who use the software to look for short-term trading opportunities across major currency pairs during each trading day. They trade once the strategy has found the right opportunity. They may or may not let the strategy automatically enter or exit trades.

- People trying out an alternative to paying managers for managing their forex trading. We talk more about managed account options in Chapter 21.

- Traders who know the ropes, but just don't have the time to trade full-time. As long as you understand forex trading and can fully test the strategy, automated trading may be a good alternative for the part-time trader. But remember, you still need to be able to evaluate how well the system is doing for you, and know which automated strategy to use when.

- Some institutions and corporations with professional money managers use these strategies to automate their forex trading.

How to Get Started with Automated Trading

The first thing you need to do if you think automated trading is something you want to try is to find a broker that offers one of the many available platforms to trade automated strategies. You can use platforms such as MT4, Mirror Trader, Strategy Runner, and Ninja Trader, just to name a few.

Some brokers charge you for using these platforms by building a fee into the spread between the bid and ask. (We talk more about the spread in Chapter 15.) Others charge you a fee directly. Be sure you know what the fees for using automated trading strategies will be before opening an account. GFT does not charge a fee for trading strategies and gives you the same spreads that they offer on their own proprietary trading platform.

There are features and benefits that come with each automated trading platform. For example, with MT4, in addition to giving you the ability to use automated trading strategies known as expert advisors on the MT4 platform, you are also able to:

- Build your own indicators and strategies.

- Analyze your trading strategy using more than 50 built-in indicators.

- Trade your forex account with multiple order types and execution options. We talk more about order types in Chapter 15.

- Place manual trades and manage open positions and pending orders that have been placed manually or by expert advisors.

- Backtest expert advisors using a variety of customizable parameters.

- Choose from an online library of available expert advisors hosted by the MT4 platform or upload your own.

If you purchase and plan to use an expert advisor, you import the script into MT4. Once you have activated an expert advisor in MT4, the strategy will enter and exit trades for you automatically, 24 hours a day. (Expert advisors will run 24 hours a day on MT4 only if you remain logged into your platform or have subscribed to a Virtual Private Server (VPS) that will keep your strategies running even if your computer is turned off or you are logged out of the system.)

Sure sounds like a dream if you want to get some sleep and still trade forex.

But don't even think about using a robot and putting your own money at risk without backtesting the system and then running some simulations using a practice demo account.

 CAPITAL CAUTIONS

Always test an automated strategy before you start using it on your trading account. Don't just believe the backtest data provided by the vendor. Run your own backtests during various market conditions and scour the results.

As previously mentioned, MT4 allows you to backtest your automated trading strategies known as expert advisors to the MT4 community. Once you have chosen the expert advisor to test, you can modify the parameters of its written script if you want and then select a time period for testing.

After the time period that you select has been run through the test, you'll get an extensive report that enables you to review the results of the test's analysis. These results will show you the type of trades that were made, such as buys and sells or limits and stops. You'll get details about the order of the trades and the size of the lots that were traded.

You'll find information on prices that were paid along with information on the profit or loss for each transaction. At the end of the test, you'll find out how this trading would have affected your account balance.

As you dig deeper into the test module, you can find out more information about the quality of the trading model, such as whether or not trades were performed throughout the test time frame. A color coding is used as part of the test program. For example, the color green is used to show the modeling quality and it becomes brighter as the modeling quality gets higher. You can use the data you collect with testing to determine the best market conditions for each robot you test. Then you can adjust your settings for trading.

As you can tell from this brief description, you need a solid understanding of trading currency pairs before the testing will actually mean anything to you.

Now that we have talked extensively about MT4, you should also know that there are other options out there:

- Mirror Trader is a platform with a library of hundreds of preselected automated trading strategies, which have to meet strict criteria that the proprietors of the platform have established. You can choose these strategies based on a ranking system developed by Mirror Trader.

- Strategy Runner is another platform that enables you to connect automated trading strategies directly to a live account with the broker of your choosing. Strategy Runner allows you to choose from hundreds of strategies for a subscription fee, in addition to building your own custom strategies as well as placing manual trades.

- Ninja Trader is yet another software program that enables you to run strategies with backtesting capabilities among the features the platform offers. These are just a few of the plethora of automated trading software vendors that are available to today's traders.

Forex Software

Automated trading strategies are just one type of software you can use to beef up your trading portfolio. One thing you must remember, though: All software marketers promise the world but don't always deliver. Do your homework and research the products. Read the online discussion boards and online reviews. Find out as much as you can before spending your hard-earned money.

CAPITAL CAUTIONS

Even if you find positive reviews online, try to find out who is behind those reviews. You may find that the reviewers have a stake in selling the product, especially those who post on community forex discussion boards. So tread carefully.

In addition to automated trade execution software, you will also find forex trading software that serves as signal generators, forecasters, indicators, and charting platforms. All of these types of software can help to automate your trading and duplicate winning results that you've developed over the years as you've honed your own trading strategies.

Before buying any forex software, be sure the vendors provide you with regular updates and downloads, as the currency market is constantly changing. The software can become quickly outdated without frequent updates. If you find a vendor willing to sell you a particular type of software cheaper than most, you may find that they charge more for updates. So when you price a new piece of software, check the price for updates as well as the cost of the program.

Forex Trading Signal Generators

This type of software provides you with signals upon which you can trade directly. You may also want to use signals to enhance your own trading strategies. Be sure to look at how these signals are provided. If you're not at your computer all day, you may want to find a signal generator that can provide signals to a mobile device.

Forex Forecast Software

This type of software gives you detail about the profit and loss you might be facing. Using this software, you'll get some figures about what your trading strategy might achieve. You'll also get clues about what to avoid, ensuring that you don't lose control of your trading. Many depend on this type of software for information about which currency to buy, sell, or avoid.

Forex forecast software will give you early notification about its forecasting information more than once a day. It will also alert you as to when to exit trades either to take profit or limit losses.

The software tracks the fluctuations of currency pairs and will change its forecast according to changing market conditions. It can help you stay on top of market changes.

Don't think you can depend on forex forecast software to give you the right signals 100 percent of the time. That's not a possibility, but good software can have an accuracy of 75 percent.

Even as you test out a software package and become more and more confident in its accuracy, don't get greedy. Keep your emotions in check and follow your trading strategies.

Forex Indicators and Charting Platforms

Most forex trading platforms include indicators and charting tools. As you pick your broker, take these tools for a test drive and see if they'll meet your expectations. Practice with these tools on a demo model before you start trading.

If during the tests you find the tools aren't right for you, move on to another broker to see if you can find what you're looking for before opening an account and trading your own money.

Now that we've looked at various types of trading platforms and trading software, let's look at how to place orders in the next chapter.

The Least You Need to Know

- Automated trading strategies are computer scripts written by experienced traders that execute trades automatically using signals generated by data analysis and technical indicators.

- The forex market can be volatile. The price fluctuation of currency pairs is a constantly moving target with infinite variations due to outside forces that will cause them to move one of three ways—up, down, or sideways.

- Not all robots are programmed for all types of trading environments, and most are not even programmed to recognize a trading environment.

- Carefully research all robots before you buy them, and be sure to backtest their results and forward test them in a demo environment before using them to trade your hard-earned money.

- To use automated trading strategies, you need to find one of the many sophisticated platforms available to the market such as MT4, Mirror Trader, Strategy Runner, or Ninja Trader, just to name a few.

- Automated trading strategies, such as expert advisors and forex robots, are not the only type of forex software available to improve trading. Every broker offers forex indicators and charting tools. Test those out as well before opening an account.

How to Place Orders

In This Chapter

- Learning the terms for trading
- Borrowing to trade
- Picking a broker or dealer
- Ordering currency
- Calculating profits and losses

As a forex trader, you'll be placing orders either to buy or sell currency. The basic process is not difficult, but you do need to understand certain terms unique to trading.

In this chapter, we review the trading terms for placing an order, explain the process of borrowing money to buy money, sort out how to pick your broker or dealer, review the basics of placing an order, and explore the types of orders.

Reviewing Key Trading Terms

If you've traded stocks, you'll find many of the terms for trading forex to be similar, but with a slightly different twist. This section covers some key terms to understand before placing an order.

Going Long or Short

When you first enter the forex market, you either go long, by buying a currency, or go short, by selling a currency. Either way, you always buy currencies in pairs. We discuss the most active trading pairs in Chapter 5. When a currency is going up, you want to buy that currency, so you go long. For example, if after researching currencies you learn that euros are expected to increase in value relative to the U.S. dollar, you would buy euros and sell U.S. dollars.

The opposite is true if your research shows that a currency is expected to decrease in relative value. Then you would short the currency by selling it and buy one that is expected to rise.

Positions

A position is an open trade. Every time you take a position in the forex market, it involves someone buying and selling each currency in the pair, while someone else has to be willing to sell and buy the corresponding currencies.

You should have no trouble trading a currency pair as long as there is liquidity in the market for that pair. If you are trading the major currencies, you should be able to find a willing buyer or seller, called a counterparty.

You will usually close out a position with your broker by reversing the original transaction. For example, if you bought Japanese yen with U.S. dollars, you would close the trade by selling Japanese yen for U.S. dollars.

Bid and Offer Prices

When you see a quote for a currency pair, you will actually see two prices. One is the price at which the forex broker or dealer is willing to sell the currency, called the offer or the ask. The other is the price at which the forex market maker is willing to buy the currency, called the bid. You can also view this in terms of the trader, where the bid is the price at which a customer can sell, and the offer is the price at which a customer can buy. The bid price is always lower than the offer price, and is listed as the first price in a quote.

Spread

The spread is the difference in pips (discussed later in this chapter) between the bid and the ask price for a currency. Forex brokers and dealers make money from the spread rather than with commissions, so you may notice a difference in the size of the spreads offered by different brokers, dealers, and banks.

WEALTH BUILDERS

Always look for a broker or dealer who consistently offers tight spreads (which means the bid and ask are close in price)—especially on the major currency pairs. It will save you money.

Most brokers and dealers advertise that you can trade forex commission-free, because they make their money on the spread. Be sure you understand how the broker or dealer is being compensated before opening an account. Most spreads result in a cost of $10 to $40 per trade. Some forex brokers hide additional fees in a wide spread, so review the spread carefully with your broker and be sure you understand your trading costs.

Exchange Rate

Exchange rates are given in terms of the base currency and pricing (or terms) currency. The base currency is always shown first in a currency pair. If you are buying the base currency, the exchange rate is the amount you would pay or receive depending on the value of the base currency in terms of the pricing currency. Conversely, if you are selling the base currency, the exchange rate is how much you'll pay or receive for one unit of that currency.

For example, if the pair is shown as USD/JPY, the U.S. dollar is the base currency and the Japanese yen is the terms currency. So a quote of USD/JPY to sell USD for JPY at a price of 82.77 would mean for each U.S. dollar you could get 82.77 Japanese yen.

In forex trading, the exchange rate will always be given as a pair when you are buying or selling, because you are always selling one currency to buy another.

Pip

A pip is the pricing unit used in forex trading. A pip is the smallest change in price that can be made in a currency. It is one unit of price change in the bid/ask price of a currency and is denoted by the last number behind the decimal point of the price. For example, if you receive a quote for the pair USD/JPY (U.S. dollar/Japanese yen) of 82.77/82.80, the spread is 3 pips.

Bull and Bear Markets

In a bull market, the general market is moving upward. If the bears are in control, then the general market is moving downward.

Using Leverage

If you want to make money trading forex, you'll most likely need to borrow money, because the price differences in currency (which are what you will make your profit or loss on) are only fractions of a cent. When you borrow money to trade, it is called leverage.

Leverage is the amount of money a forex broker or dealer lends you for your trading activities. A common leverage option is 50 to 1. That means for every unit you use of your own capital, the broker lends you 50 units. So for an account with $5,000, you can trade up to $250,000 of currency.

CAPITAL CAUTIONS

Margin accounts can make you responsible for losses that exceed the dollar amount you put into the account. Don't trade on margin unless you understand how much money you are putting at risk. Be prepared to accept losses that can exceed the amount of money you put into a margin account. Although some brokers or dealers have policies in place to take you out of the market before you reach a negative balance, it cannot always be avoided during market gaps.

It might sound exciting that you can trade a quarter of a million dollars for just $5,000, but remember: although leverage does help you maximize your profits, it also increases your risk for substantial losses. When you're first getting started in forex, it's a good idea to start much smaller.

To avoid taking on too much risk and to be sure you'll have enough money to cover any losses, it's a good idea to limit each trade to just 5 percent of your useable margin. That way, if you do take a sizeable loss, you'll have enough in your account to cover it without having to dig deeper into your pockets.

Watch your useable margin as you trade. As you build your account, you'll be able to buy more lots, but if you take it slowly and follow the basic rule of not putting more than 5 to 10 percent of your useable margin in one basket, you'll minimize your risk. This will allow you to diversify your currency pairs and keep better control on your loss potential. You may also have a better chance of building your account with steady profits.

If your useable funds go into the negative, you will get a margin call. This means that if you don't deposit more money into your account quickly, the positions you hold will be sold to cover your losses.

WEALTH BUILDERS

Be patient as you build your forex account and don't put too much of your money into one currency pair. Follow the rule of trading no more than 5 percent of your useable margin on one transaction. You can minimize your risk and work toward steadily building your profits.

Most forex dealers give their clients between two and five days to cover a margin call. If you cannot bring your account up to the specified minimum, your broker or dealer has the right to sell your positions to cover your account balance. A margin call is not a bad thing—its purpose is to protect you and your capital. Be sure you read the fine print on your margin account contract. Also, discuss with your dealer how margin calls are handled and how much time you have to answer a call.

When your useable margin drops too low (that level is set by your broker when you open an account), you won't be able to trade on your current positions. You'll get a message on your screen such as "account in untradeable condition." You'll probably need to put more money into your account in order to trade.

CAPITAL CAUTIONS

You can lose your entire account balance if you're not careful, but you aren't likely to lose your house on a margin call. By putting on the brakes when your useable margin falls below a certain point, a good broker is actually protecting you from a more significant loss. Although you may initially get angry when you can't trade, it's a good thing, and for your own protection.

Many forex dealers no longer use a margin call system because the market moves too fast for traders to respond. All money could be lost too quickly. Instead, dealers set a minimum margin percent requirement, such as 25 percent of the account equity. If the account falls below that percentage, all holdings are liquidated. This protects the trader from losing everything. That way the trader will have enough money left after liquidation to begin trading again.

Choosing a Broker or Dealer

When you start looking for a company to open an account with, you'll find there are hundreds of websites promising quick riches. Most will promise you commission-free trades, but watch out for the hidden costs and those that are not so hidden. Remember that the way most brokers or dealers make money is based on the spread between the bid and ask price. Always look for tight spreads to save money.

But more important, you need to find an established and reputable dealer. Forex dealers have relationships with large banks or financial institutions because of the large sums of capital that are involved. Your best bet is to work with a dealer that has Futures Commission Merchant (FCM) status and can cut the middleman out of the equation. Co-author Gary Tilkin's company, GFT, provides this type of service. Dealers can save you fees that you may pay with a broker.

If you do decide to work with a broker, be sure you find one that is affiliated with an FCM. An FCM can handle futures contract orders, and can extend credit to customers. If based in the United States, your broker should also be registered with the Commodity Futures Trading Commission (CFTC) and can be a member of the National Futures Association (NFA).

WEALTH BUILDERS

In rare cases, some brokers are not regulated at all. Stay away from them. Any person can advertise himself as a forex broker without becoming registered with the regulatory agencies, so do your homework. Make sure that your broker has gone through the hoops to become registered. You can find out very quickly by using the National Futures Association's Background Affiliation Status Information Center at www.nfa.futures.org/basicnet.

In Chapter 13, we discuss trading platforms and some of the top online dealers that provide services to individual forex traders.

Exploring Order Types

You can use several different types of orders to trade forex. We're going to introduce you to the five key types—market orders, limit orders, stop orders, stop-limit orders, and order cancels order.

Market Order

A market order is the simplest and most basic order you can place. You see a trade you want and place an order to make the trade.

The problem with a market order is that you are not always guaranteed that the actual trade your broker completes will match the precise entry point that you saw on your screen. The forex market moves so fast that by the time your trade is executed, even if it is less than a second later, the quotes you see on your screen may not be accurate and the price you saw may no longer exist. If you are trying to guarantee a particular price on execution, a market order is not a good selection.

Limit Order

A better type of order to place when buying or selling a currency is called a limit order. This allows you to specify the price at which you want to buy or sell the currency pair.

If you are looking to buy a currency, you would place a limit order specifying that you will buy the currency at a specific price or lower. That way you won't end up paying more for the currency than you specified as the appropriate entry point.

If you are looking to sell a currency, you would place a limit order specifying that you will sell the currency at a specific price or higher. That way you won't end up with less than the price that you chose as the appropriate exit point.

WEALTH BUILDERS

Some brokers may charge more for a limit order than a market order, but this is not a place where you should be thrifty. In this type of fast-moving market, you want the extra protection of a limit order. If your broker charges too much for limit orders, find another broker, but don't cut corners by placing market orders. Most dealers, including GFT, offer limit orders at no additional charge.

You can place two types of limit orders: good 'til canceled and good for the day.

- Good 'til canceled (GTC) orders remain in play until you decide to cancel the order. You have the responsibility to monitor your outstanding orders, so pay close attention to your standing limit orders to be sure you do still want them to be executed.

- Good for the day (GFD) orders remain in play through the day and are automatically removed by your broker at the end of the day. Because the forex market has the advantage of being a 24-hour market, a variation of GFD in forex is "good until close of." With this added twist you indicate which currency pair you want as GFD and what geographical market you want it to correspond to. For example, you might want your EUR/USD order to be canceled when the London market closes.

Stop Order

When you place a stop order, you set in place an order that will automatically be executed when your price is hit. When the price is hit, the order becomes a market order and will be executed as soon as possible.

Stop orders are used by traders to lock in profits or limit losses. For example, suppose you decided that you wanted to trade the currency pair USD/JPY. After researching your numbers, you saw that the best entry point was 82. You placed a limit order and purchased the yen for 82.

You expect the yen to gain in relative value and you want to liquidate your position when it hits 78. You see that the yen moves to a price of 80. You've picked the right direction for the currency and want to lock in your profits. You would then place a stop order at 80.5 to protect your profit in case the yen starts moving in the other direction. If the yen does end up losing value and heads back up to 82, your broker would automatically execute the stop order and protect your profits between 82 and 80.5.

If the currency is very volatile and moving up and down between 82 and 78, your stop order could be executed too soon. The market might make it down to your target exit point of 78, but after your stop is already executed.

Also, your stop order is not a guaranteed exit price. When the stop price is hit, it becomes a market order and will be executed at the best possible price as quickly as possible. So if the market is moving rapidly, you could end up with an order executed at a price significantly different from the price you specified in your stop order.

Stop-Limit Order

Your best bet if you want to guarantee a price is to place an order that uses the benefits of both a stop order and a limit order, called a stop-limit order. If you place a stop order, but are worried that the market may move too quickly for the order to be executed in time, then you can include a limit order as part of the stop order.

When you use a stop-limit order, the stop becomes a limit order rather than a market order and won't be executed unless your broker can get the price you specified or better.

Remember, a limit order does prevent the trade from being executed. If the market is moving so fast that your broker or dealer doesn't have enough time to execute the order at the price you specified, you could end up completely missing the opportunity for your order to be executed.

Order Cancels Order

Sometimes you'll want to use a more complicated order that actually allows you to place two limit or two stop orders at the same time. You can place one order to buy a currency at a specific price and one order to sell the same currency at a specific price.

For example, suppose you see the pair USD/JPY at a price of 82. In researching the currency, you saw some data indicating that there may be a breakout increasing the value of the yen to 83 and other data indicating that the yen may drop in value to 81. In this case, you might place a buy limit order at 81.5 and a sell limit order at 82.5. If the market moves toward 83, the sell limit order would be executed and the buy limit ordered would be canceled.

Trailing Stop Order

With a trailing stop order, you can set your stop order to continue to follow the price movement (in real time) by specifying the distance, in pips, you would like your stop to move—depending on the market direction and type of stop order placed.

For example, you have an open position where you bought (went long) one lot (100,000 units) of USD/JPY at 74.5. You are expecting the pair to move 50 pips to 75 but want to limit your loss should volatile market conditions move against you. You could set up an automatic trailing stop to exit your position at 74.7 (thus automatically stopping a loss).

Placing Trades: GFT's DealBook® 360 Example

By now you've realized that placing a forex order requires you to understand a lot about the currency you trade, as well as the type of order you want to place. The actual process of placing an order is pretty simple, but do pay close attention to the details. You usually can't call your dealer and say you made a mistake. By the time you do, the price will have changed numerous times and your order likely can't be reversed. This can be even worse if you are dealing with a broker who is not a primary market maker.

Now we'll take you through the steps of actually placing an order using GFT's DealBook® 360.

 CAPITAL CAUTIONS

The quickest way to lose money when trading forex is to make a mistake when you place your order. Every type of ordering system for forex provides some way to confirm your order. Don't quickly click "Yes" at the bottom of the screen; read your orders carefully before confirming them.

Step 1: Pick the currency pair you want to trade. After clicking on New Order, your first step is to pick the currency pair you want to trade. In the following figure, we show you how you click on the arrow next to the symbol box and a drop-down menu will give you the currency options. In this example, we scrolled down the list to USD/JPY.

Step 1: Pick the currency pair you want to trade.

Step 2: Pick the order type you want to place. Next, pick the type of order that you want to place. Click on the arrow next to order type and you'll get a drop-down menu. In the following figure, we show you the drop-down order menu that includes Market order, Limit order, stop order, OCO (order cancels order) parent and contingents, training stop, and scale out. In this example, we picked OCO.

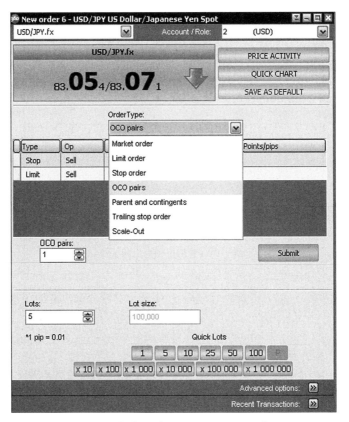

Step 2: Pick the order type you want to place.

Step 3: Set your entry or exit points. You will need to indicate whether you want to buy or sell the currency pair and at what price you want to do that. You can make those changes in the order options section of the new order form.

In the figure that follows, we show you that by clicking on the arrow to the right of Sell you get a drop-down menu that lets you choose whether or not you want to buy or sell the currency. To the left you will see another drop-down menu where you can indicate a limit or stop order. In the middle of that line is where you see the currency price. You just click on the price to change the price to your desired entry or exit point.

Note that at the top of the following Step 3 figure, the price for the currency pair is shown as 83.064/83.079. The smaller number to the left of the larger numbers represents the fractional pip. If you click the button next to Advanced Options, you'll see additional options. If you uncheck Display Handle, you can view the price as 064/079. This indicates the pip spread.

Step 3: Set up your entry or exit points.

Step 4: Indicate number of lots and advanced options. Indicate how many lots you want to buy or sell and the lot size. We've set it to 1 lot of 100,000 in the next figure. We've also opened the advanced options section to set up a time limit for the order. You can see at the bottom of the order screen there are two options for time limit—"Good until Canceled" or "Good until Close of" and then you are given a list of market close possibilities. We've highlighted Europe/London.

Also note that the price quote for the pair is 83.057/83.080. This screenshot was created several seconds later and the price for the pair moved. We set the final OCO order as a stop order to sell at 82.974 and a limit order to sell at 83.144.

Step 4: You can see that the number of lots to be sold in this image is one lot of 100,000. Also, we show you how to select a time limit for the order. In this image, we select Good until Close of the Europe/London market.

Step 5: Confirm your order. Once you're sure you've checked all aspects of your order, hit the submit button. You will get a box asking you to confirm your order. In the Step 5 figure, we show you a Confirm Order box. You should check the order to be sure that is what you want. If it is, you would hit Yes and the order would be placed. If you want to make changes, you would hit No and go back to the order form to make changes.

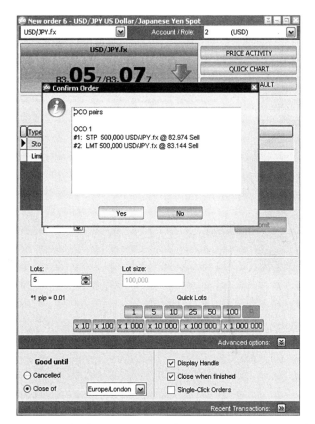

Step 5: This shows a Confirm Order box. If you click Yes, the order will be placed. If you click No, the order will not be placed and you will be able to make changes to the order.

Calculating Profits and Losses

Next, we show you how to calculate your profits or losses. After closing out a position, you take the price you paid to sell the base currency and subtract the price you paid to buy back the base currency, then multiply the difference by the transaction size. That will give you the gain or loss in the currency traded. You would then have to multiply that amount by the conversion rate of that currency to dollars to find out your gain or loss in U.S. dollars.

For example, suppose you bought USD/JPY at 80.66 and sold at 80.57. Also suppose the conversion rate from 1 yen to dollars is .0119. Here is how you would calculate your gain in yen and then convert it to dollars.

- Step 1: Subtract 80.57 – 80.66 = .09 pips
- Step 2: Multiply .09 × 100,000 = Gain of 9,000 yen
- Step 3: Multiply 9,000 × .0119 = Gain of $107.10

When you have a profit, you subtract any broker's fees to calculate your profit.

If the numbers were reversed and you had bought yen for 80.57 and sold it for 80.66, then you would have had a loss of 9,000 yen or $107.10.

The Least You Need to Know

- Be sure you understand the key trading terms before you start placing your orders.
- Use leverage to make money trading currency pairs because currencies are traded in fractions of a cent.
- Choose a reputable broker that is registered with the CFTC and the NFA.
- Be certain you know how to place the various order types and how each type impacts the execution of your order.
- Take the time to learn how to place an order using your broker's software. You can practice placing orders using GFT's DealBook® 360.

Managing Your Trade

In This Chapter

- Monitoring forex market news
- Keeping track of other key markets
- Charting tools
- Updating order levels

You developed your trading plan and placed your trade with entry and exit points. Now you can sit back and relax, right? Not quite.

As we've discussed, forex is like riding a roller coaster with many, many surprising twists and turns. Even if you've carefully developed a trading plan and tested your plan using practice accounts, you still need to manage a trade once the ride starts.

In this chapter, we review the key things you should be doing whenever you have a forex position open.

Keep an Eye on the Market

Whenever you have open positions, it's critical that you keep an eye on the market and monitor its ups and downs, not only price news but also news about related financial markets. If the market moves in a different way than you anticipated in your trading plan, you may need to adjust your stop-loss position to preserve a profit or prevent even more loss.

Even when positive change happens and the markets move more quickly in the direction you expected, you may need to take a profit earlier and avoid risking a change in direction that could change a profit into a loss.

Set Rate Alerts

As you monitor the markets, be sure you don't miss any major price shifts. Set *rate alerts* using your charting system or trading pattern.

DEFINITION

Rate alerts are electronic messages that alert you when the currency pair you've chosen has hit your specified price. They help you monitor how your trade is progressing.

Charting systems only have the capability of alerting about price developments when your computer is on and you're sitting in front of it, but some forex brokers offer you rate alerts that can be sent via e-mail or text message to your cell phone or other mobile device.

If you're planning to leave your computer regularly after placing trades—remember, it's a 24-hour marketplace—then finding a broker that offers a trading platform that includes rate alerts to your mobile devices will be critical to your ability to monitor your open positions. As you select your broker, be sure you have mobile devices that will be compatible with your broker's trading platform.

Even if you have set rate alerts, don't think you can avoid using stop-loss orders. Sometimes the market moves too quickly for you to even react to avoid a major loss. If you wait for that rate alert, you'll then need to log on to your trading platform or call your broker—and you could lose everything in the minutes it takes to react.

Always be sure to set your stop-loss orders at the same time as you open a trading position. Don't count on rate alerts to warn you in time. Their primary purpose is to help you monitor what's happening with open positions and be sure the trade is moving in the direction you anticipated.

Monitor Market-Moving News on Your Open Positions

Price changes are not the only thing you need to watch when you have an open trade. You also want to keep abreast of any news that could impact your trade. In Chapter 5, we talk about the market-moving economic releases that are important for each major currency, such as data releases about consumer prices or jobs reports. If you're not familiar with these releases, we explain what they are in greater detail in Chapter 8 when we talk about the key fundamental analysis tools.

Even before you open a position, be sure you know what types of market-moving releases will be announced while your position is open. Also watch for news of any major speeches or testimony by key central bankers, such as a speech by the chairman of the Federal Reserve if you're trading with a currency pair involving the U.S. dollar.

WEALTH BUILDERS

You can get advance notice of speeches and Congressional testimony by governors or the chairman of the Federal Reserve by monitoring the news and events page at the Federal Reserve website (www.federalreserve.gov/newsevents/default.htm).

If an economic release is expected during your open position, watch for stories in the financial press that speculate on what that news will be. For example, days before the Federal Open Market Committee meets, financial analysts will talk about whether they expect interest rates to change and in what direction. That speculation could drive the price of the U.S. dollar up or down prior to the actual decision announcement.

As you developed your trading plan, you might have used the anticipated news that interest rates will increase to determine your entry and exit points. If the analysts are wrong and interest rates don't rise, your trade could quickly move in the opposite direction than you expected. Keeping an eye on this news allows you to change your plan before you lose everything.

When developing your trading plan, always write down your expectations for key market-moving news as part of that plan. Whenever one of those expectations does not come true, be ready to move quickly.

Monitor Political News

Economic news is not the only news that can torpedo your trading plan. Political turmoil can also rapidly change the direction of a currency pair both in the short and long term.

Don't forget to continue tracking fundamental forces, such as political and social news, that can drive the supply and demand of the currencies you trade. This type of news can drive the value of a currency up or down.

Some traders enjoy trading on breaking news; others prefer to stay out of the market if they think the news makes the market too unpredictable. That's your call. Whatever you decide, be certain you know your preference before you open your position and start trading.

Monitor Other Financial Markets

Forex markets don't operate in a vacuum. Other major financial markets can impact the price of currency as well, including gold prices, oil prices, stock prices, and bond yields. Keeping an eye on what's happening in these other markets can also help you protect your profits—or make even more.

Although there isn't a direct statistical correlation between these other financial markets and the forex marketplace, psychologically, if one of the markets is facing a major price shift, you will need to assess its impact on your forex position.

Gold

Many people think of gold as a safe place to be when there are doubts about the U.S. dollar, so if you're trading in U.S. dollars, monitoring sentiment about gold can be crucial. Gold prices tend to move in the opposite direction of the U.S. dollar, but there are no guarantees.

You can expect gold to move based on news about the U.S. dollar, but sometimes it takes its own course corrections and market twists. As a forex trader, keep an eye on the gold market and see if its moves are impacting the direction of any open positions you have. Plan a course correction if gold is throwing you some surprises.

Oil

News about oil prices tends to impact economic news, such as interest rate speculation and inflation rates. Some believe that oil news can directly impact currencies, but no one has proven it statistically. Again, you're not worried about statistics when trading currencies, because the market moves much faster based on the psychological responses to the news than what will ultimately be the real impact on the economy.

Just remember that higher oil prices tend to be a warning that inflation is on the way, which could mean interest rates will move higher. Oil price spikes also could lead to slower economic growth. Of course, either impact will likely take months to truly be seen in the economy, but the economic news about what might happen drives the quick-moving forex market.

 CURRENCY COIN

A classic example of how oil prices can impact currency is what happened to various currency pairs between October 2007 and July 2008 when oil prices dropped more than 50 percent. In that time frame, key pairs—EUR/USD, GBP/JPY and USD/JPY—fell about 20 percent. The daily trading ranges increased significantly as few-hundred point swings in the Dow became the norm. The same was true for currencies, where the average daily range expanded significantly. The average true range for many currency pairs doubled in that period.

Stocks

There's not much correlation between stock prices and currency prices, but when a major stock exchange drops by a significant amount, such as 2 to 5 percent, you can expect forex traders to quickly jump out of the currency, putting downward pressure on that currency's price.

For example, when the U.S. stock market drops 2 percent or more, you can expect to see some downward pressure on the price of the dollar. The greater the drop, the greater pressure you'll likely see on the price of the dollar.

Bonds

Government bond yields give you a window into the direction of interest rates and what bond traders expect that government to do. For example, if U.S. Treasury bond yields go up, that's an indication that news about the dollar will be positive. When U.S. Treasury bond yields go down, bad news about the dollar will likely follow.

You do still need to understand why bond yields are shifting. If it's because of expected bad news from the Fed on interest rates, the impact on the dollar could be significant. But if the bad news on bonds is related to a problem with emerging market defaults, then the impact on the dollar may not be as clear.

You won't likely see a big impact on the forex market if the yield change is 1 to 2 basis points, but any change of 3 basis points or more will likely put pressure on the price of the dollar.

Trend or a Range?

Once you open a trade, it's critical to understand whether the market is in a trend or trading in a range. In a trend the market may move quickly up or down, but if it's trading in a range then the moves will be slower and will remain between two points.

Two common technical indicators can help you determine the difference between these two market conditions—Bollinger Bands and ADX.

Bollinger Bands

Bollinger Bands are great tools to determine when a currency pair enters or exits a trend. You can watch for when a trade exits a buy or sell zone to open your position if you are a range trader.

Bollinger Bands are typically used to determine volatility, but they also help you to gauge trends. We talk more about Bollinger Bands and their role in trend spotting in Chapter 10. In the following chart, we plotted a standard Bollinger Band using the settings 20, 2. The 2 means two standard deviations away from the 20-day moving average. Then we added a set of 20, 1. This second set was plotted based on 1 standard deviation away from the 20-day moving average. Most charting programs enable you to do Bollinger Bands.

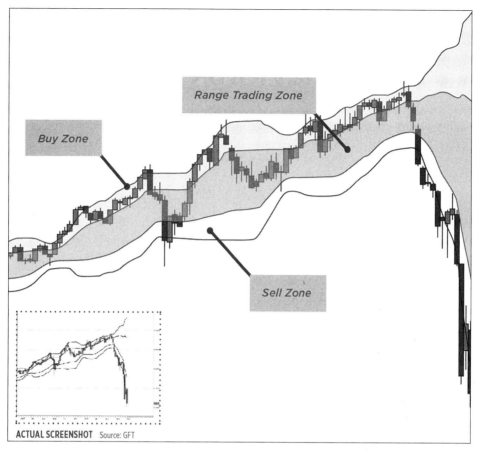

Traders use Bollinger Bands to monitor their trades when the position is open as well as when they develop their plans.

This Bollinger Band helps us find our buy zone and sell zone. The buy zone is the zone between the upper Bollinger Band of two standard deviations and the upper Bollinger Band of one standard deviation. The sell zone is the zone between the lower Bollinger Band of two standard deviations and the lower Bollinger Band of one standard deviation.

If the currency pair closes below the buy zone or above the sell zone, we say that the pair has entered its range-trading zone.

ADX

The Average Directional Index (ADX) is a classic measure of a trend's strength. Trend traders like to use this technical analysis tool when planning their trades and monitoring them after the position is open.

ADX, which looks at moving averages, can help define the direction of the trend. The ADX measures whether the trend is strong or weak. The index is displayed on a scale of 0 to 100 as an oscillator in a separate box below the price.

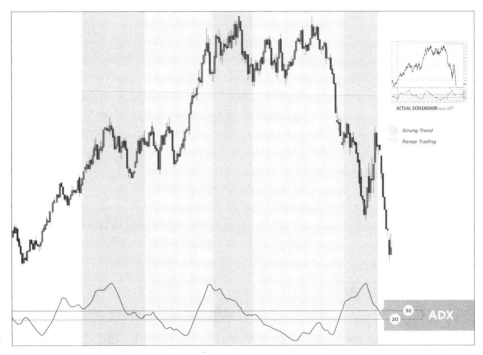

ADX charts help the trader determine the strength of the trend. When the ADX is greater than 30, the trend is strong. If ADX is below 20, a trend is weak. In a strong trend, you want to see the ADX sloping upward.

In the chart above, the ADX crossed above the 30 mark when the currency pair was trading at 1.52. Over the next month, the currency pair gained strength at a rapid pace, hitting a high above 1.60. When the ADX crossed back below the 30 mark, the currency pair ended up range trading for the next few months before breaking lower.

Whether you like using these two technical analysis tools or find others that help you monitor your trades, always use charting to follow an open trade. Don't just depend on the research you did while developing your trading plan.

Managing Your Target Price

You may find that you need to make adjustments to your trading plan once you've opened a position. If the market moves in your favor, you may decide to adjust your target price for taking profits, but if you do, be sure you adjust your stop-loss orders to protect your profits on the way.

Always remember to adjust your take-profit target and your stop-loss target at the same time. You don't want to risk giving back profit you've already gotten just to try to ride the roller coaster a little higher.

Reasons You May Increase Profit Targets

We've talked about how it's important to develop your trading plan and stick to it. Don't let emotion get the best of you. However, there may be some situations where you can make a rational decision to change the plan, as long as you do so by protecting your profits at the same time.

Here are three key reasons you may want to reassess your profit-taking position in your trading plan:

- **Surprisingly positive market news:** This can include unexpected news from a major central bank, such as the Federal Reserve or the European Central Bank. Or it may be news from the U.S. Treasury secretary or an unexpected agreement by the G7. Wherever the surprising news comes from, if it's at odds with the expectations of analysts and other news sources, the chances are greater that it will result in a major price move.

- **Less liquidity than expected:** If less supply is on the market than expected, prices may go up for your currency. You can look for this possibility most often during national holidays, seasonal periods (such as Christmas and New Year's), but you may also see some liquidity pressure at the end of a month or quarter.

- **Major break in technical trends:** As you watch your charts, you may see a major breakout from your previously anticipated position. If the trend indicates more profits, consider changing both your profit-taking point and your stop-loss point, but do so at the same time.

Generally, we don't recommend that you change your profit-taking plans, but you may want to if the market moves surprisingly in your favor. Just keep your emotions in check and be sure to protect the profit you've already made.

Protecting Profits by Tightening Stop-Loss Orders

When it comes to protecting gains, we have no hesitation in recommending that you tighten your stop-losses and change your trading plan. Taking steps to protect your profits is always a good thing to do, even if it means missing some profits. You're better off being cautious and having the money you need to trade another day than sticking to a plan that could result in risking that hard-earned profit.

Stay focused on the daily trend-line levels that you expected when you developed the plan, as we discussed in Chapter 10. Know your daily highs/lows and your Fibonacci retracement levels. If you see a major change in these trends, don't hesitate to pull the trigger and tighten your stop.

The one risk you do face if you adjust your stops too aggressively is that you could sell more quickly than anticipated; but as long as you have a profit, no matter how small, you'll be around to trade another day.

As you become more confident in your trading plan, you may find that you get less nervous about tightening those stop-loss orders. But, until you do feel confident, don't ever hesitate to take a profit and think you made the wrong decision.

When to Get Out

Timing is everything. Getting out at the right time can be the difference between making a profit and taking a loss. Finding that right time depends on your trading strategy.

For example, if you're trading before a major data release, such as a Federal Open Market Committee interest rate decision, be aware that the majority of the price action will be prior to the decision when everyone is speculating on the result.

You can't be sure how everyone will react before the final announcement of FOMC's decision, but you can certainly figure out which way prices will go if the Fed decides to raise interest rates. You can be certain the price of the U.S. dollar will go up. But if speculators thought the Fed was going to raise interest rates and it didn't, you can be certain the price of the U.S. dollar will go down rapidly. Getting out before the announcement can sometimes be your best timing.

The key to timing an exit is setting that goal before you even place a trade by setting your exit point with a stop-loss. Only adjust that stop-loss when you decide to tighten to preserve profit, or if you think there is more profit to be made and you decide to change your profit target. If the market has moved more quickly in the direction you anticipated, you may want to reconsider the plan and increase your profit target, but be sure you set your stop-loss to preserve already won profits.

Another common trading strategy is to plan your trades based on the time of day. For example, if you plan a trade based on a directional price move you see in the morning in New York, be sure to be ready for a price reaction as European traders begin to wind up their day and close out positions.

Sometimes when London closes you can see a price move in the direction you were expecting and sometimes you'll see a surprise reversal. Timing your exit prior to the close, determining the impact, and then deciding your next move may be your best bet—especially if you're seeing signs of a reversal. If you want to stay in the market and you have a nice profit, you may want to tighten your stop before the London close.

You also may be a trader who likes to trade based on the day of the week. You've tracked liquidity conditions and you plan a trade based on a holiday weekend, a month end, a quarter end, or just based on a Friday close. Every Friday you know the market will close for the weekend in a matter of hours. Yes, forex is a 24/7 market, but many traders do take the weekend off. If you hold your position, you could get caught up in unexpected position adjustments just before the weekly close as traders close out their open positions. So you may want to time your exit just before the adjustments.

The calendar is your friend when developing trading strategies and entry and exit points. Although it's important to set those exit points with a stop-loss order when you place the trade, always watch those critical times of day or days of week and adjust your exit accordingly.

Prices also can give you clues about the time to exit a position. When you see a sharp price increase, that's usually a sign that there's significant interest in that pair or one of its currencies.

Monitor your positions, and if you see a quick reversal or price gap, then you can also expect to find news or rumors driving that change. Sometimes it can just be temporary illiquidity for that pair. Whatever the reason, if there is a sharp change in the price, especially if it starts to move in the opposite direction than you planned, getting out can be your safest bet. Adjust your stop-loss and preserve your cash.

You learn how to trade by doing it and keeping track of what you did, so you can review your successes as well as your failures. In the next chapter, we talk about evaluating your trades and how to use that to improve your results.

The Least You Need to Know

- Just because you developed a trading plan, it doesn't mean you can just sit back and relax. Monitoring trades that are open is critical to your success.
- You must monitor economic news related to any open position, but don't forget to watch the political and social news as well.
- Use technical analysis tools to watch your ranges and your trends.
- Generally we think you should stick to your trading plan, but some surprises could warrant a change while a position is open.
- Exits can be timed to the time of day, day of week, or even market-moving news. Learning to time your exits can be the difference between making a profit and taking a loss.

Evaluating Your Results

In This Chapter

- Taking notes
- Using your journal
- Honing your strategies
- Getting to know your strengths

As the old adage goes, if you forget your mistakes, you're doomed to repeat them. The quicker you learn from your past successes *and* failures, the better your chances of becoming a successful trader. As you finish your trading day, take the time to evaluate how you did, and make some notes about what you did wrong and what you did right.

In this chapter, we talk about how to evaluate your trading and keep a journal you can use as a tool to hone your skills and improve your strategies. We also talk about how to take advantage of your strengths and get control of your weaknesses.

Noting Your Wins and Losses

At the end of a trading day, you're probably exhausted from the highs and lows of the market, but don't consider the day complete until you evaluate how you did. You can do that by just sitting down and thinking about what went wrong and what went right, but you're much better off writing everything down so you have a permanent record you can review later.

CAPITAL CAUTIONS

Don't get lazy. Take the time to evaluate every trade by keeping a journal. Without it you tend to remember the positives and glaze over the negatives.

The best way to do this is by keeping notes of your trades in a trading journal. Use a loose-leaf binder so you can then section it off based on your trading strategy. You may have sections organized by trading pair. For example, most traders will choose to concentrate on two or three trading pairs. You can make a section for each pair. Other traders prefer to develop their trading strategies by the time of day they trade. You may find it more useful to develop sections based on the time of day or day of month.

The big advantage of using a loose-leaf binder is that, as you hone your skills, if you do decide to change your trading strategies, it's much easier to reorganize the journal into sections that match your current trading strategies. For example, suppose you organized your journal by pairs, but find that the day of the week you trade is more critical to your successes. You can easily reorganize the pages into day-of-the-week sections.

What to Keep in Your Journal

Generally you want to keep a record of the key decision points that you made before placing the trade and then the key decision points that you made to exit the trade. Here are some key points to track for any trade:

- **Macroeconomic conditions:** List the world economic conditions that you considered before the trade, such as wars, oil prices, trade agreements among nations, storms, earthquakes, or holiday shopping.

- **Money-market conditions:** List any key money-market movers that you included when developing your trading plan, such as an anticipated rate announcement from a central bank or news about jobs. If you read an article that influenced your decision to trade based on market conditions, make a copy and keep it in your journal.

- **Currency pair:** Jot down why you chose to trade the currency pair. Did you choose the pair because of economic or market conditions? Were you expecting the pair to move in a particular direction? Write down your expectations and then briefly indicate whether you guessed right or wrong. If you read a good article about the pair in making your decisions, make a copy and keep it in your journal.

- **Technical analysis:** Write down which tools you used to determine your entry and exit points. Did they help you to determine the correct entry and exit points? Indicate which tools gave you the most accurate picture of what actually happened. If you read the charts wrong, keep notes about what you thought would happen and what did happen. This will help you hone your chart-reading skills. Make copies of the key charts you used and keep them in your journal.

- **Entry and exit points:** Write down the actual entry and exit points you picked before the trade and any changes you made during the trade. Were your initial entry and exit points the best ones? If not, keep notes on what you did wrong so you can hone your skills to improve your selection of entry and exit points.

- **Actual exit of position:** Jot down why you finally decided to exit the position. Was it automatic based on the initial exit point you set, or did you change the exit point during the trade? If you did change the exit point during the trade, why did you do so? Was it a mistake to change the exit point or did you benefit from the change?

- **Profit or Loss:** Write down your percentage gain or loss from the trade, as well as the dollar values.

- **Note your emotions:** Keep track of how you felt during the trade with some notes about any thoughts, hopes, or fears that you had before opening the trade, while the trade was opened, and after you exited the position.

- **Evaluate your results:** Finally, evaluate how you did. Write down what went right and what went wrong. Note how you could have done things differently to get better results. Identify any signals you used to enter or exit the trade and how well they worked.

Using Your Journal

Keeping a journal only works if you use it to learn from your past mistakes and successes. Review it regularly, especially before mapping out your next trading strategy. Read what worked and what didn't for the currency pairs you're thinking of trading again. As you get more experience trading a pair, you'll get better at picking the right entry and exit points. Your charting skills will also improve, but to do so you need to keep a record of what charts you looked at and how you read those charts versus what actually did happen.

Take the time to review your journal at least once a week or once a month, depending on how frequently you trade. That way you'll be able to pinpoint any consistent mistakes or missed opportunities and improve your planning strategies.

Improving Your Trading Strategies

As your journal grows, you'll start to see that some things work better for you than others. Initially you should definitely use both fundamental and technical analysis to plan your trade, but as you become more experienced you'll find some things work better for you than others.

 WEALTH BUILDERS

Get to know whether fundamental or technical analysis works better for you. Hone those skills that give you your greatest successes.

If you find more of your winning trades were planned using a particular charting tool, then you'll want to spend more time and energy learning to use that tool most effectively. Don't stop learning and using other tools, but do hone your skills with the tools that work best for you. You may be most successful trading at a particular time of day or day of week. Review your journal and see what patterns result in the most successful trades. You should then work to develop your strategies to take advantage of the ones that are getting you the best results.

Successful trading is not only based on how you trade, but also how large your position was. As you review your profits and losses, you need to consider whether the amount you're trading is too large or too small. If it's too small you might not make much money, but if it's too large you could lose all you have with just one trade gone wrong. Finding that proper balance takes time.

There are no right or wrong answers when you're working on improving your trading strategies. The key is what works for you based on your financial position as well as your emotional involvement. Some people are able to trade almost like a computer, with no emotional involvement, but they are rare. Most people do find their emotions impact their decision making, especially when trades go very wrong—or very right.

When a trade goes bad, they may jump out at the wrong time and miss an opportunity, or they may hold on, hoping things will go according to the original trading plan if they just give it a bit more time. That's why we insist that you set an exit point at the same time as you set an entry point. That helps to alleviate some of the problems of being driven by emotions.

When a trade goes very right, a trader can get so excited that they stay with a winning trade only to let it turn into a loser. If you do decide to change an exit point and let the trade ride, always set a new exit point at a level more beneficial to you than your original exit point, so you can preserve any profits you've already won.

Getting the Most Out of Your Journal

You may think that journaling is just too much trouble, but let us guarantee you that your memories of individual trades will fade. Unless you write down the details, you'll likely forget some, especially those things that didn't go right.

We all like to gloss over our failures at times. But many successful people will tell you that you learn more from your failures than your successes. You need to have the hard facts to review as you hone skills.

 CURRENCY COIN

"An expert is a person who has made all the mistakes that can be made in a very narrow field."

—Niels Bohr, Danish physicist, born 1882

As you evaluate your wins and losses, you'll find that you use the journal differently depending upon whether you are a long-term or medium-term trader versus a short-term trader.

Long-Term or Medium-Term Traders

You'll likely have fewer trades to review than short-term traders. You'll also be more likely to focus on the longer-term impacts of fundamental analysis, taking a close look at economic news, money market news, and political or social changes within the countries of the currency pairs you are trading. Technical analysis will be important to you, but you'll be looking at longer-term charts and longer-term trends.

In addition to looking at the fundamental and technical analysis you did before a trade, you also need to track your actual wins and losses. Total your number of winning trades and the number of losing trades. Also total your profits and losses.

You can judge how well you are doing by dividing your total profits by the number of winning trades to find out your average profit per trade. You should do the same thing with your losses.

As a long- or medium-term trader, you'll probably want to do this on a monthly basis. These calculations will let you see your trading trends. If your average wins are not improving, it's time to revisit your trading strategy completely.

Short-Term Traders

As a short-term trader, you'll probably have a lot more trades because you'll tend to open and close trades every day or every couple of days. You'll need to measure your results every day or at the very least once a week, depending on how many trades you place every day.

If you're only placing one or two trades a day, calculating results once a week should be enough for you to watch your profit and loss trends; but if you trade several times a day, you'll be better off doing the profit/loss calculations every day.

The basic process is the same as for long-term and medium-term trades. Add up the total number of wins in a day or in a week. Also add up the total profits in a day or in a week. Then divide your total profits by your total number of winning trades to get an average profit per trade. Do the same calculations with your losses to find an average loss.

CAPITAL CAUTIONS

If your trading results are not showing an improving trend in profits, it's time to revisit your trading strategies and see what's working and what isn't.

Generally, no matter what kind of trader you are, if you have more winning trades than losing trades, you're on the right track. You're getting better and better at spotting trading opportunities, as well as picking the proper entry and exit points. But if you have more losing trades than winning trades, something is seriously wrong. You need to go back to the drawing board and develop new trading strategies or improve the ones you're currently using.

Check on Your Timing

As you work to develop even stronger trading strategies, look at your winning and losing trades in different ways. You may find that you do better trading a particular time of day or day of week. Or you may find that you do better trading certain pairs than others.

For example, see if most of your winning trades happen at a particular time of day or day of the week. Also, review your losing trades for the same information. If you find most of your winning trades happen on Tuesday and Wednesday and most of your losing trades happen on Monday and Friday, you need to find out what it is about your trading strategy that only works on certain days. Or maybe you want to decide to hone the strategies for the days you do well and skip trading on the days you don't. For the days you don't do well you may need to develop an entirely new trading strategy.

You may find that as you review your trades you do well trading certain pairs and lose most of the time you trade others. If that's the case, focus on the ones that you do well trading, then decide whether you want to continue trading your losing pairs at all.

Keeping Your Emotions in Check

The key to successful trading will always be to get a check on your emotions and trade as analytically as you can. Learn to evaluate how much your emotions impacted your decisions before, during, and after a trade. Get a handle on those emotions and work toward trading with your analytical tools as the primary driver.

- **Don't lie to yourself.** Some people tend to only want to concentrate on their successes and forget their failures. That will be your downfall in forex trading. Always remember what went wrong as well as what went right.

- **Learn to spot your trading habits.** Everyone tends to fall into a particular habit, especially if the habit is working. If you're regularly winning, then you have good habits—but don't get overconfident. Continue to keep your journals and watch your trends. If you're losing more than you're winning, review your trading habits carefully and see what may be holding you back from success. You also want to be careful if you become too successful. For example, if you're winning on more days than you're losing, you may get overconfident and start developing bad trading habits that could come back to haunt you. You may start overextending the amount you trade and eventually take a big loss.

- **Trade on your strengths.** Take the time to identify your strengths and weaknesses. Over time you'll find that you're best at certain aspects, whether its spotting good market conditions or charting trends. Focus on those areas where you find the most success and hone those skills. Don't ignore your weaknesses, though. Know where they are and adjust your trading strategy to protect yourself from decisions made based on those weaknesses.

- **Pick your times and your pairs.** As you get more experience trading forex, you'll find that you do better with certain pairs. You'll also likely find that you do better trading at a particular time of day or day of week. Get to know what works best and hone your skills based on what works for you.

We've said numerous times that forex trading is like riding a roller coaster with unexpected twists and turns, but you can harness that roller coaster by knowing your strengths and avoiding your weaknesses. The best way to get a handle on those strengths and weaknesses is to keep a journal and review it regularly.

You also want to know how to avoid a dangerous and costly ride trading forex, by getting caught up in a money fraud. In the next chapter, we take a closer look at what you must avoid.

The Least You Need to Know

- Get into the habit of evaluating every trade by keeping a journal.
- Don't just keep a journal, review it regularly to hone your skills.
- Watch your winning and losing trends. Focus on what's working and avoid what's not.
- Get control of your emotions. Build on your strengths and avoid your weaknesses.

Trading Options

We introduce you to various forex trading options in this last section of the book. We start by talking about how to avoid money fraud.

Then we introduce you to mini accounts that help you start small, and standard-sized accounts that you may want to use when you become more experienced.

If you don't want to actually trade currency yourself, you don't have to do so. You can choose to let a professional money manager handle your forex trading or you can choose to trade options.

Finally we talk about how to set up your forex business and where to find good sources for forex news.

Avoiding Money Fraud

Chapter

18

In This Chapter

- Exposing the lies
- Researching offers
- Protecting yourself
- Seeking advice
- Resolving disputes

You may hear get-rich-quick promises in late-night television ads or infomercials. You may also see promotions about ways to get rich quick on the Internet by trading in foreign currency. Don't believe any of them. Forex trading is risky and requires a significant amount of time to learn to do properly.

Avoid getting caught up in forex fraud schemes. In this chapter, we talk about the common types of fraudulent claims you might see and what you can do to protect yourself from becoming a victim.

Believe It: Forex Trading Is Risky

Forex scammers use many different pitches to lure you in and make you think you can get rich quick. Your parents probably told you if something sounds too good to be true, it probably is. Remember that phrase as you read any offer to trade forex.

You must be even more aware of scams if you suddenly acquire a large sum of cash from an inheritance, insurance settlement, or retirement funds that could attract fraudulent operators. Once the money is gone, it's very difficult, if not impossible, to recover.

Here we review some of the key claims you may hear via phone, mail, or e-mail. These claims were gathered by the United States Commodity Futures Trading Commission (CFTC) during its investigations of fraudulent forex operators.

Beware of Claims Predicting Large Profits

Be cautious whenever you hear or read these claims:

- "Whether the market moves up or down in the currency market, you will make a profit."

- "Make $1,000 per week, every week."

- "We are outperforming 90 percent of domestic investments."

- "The main advantage of the forex markets is that there is no bear market."

- "We guarantee you will make at least a 30 to 40 percent rate of return within two months."

You should be careful anytime someone promises you extremely high performance. Usually these claims are false.

Question Claims Promising No Risk

Anytime someone encourages you to trade forex with a claim that there is little or no financial risk, it's false. Here are some common claims the CFTC has seen in fraudulent scams:

- "With a $10,000 deposit, the maximum you can lose is $200 to $250 per day."

- "We promise to recover any losses you have."

- "Your investment is secure."

Any attempt made by a company to downplay the risks you will take trading forex is likely a scam. Don't trust anyone who tells you that the written risk disclosure statement you see in the mailing you received or on their website you are reading is just a required formality of a government agency.

You must accept that the currency markets are volatile and risks can be substantial, especially for inexperienced customers. Scammers look for unsuspecting folks who will deposit their money and quickly lose it. The scammers protect themselves from losses by putting automatic stops in as your money disappears. In Chapter 15, we talk more about how forex trading is done on margin and the risks involved.

Avoid Firms That Promise Trading on the "Interbank Market"

Any firms that claim you can trade in the "interbank market" (where the big boys play) or that they will do it for you (other than a reputable managed account) are likely setting you up for a fall. Unregulated, fraudulent currency trading firms often tell their potential customers that their funds are traded in the "interbank market" to get you the best prices.

The only types of firms that do trade money on the interbank market are banks, investment banks, and large corporations. You won't be able to trade, and anyone who claims you can is not telling you the truth—unless, of course, you are planning to trade using the services of a major bank or investment bank, and with a very significant amount of capital. As long as you are working directly with a well-known bank, you are likely trading with an institution that is regulated by the government and not a scam artist.

Be Cautious About Trading Online

Although you will find reputable firms that do offer online trading services, be sure you know a lot more about the firm than what's on its website. Once you send funds electronically, it will likely be impossible to get them back if you later find out that the company is a fraudulent operator.

 CAPITAL CAUTIONS

An enticing Internet site can look very professional. But remember it can cost an Internet advertiser just pennies per day to reach a potential audience of millions of people. Fraudulent currency trading firms have learned that the Internet is an inexpensive and effective way to reach a large pool of potential customers.

Many fraudulent forex Internet scammers are not even located in the United States. You may not even find an address or other information identifying their nationality or location. If you do transfer funds to a foreign firm, you have even less of a chance to recover your money. Be sure you know exactly where your funds will be held when you open an account.

Be Aware of Scams Targeting Ethnic Minorities

Some forex scammers find that a great way to get new customers is to target people in ethnic communities. The CFTC found that people in Russian, Chinese, and Indian immigrant communities are targeted through advertisements in their ethnic newspapers and through television "infomercials" on stations that serve those communities.

CAPITAL CAUTIONS

Sophisticated fraud operators may give you a beautifully designed glossy brochure with impressive-looking charts. Don't depend on it. The information may be false. Always research a firm's claims no matter how good the information looks.

One common scam in these communities is to advertise as though the company is offering you a "job opportunity" for an "account executive" to trade foreign currencies. When you get to the job, you find out that you must use your own money for trading. You likely will also be encouraged to recruit family and friends. You could be lured into a trap not only to lose your own money, but to encourage your family members and friends to lose theirs.

Don't Open an Account if You Can't Check a Firm's Background

Any firm that won't give you enough information to check its background is probably a fraudulent operator. Don't just accept the information you're given; be sure to carefully check it all out with the regulatory agencies at the federal and state level. We talk more about how to do that in the following section on regulatory agencies. We also provide full details about the regulatory agencies in Appendix C.

When you do get information about a firm's background, don't depend on verbal statements you get from its employees. Be sure you get all the information in written form. If you are not able to verify the information you are given, it's a sure sign you're dealing with a questionable firm. Don't do business with any firm that you can't prove is legitimate.

Don't Make Quick Decisions

A favorite tactic of many forex scammers is to tell you by phone or e-mail that you must respond within a number of minutes or hours in order to get the deal promised. Don't fall for that tactic.

Always take the time to research the firm that approached you. You should be sure that the firm is legitimate and one that you would be comfortable using as your broker. Also, you should always independently research any tip or idea. If you don't understand the tip or why it's worth acting upon, don't take the action.

Get Everything in Writing

You may hate to read the fine print, but be sure you get everything that is promised to you in writing. Read all documentation carefully and be sure that you understand it. Before opening an account, you should get a contract that spells out all the trading rules, referred to as the customer or account agreement. You should also get a risk disclosure statement that clearly spells out the risks of trading forex.

In the customer or account agreement, you should find details about the laws and regulations under which the firm operates, the deposit requirements, details about trading on margin, and what happens if your account falls short. You should get information on how trades will be liquidated. You should also get a full listing of services provided and any fees and charges for those services. Be sure that you understand all fees and the basis for each of these charges.

If you do plan to trade online, there will likely be a separate agreement for electronic order entry and access that spells out how to access your account online and how it will be managed. Your entire relationship with your forex broker will be governed by this customer or account agreement. Be sure you understand your rights and responsibilities, as well as the firm's rights and responsibilities, before signing anything.

If you don't understand something, ask about it and be sure that you do understand all provisions before signing the document. If the answer seems to differ from what you are seeing, be sure you get all promises in writing.

A Money Manager Should Have a Track Record

If you choose to go with a money manager to handle your forex account, you should always seek as much information as you can about its past performance. Be aware that the information you receive may not always be reliable, and can be very difficult to verify. Fraudulent money managers have been found to indicate that their performance track record is audited by an independent accounting firm, even though that information is itself fraudulent.

 WEALTH BUILDERS

Remember that anything a salesperson promises may not actually be honored if you don't get it in writing. If a salesperson hedges on putting something in writing, the claim likely is not true.

Money managers are not required to provide this information, but be leery of any that refuse to give you information about their performance track record. And, of course, always look for a money manager with a long history and a reliable positive performance record.

Check with Regulatory Agencies

Before you even open an account, here are the key steps you should take to research the company to make sure it's legitimate.

CFTC

Your first stop should be the CFTC's consumer protection web page. You can access that by going to www.cftc.gov and clicking on the link to consumer protection. There you will find the most current advisories on forex fraud operations that the CFTC is investigating. You'll also get links to consumer advisories, as well as be able to report information about any questionable offers that you receive.

National Futures Association (NFA)

Your next stop should be the website of the National Futures Association. There you can use the NFA's Background Affiliation Status Information Center—BASIC—(www.nfa.futures.org/basicnet) to find out whether the company is registered with the CFTC and is a member of the NFA.

You are much safer working with a firm that is registered with the CFTC and is a member of the NFA. These firms must follow government regulations, and you have access to account discrepancy resources if problems arise. (We talk more about dispute resolution later in this chapter.)

CAPITAL CAUTIONS

Firms not registered with the CFTC could be questionable. Any forex broker who solicits to customers must be registered with the CFTC. If the company only trades for itself or its directors, then it does not have to be registered.

You should also check whether or not there has been disciplinary action against the firm. You can find out a firm's or an individual's status and disciplinary record using the BASIC database at NFA's website.

Contact State Authorities

If you've had no success finding the information you need, you can contact your state authorities. You should also research the firm's background information further to be sure there aren't any problems noticed by your state's agencies. Here are a few contacts you should make:

- Your state's securities commissioner, which you can find online using the database at the North American Securities Administrators Association (www. nasaa.org/QuickLinks/ContactYourRegulator.cfm).

- Your state attorney general's consumer protection bureau, which you can find online using the database at the website of the National Association of Attorneys General, www.naag.org. In the middle of the page you'll see a map you can use to locate the attorney general for your state. You'll then be able to get to his or her information page, where you'll find a link to the attorney general's consumer protection website.

- The Better Business Bureau. As with any company you plan to do business with, it's a good idea to check with the Better Business Bureau to find out if any claims have been filed against the firm. On the national Better Business Bureau website (www.bbb.org) you will find links to access the national database of businesses, as well as information to contact your local Better Business Bureau or to access its website.

If the firm you are researching is located in another state, you should also contact the securities commissioner, attorney general, and Better Business Bureau for the state in which the business is located. There may be complaints filed in the firm's home state that are not known by your state officials.

Seek Professional Advice from an Independent Third Party

It's always a good idea to seek advice from an independent third party that won't benefit financially from your decision to do business with a firm, especially when you are thinking of risking a lot of money. If you do want to get involved in forex trading, talk with your local banker or accountant. He or she may be able to recommend a number of good firms to work with or possibly even a contact within your own bank.

You don't have to work with your bank, but it can't hurt to sit down and talk with someone as you gather information about your forex trading options.

Resolving Problems with Your Forex Account

You may from time to time find that you are having a problem resolving an issue with your forex broker or dealer. Your first step should be to try to resolve the issue directly with the firm, but if you are not successful you may be able to seek the help of the CFTC and NFA in resolving your dispute.

NFA Dispute Resolution Program

The NFA offers a dispute resolution program to help customers and members of the NFA resolve disputes. As long as the firm you are dealing with is a member of the NFA, you can seek their assistance. That's one of the key reasons to do your research up front and only work with forex trading companies that are members of the NFA.

The NFA offers both arbitration and mediation. Arbitration involves a process where the NFA member and the client present their arguments and any supporting evidence to an impartial third party or panel. The impartial third party or panel decides how the matter should be resolved.

WEALTH BUILDERS

You can get information about NFA's Dispute Resolution program by calling 1-800-621-3570. You can also read more about the program at www.nfa.futures. org. You will find a link to file a complaint at the top of the page.

Mediation involves a process where the two parties in dispute work with an independent third party called a mediator to resolve the dispute in a way that is mutually agreeable. The mediator does not decide who is right or wrong, but tries to get both parties to come to an agreement.

CFTC Reparations Program

The CFTC offers a reparations program for resolving disputes, which you can find online at www.cftc.gov/ConsumerProtection/RedressReparations/index.htm. This program serves people who have suffered a loss as a result of a commodity law violation. Currency is one of the many commodities the CFTC regulates. In order for the CFTC to get involved, the alleged violation must have been committed by a futures professional, which includes forex brokers and dealers, provided they have registered with the CFTC. There are three types of reparations proceedings:

- Voluntary proceedings, which cost $50 to file, are the quickest. These do not involve hearings or appeals. Complaints are dealt with solely on the basis of written submissions and any supporting evidence provided by the parties involved. If you choose to use this method, you do waive your right to appeal. All parties must consent to the rules of a voluntary proceeding before a case can go forward using this method. The decision of a voluntary proceeding cannot be appealed. There will be no factual findings or a discussion of how the decision was reached when a person choosing to file using voluntary proceedings and the parties involved accept this type of proceeding. There is no dollar limit in a voluntary proceeding.

- Summary proceedings, which cost $125 to file, are used to resolve claims for $30,000 or less. These proceedings are conducted orally by conference call if a judge decides a hearing is needed. The results of a summary judgment can be appealed. The initial decision will include factual findings and a discussion of the basis for the decision. The party that loses in the summary proceedings has the right to appeal the decision first to the full CFTC commission and then to the Federal Court of Appeals.

- Formal proceedings, which cost $250 to file, are used to resolve claims over $30,000 and involve an in-person hearing. The initial decision can be appealed and will include factual findings and a discussion of the basis for the legal conclusions. The party that loses in the formal proceedings has the right to appeal the decision first to the full CFTC commission and then to the Federal Court of Appeals.

In any of these types of proceedings, the customer can seek actual damages, which include all out-of-pocket trading losses. If the customer wins, he or she can recover his or her losses as well as the filing fee. Customers may represent themselves or may be represented by a lawyer.

You must file your reparations complaint within two years of the date that your cause of action occurs. This means two years from the date you know or should have known that there was wrongdoing. If you think you have been harmed by a violation of commodity laws, you should file with the CFTC as soon as possible to protect your rights.

You may be wondering what you need to file a complaint. Here are the key points on the CFTC's checklist:

- Was the broker, dealer, or firm registered with the CFTC at the time of the alleged violations? If you did your research before opening the account, you should have a record of this.

- Does the issue in question fall under the jurisdiction of the reparations program? Did you suffer a loss as a result of commodity law violation?

- List the names, addresses, and telephone numbers of each individual firm alleged in the complaint.

- Provide a complete description of your case, including a chronological account of the acts involved, the names of the persons who committed each act, the date and place of each act, and the way in which these acts harmed you.

- Provide an explanation for the amount of damages you are seeking and how you calculated those damages.

- Attach all supporting documents, such as account statements and account opening documents.

- Include a statement about other legal actions you may already have taken, including any arbitration proceeding or civil court litigation you have filed.

- Include a statement indicating if any of the parties named are in pending receivership or bankruptcy proceedings.

You will also need to state under which type of proceeding you are filing—voluntary, summary, or formal—and pay the required filing fee.

If you do have a problem with an account, provided you've done your research up front you should be protected. Be sure to find out whether the broker or dealer you plan to use is registered with the CFTC and a member of the NFA. This research will be very valuable later and will put you in a strong position to protect yourself. If you failed to do this research, you may be out of luck trying to get your money back from a fraudulent operator.

Don't Trade More Than You Can Afford to Lose

Rule number one for forex trading is to never risk more than you can afford to lose. We know that we've said this numerous times in the book, but it is the most important thing for you to remember as you enter the exciting world of forex trading.

The Least You Need to Know

- Familiarize yourself with the typical fraudulent claims and avoid getting lured in by them.

- Read everything carefully before you sign it and make sure that all promises you receive verbally are made in writing.

- Carefully research any firm you plan to work with through both federal and state agencies.

- You can get help if you are harmed by a forex broker or dealer that is registered with the CFTC and a member of the NFA, so be sure you are dealing with someone who is registered with the CFTC and a member of the NFA.

Using Mini Accounts

In This Chapter

- Taking tiny steps
- Borrowing too heavily
- Understanding your risk
- Recognizing your potential losses

When just getting started with forex, many people prefer to start slowly by taking tiny steps. You can do that through a mini account. But be careful. Many mini accounts allow much higher leverage. You can lose your entire deposit in a matter of hours.

In this chapter, we explain how mini accounts work and the dangers of leveraging too much.

Starting Small

A standard lot in forex is 100,000 units of the base currency of a currency pair (you can find out more about base currency in Chapter 3). So if you buy one standard lot of EUR/USD with a price of $1.2155, you would control $121,550 worth of euros.

$$\$1.2155 \times 100{,}000 = \$121{,}550$$

Most forex dealers allow you to buy this lot on a margin account with leverage of 50:1, which translates into a 2 percent margin deposit. So you would need $2,431.00 in your forex trading account to make this trade.

$121,550 × .02 = $2,431.00

If you're new to forex, that may still be more than you are ready to risk on your first purchase. It's very important to keep your own risk tolerance in mind. To make it easier and less risky for you as a new trader, many brokers and dealers offer what is called a *mini account*.

DEFINITION

A forex **mini account** allows you to trade a smaller amount of currencies with smaller minimum deposits by using a mini lot. A mini lot is 10,000 units of currency, which is just a tenth of the size of a standard lot of 100,000 units. Mini accounts offer higher leverage, so you can control more currency with a lower deposit.

With a mini account you can buy a mini lot, which is just 10,000 units of the base currency. So for the same currency exchange example discussed here you would need only a $243.10 security deposit in your account:

$1.2155 × 10,000 = $12,155

$12,155 × .02 = $243.10

Now, suppose the market moved 100 pips against you to $1.2055; then you would have just $12,055, which would be a loss of $100.

This type of movement in the forex market can happen over a matter of hours and you can quickly lose the amount you deposited; but at least the loss on a mini account is much less than it would be for a standard lot.

In looking at the same scenario with a standard lot of EUR/USD, you would initially control $121,550 with a deposit of $2,431.00. If the market moved in your favor by 100 pips, the lot would be worth:

1.2255 × 100,000 = $122,550

Your profit would be $1,000 less any broker fess.

But just as quickly, the market could move against you by 100 pips to 1.2055, and then your lot would be worth:

$1.2055 \times 100,000 = \$120,550$

Your loss would be $1,000 plus any broker fees.

You may not be ready to take that much risk if you're just starting out with forex trading. You're better off using a mini account initially and making your mistakes by taking less risk. You won't gain much, but you can use the time trading in a mini account to learn the ropes and test your trading strategies.

 WEALTH BUILDERS

Mini accounts allow you to start small, but don't use that advantage to leverage your purchases too much. Although some brokers or dealers allow you to leverage 400:1, don't do it unless you're confident that you know what you are doing. With leverage that high, you can quickly lose more than you spent to initially enter the trade.

By using smaller lot sizes, you build up your account slowly. But if you do things right, you can build your trading account to a sizeable amount while building the confidence to try your strategies trading standard account sizes.

Don't Start Too Small!

If you're not ready to put at least $2,500 into starting your forex trading business, start practicing with a demonstration account and wait until you are ready to make at least that level of commitment.

But don't ever go deeper into your pockets and use money that you intended for your child's education or your retirement in such a risky venture. You must always be ready to lose all the money in a forex account, especially when you are first beginning and learning all the tools you'll need—fundamental analysis, technical analysis, and charting.

Take the time to learn and save your risk capital. It will be time well spent to get yourself ready for this opportunity to make a lot of money trading money. But be ready to lose a lot at times, too. Even the most experienced traders can take a loss when the market moves against their expectations. You can never be immune to periodic losses if you choose to trade forex.

Some brokers who offer mini accounts will even allow inexperienced traders to open an account using a credit card. This can be extremely risky. Not only can you lose all the money you deposit using a cash advance from your credit card, you would then also be paying high interest rates as you pay back your credit card company, increasing your potential for loss.

Always trade forex using cash you have deposited. If you use your credit card, you could lose the money you deposited even before you get your credit card bill.

Carefully Check Out Your Loss Potential

When you sign up with a broker, check the small print on your account agreement. Be sure the agreement limits your losses to the amount that you deposit. That means that you should never lose more than you put into your account, except in times of extreme market gapping, when the market is very volatile, such as after a major earthquake.

Before depositing any money, read all the fine print carefully. You must understand your rights and responsibilities, as well as the obligations of your broker.

 CAPITAL CAUTIONS

Some brokers promoting mini accounts do so to lure unsuspecting clients into taking more risk than they can truly afford. These brokers often don't have the training or the financial ability to even understand how speculative the forex market truly can be. Don't be one of their victims. Educate yourself fully before beginning to trade.

If you're drawn into the market by high-pressure sales without taking the time to truly learn how to trade forex successfully, you're doomed to fail and lose all the money you deposit. You could even possibly lose more than you deposit.

Many forex brokers that offer these low minimum accounts limit their risks but increase yours. Their computer trading software includes built-in liquidation stop-losses. If your trade moves against you, the broker's software is written to automatically limit its risk. When your account falls below a certain level (also known as a margin call, which we discuss in greater depth in Chapter 15), the broker's computer software is programmed to automatically sell your positions to cover your margin call.

When you get a margin call, your holdings can be closed immediately if your account agreement is set up that way. You could lose your entire account in minutes. Your broker won't lose, though. Brokers protect themselves by putting in these automatic stop-losses.

Your losses are locked in because your positions were closed. Your broker is fully protected with the automatic stop-losses.

Very high leverage can help you build your small account in a hurry. But it's a double-edged sword. You can also end up burning through your deposit just as quickly if the market moves against you. Concentrate on the size of the risk you are taking on each trade rather than the amount of currency you're going to control.

Test out a number of scenarios based on the way the market may move, just as we did previously. Run the numbers for a 100, 200, or 300 pip gain or loss. Be sure you can handle that level of loss and still be able to trade again. If not, you're probably leveraging too high. Take it slower.

Learn, make your mistakes without taking on too much risk, and give yourself the time to become an experienced, successful forex trader. You will always find currency to trade. It's much harder to rebuild an account that you've lost completely to trading mistakes.

GFT's Unique Option

GFT, the company owned by co-author Gary Tilkin, offers mini accounts with a minimum deposit of $200, and maximum leverage of 50:1.

The Least You Need to Know

- You can open a mini forex account with as little as $250, but make sure you think carefully and manage your leverage wisely.
- You can trade mini forex lots that are only 10,000 units of a currency rather than a standard lot of 100,000 units.
- If you are going to start small, don't start small and leverage your trade to the point that you can lose more than you deposit in your account.

Trading with Standard Accounts

Chapter 20

In This Chapter

- Exploring standard lots
- Counting the profits
- Finding the right broker

After you've been trading for a while and have honed your trading skills, you may be ready to take on more risk for the potential of more reward. You likely were attracted to trading forex for its potential to make money. But remember, there is equal potential to lose money.

In this chapter, we look at the pros and cons of standard lots and help you to understand how much you put at risk to trade with the big boys.

Understanding a Standard Lot

As we discussed in Chapter 18, a standard lot in forex is 100,000 units of a specific currency. So, for example, if you buy one standard lot of EUR/USD with a price of $1.2155, you would control $121,550 worth of euros.

$$\$1.2155 \times 100{,}000 = \$121{,}550$$

Most forex dealers allow you to buy this lot on a margin account with leverage of 50:1, which translates into a 2 percent margin deposit. So you would need $2,431.00 in your forex trading account to make this trade.

$$\$121{,}550 \times .02 = \$2{,}431.00$$

Although this is less than the minimum deposit for standard accounts (minimum deposits typically range from $2,000 to $10,000), if you're new to forex, that may still be more than you are ready to risk on your first purchase. Generally, traders will tell you never to risk more than 10 percent of your cash on a trade, so for a trade of this size, you should have at least $12,200 in your account.

Determining How Much Can You Make

When trading a standard-sized lot, you may wonder how much more you could make on a trade. Remember, with currency trading you are trading based on the movement in pips, which is the smallest change in currency price.

These movements are really just fractions of a cent. For example, for a currency pair to move just 1 cent from 1.5000 to 1.5100, it will actually move by 100 pips. A 100 pip move would be worth $1,000 to you as a standard lot trader, as long as the market moved in the direction you expect, but a 1 cent move in the wrong direction could result in a $1,000 loss.

Once you have enough experience, you may want to consider trading in standard lots, but even if you feel you have developed a good trading strategy, don't consider it until you've built up a large enough cash account to take the risk. To trade in standard lots, you must have adequate up-front capital—that means at least $2,000 but more likely $10,000 to open an account. Because you have more money to invest, you can expect to get more services and perks. If you do decide to move up to a standard lot size, you may want to change brokers based on services offered.

Finding the Right Broker

So what should you look for when you're ready to trade with the big boys? Your first priority should always be the safety of your account. After that, consider the commissions and spreads, how much you must deposit initially, what trading platforms and software are offered by each broker you consider, what currency pairs are offered, and whether the broker offers good, 24-hour customer support. Let's take a close look at each of these requirements.

Regulation and Safety

Your first consideration should always be the honesty of each broker. If you fail at this step, you're likely to lose before you ever get started. The basic guidelines for finding a safe broker are simple. You should check out a firm's background, review comments from other traders on forex discussion boards about a broker's services, and ask questions of the brokers you are considering directly.

However, even after doing all these things, be sure that government authorities regulate the broker (see Chapter 18). Also review the technologies offered for ensuring the safety of your personal information and account details from unauthorized access. For example, technologies like *SSL-encryption* are standard in business today. If you don't see them implemented, find a different broker.

DEFINITION

SSL-encryption is short for secured sockets layer, which protects the security of information you transmit over the Internet. When there is no SSL-encryption, you will see an open padlock on your browser. When SSL-encryption is enabled, the padlock will close. Click on the padlock and you can get information about the SSL certificate provider.

The two key regulatory bodies in the United States are the National Futures Association (NFA) and the U.S. Commodities Futures Trading Commission (CFTC). When you go to the website of any broker you are considering, your first stop should be at the broker's "About Us" section to find out who regulates the broker. A broker should also post at the bottom of its website pages that it's a member of the NFA and subject to regulations of the CFTC. We provide full information about the regulators in Appendix C.

If you are considering trading through a foreign broker, research which regulatory body oversees the broker's operations. Each European nation has its own regulatory body. For example, in the United Kingdom, the regulator is the Financial Services Authority (www.fsa.gov.uk).

WEALTH BUILDERS

If you are thinking of using a foreign broker, contact the central bank for the country in which the broker is located and find out more about how that country regulates brokers. You can get a list of central banks at the Bank for International Settlements (www.bis.org/cbanks.htm).

You definitely want to avoid signing up with a fraudulent broker. We talk more about how to avoid money fraud and spot the dangers in Chapter 18.

Commissions and Spreads

Obviously, the lower the commissions the better you are. Forex brokers and dealers make money from the spread rather than from commissions. So the key thing to watch is the size of the spreads offered by different brokers, dealers, and banks.

Although brokers and dealers advertise that you can trade forex commission-free, because they make their money on the spread, be sure you understand how the broker or dealer is being compensated before opening an account. Most spreads result in a cost of $10 to $40 per trade. Some forex brokers hide additional fees in a wide spread, so review the spread carefully with your broker and be sure you understand your trading costs.

For example, when you see a quote for a currency pair, you will actually see two prices. One is the price at which the forex broker or dealer is willing to sell the currency, which is called the offer or the ask. The other is the price at which the forex market maker is willing to buy the currency, which is called the bid. This can also be viewed in terms of the trader, where the bid is the price at which a customer can sell, and the offer is the price at which a customer can buy. The bid price is always lower than the offer price, and is listed as the first price in a quote.

The difference between the bid and the ask is the spread. Look carefully at the promised spread, which will differ by currency pair. The most commonly traded pairs, such as the EUR/USD, will usually have tighter spreads, which means your costs of trading will be lower.

Look at the promised spreads for the same currency pair on the websites of each broker you are considering. If one broker consistently charges more, then you need to investigate whether her services warrant the higher costs. Call and ask the broker why her costs are higher and ask what services she offers to justify those higher costs.

Initial Deposit

Each broker will have his own rules about the required deposit to open a standard account. Some will allow deposits as low as $2,000, but others may require $10,000 to trade standard lots.

Brokers may also differ in how you open the account. Some may allow you to use a credit card, some may require a wire transfer, and some will work with PayPal accounts. The ease with which you can add cash to your account may be a determining factor for you.

Margin Requirements

Read the fine print carefully about the margin requirements for each broker before opening a trading account. Your initial deposit becomes your opening margin balance and the basis for your trading.

Forex brokers do not issue margin calls, as stock brokers do. When a stock broker issues a margin call, he or she expects you to deposit more cash. Instead of a margin call, Forex brokers establish ratios based on margin balances that must be maintained at all times.

If your account's margin balance falls below the ratio established by your broker, even for just a few seconds, your broker's agreement likely gives her the right to close out your positions and lock in your losses before she even notifies you that you exceeded your allowed ratio.

CAPITAL CAUTIONS

You can lose all your money quickly if you exceed your allowed margin ratio in a forex account. Your broker likely has the right to sell all your losing positions before even contacting you, locking in your losses before you have time to act.

Compare the fine print of the brokers you are considering and be sure you completely understand each broker's margin requirements and liquidation policies. These can vary by account size and lot size.

Trading Platforms and Software

Nothing is more important than a good forex trading platform (which we discuss in greater detail in Chapter 13), but whether or not a trading platform is good for you will depend on your trading style and your risk tolerance. Each broker offers his own trading platform, and there is a vast selection of forex platforms to choose from, so be sure to take each platform for a test drive using practice or demo accounts before choosing a broker.

Generally, you want to look for an interface that is comfortable to you. This can include a color selection that helps you perform better. You also want to consider what customization options are available and whether you can adapt your trading style to the trading platform.

Here are some key things you want to be sure the trading platform includes:

- Ability to facilitate automated trading
- A good charting package
- Your favorite technical trading tools
- News about key fundamental movers from credible financial news providers
- Types of trade alerts available, such as mobile alerts or computer alerts

As you trade, you may find other key features you want in your forex platform. This will vary by your trading style. Never hesitate to read the forex forums where they discuss trading platform features to learn more about what's out there and what you may want to look for from your broker's platform.

But before you change brokers, be sure you understand not only the trading platform that you'll be getting, but the other key aspects of safe and profitable trading we've discussed here. Yes, your trading platform is important, but if your account details are not secure, you'll likely take a loss even with the best trading platform in the world.

Currency Pairs Offered

As long as you're planning to trade only the major currency pairs, you can be fairly certain that you won't have a problem with any broker you choose. But if you prefer to trade emerging currencies, you may need to do more intensive research to find a broker that enables you to trade the currencies you want to trade.

Always review the list of currency pairs allowed by a broker you are considering, just to be sure you are able to employ the trading strategies you've spent time developing. Pegged currencies, such as the Hong Kong dollar, Danish krone, or Chinese renminbi may not be available through all brokers.

Customer Support

When you start trading standard forex, you're placing a lot more money at risk and you want to be sure customer support is friendly, patient, and understanding if you have a problem. Obviously you hope nothing will ever go wrong, but you want to be sure your broker has the systems in place to correct any problems.

Generally the best forex brokers have systems that run smoothly, and if there's a technical error, will be able to swiftly recognize the problem and fix it. This may even happen on its own without requiring a call from you.

But to make sure that you're safe, it is always a good idea to make a call, even before you have any real intention of opening an account, to test the quality and helpfulness of the customer support staff. If you're thinking of trading standard lots, you should have enough experience to know what kinds of errors can happen. Test customer service by asking how they would handle certain types of errors you've experienced in the past.

Also, of course, you want to be sure customer support is available 24 hours a day. The forex market is active 24 hours a day and you may need help outside of normal business hours. Be sure customer service will be there for you whatever time of day you need help.

You may decide after trading for a while that you want to include forex trading in your investment portfolio, but you just don't have the abilities or the emotional stamina to handle the rapid ups and downs.

You don't have to trade forex yourself. You can instead consider working with a professional trader. In the next chapter, we take a closer look at that option.

The Least You Need to Know

- A standard lot on 50:1 leverage means that for $2,000 of your cash you can trade $100,000 worth of a currency.
- A movement of just one cent in a currency pair can be a loss or a gain of $1,000.
- The safety and security of your account should be your number one concern when choosing a broker.
- Forex is a 24-hour-a-day business, so you want to be sure your broker offers 24-hour-a-day customer service.

Managed Forex and Trading Systems

In This Chapter

- Getting help from the professionals
- Hedging with managed funds
- Using trading systems or managed accounts

You might be interested in trying forex trading, but you don't have the time to research and manage a forex account by yourself. You do have several options— working with a professional manager, opening an account with a hedge fund that specializes in trading forex, or using a managed trading system.

In this chapter, we review the pros and cons of the managed forex options.

Professional Forex Managers

Professional forex managers used to be available only to individuals who had at least $100,000 in their forex account. Today, some dealers can make arrangements for you to open an account with a professional forex manager with an initial deposit of as little as $2,000.

Trading forex requires you to research not only the actual currencies you want to trade, but also all the countries involved in those trades. It can be an enormous task and requires a full-time commitment if you want to succeed at forex trading and make money.

Picking a well-respected professional forex manager can help you develop a well-diversified forex portfolio using disciplined and proven trading skills. Your manager will have experience seeing profits in both rising and falling markets.

The key, of course, is to find the right manager. Don't try to do that just by researching options on your own using the Internet. You'll find hundreds of websites promising professional forex management, but many are scams. We talk more about the types of scams you may find on the Internet and how to recognize them in Chapter 18.

Seek out advice from trusted friends and associates who have worked with a professional forex manager and can recommend him or her highly. Also get recommendations from forex brokers with whom you are considering opening an account. Research the brokers or dealers before even considering their recommendations through the National Futures Association database (www.nfa.futures.org/basicnet).

CAPITAL CAUTIONS

Don't ever choose a professional forex manager solely by doing an Internet search, finding an interesting website, and opening a new account online. Be sure to do extensive research on the broker or dealer who has the site as well as the professional forex manager recommended.

Seek out a professional manager who has years of consistent forex trading experience, as well as a solid group of traders working for him. Many top professional forex managers have developed proprietary technical trading strategies that analyze and predict various trends in the foreign exchange markets.

As you research potential forex managers, be sure you understand their strategies and whether they might work well for you. For example, a professional manager's experience and research may enable him to spot recurring price patterns that he has learned to take advantage of to make profits.

Most professional forex managers have complex computer programs that help them manage the funds. These programs automatically monitor holdings for predetermined risk-management factors. These factors will provide a signal for entering and exiting positions at the appropriate time based on the parameters set by the manager. Research how long the manager usually holds on to his trades. You will find some managers who are day traders closing out all positions at the end of the trading day, some who hold trades 1 to 5 days, and some who keep positions open up to 20 days or longer.

Of course, you will have to pay a fee to the manager. A common fee structure is 25 percent of trading profits plus a 2 percent annual management fee. Be prepared to give up a significant portion of your gains, because convenience comes at a cost. Be sure you understand the fees you will pay before opening an account with a professional manager.

Hedge Funds

You can also get into the forex market by seeking out hedge funds that specialize in trading forex. Hedge funds are not regulated in the same way as mutual funds, so when choosing a hedge fund, research it carefully. The government regulations for hedge funds are minimal and do little to protect the investor up front. We talk more about cases involving forex hedge fund scam operators in Chapter 18.

WEALTH BUILDERS

You can research hedge funds online through an excellent database called Eurekahedge. Its databases focus on various places around the globe. For example, to find out more information about North American hedge funds, go to www.eurekahedge.com/database/northamericanhedgefunddirectory.asp.

You will most likely need at least $100,000 to buy into a managed hedge fund account. In other words, hedge funds are only for people who can afford to risk a sizeable amount of their cash. You will hear stories of people investing hundreds of thousands of dollars, or even millions, in a hedge fund that goes broke and they lose everything. These are highly risky investment vehicles.

CAPITAL CAUTIONS

Don't open an account with a forex-managed hedge fund with money you can't afford to lose. The profit potential is high, but so is the risk.

Hedge funds, like professional forex managers, expect significant rewards for their services. Expect fund fees of 25 percent of net profits, which means that you subtract unrealized losses from unrealized gains to find the net profit. They also usually get a 2 percent annual fee for managing the hedge fund portfolio.

The primary benefit of a hedge fund is its diversification, which means the variety of currency pairs and other investments they may hold at any given time. You will find a statement of methodology when you begin researching the hedge fund. That's where you'll discover the fund manager's trading style.

When you get information from the hedge fund, look for details about how many different currency pairs are traded by the fund and in what geographic areas the fund concentrates its research. Be sure the regional areas that are traded by the hedge fund match your trading goals.

For example, if you want to focus on currency trades in the European market, you don't want to open an account with a hedge fund that focuses on the Asian market with only a small portion of its portfolio in the European market. In addition, you should find out how long the fund usually holds on to its trades. A fund that closes out its trades daily will likely be more volatile than one that tends to hold winning trades for a longer period of time.

You should also see a statement about how the manager controls risk and what strategies he or she uses to minimize risk. All forex trading is risky, but you can follow strategies to minimize that risk. You also should look for some discussion about the volatility of the fund. Can you live with those ups and downs? Or will the fund's volatility make you so nervous that you ask to get out at one of the worst times of performance?

Managed Accounts and Trading Systems

Another way to get into the forex market if you're not ready or able to make the full-time commitment to trade is by using trading systems or managed accounts. Automated trading systems will give you a signal when it's a good time to enter or exit a trade.

Managed Accounts

Managed accounts can be an alternative to hiring a professional manager or buying into a hedge fund. For these types of accounts, you open an account in your name and then take advantage of an automated trading system developed by the account manager.

Managed forex accounts are not registered as separate investment products with the U.S. Securities and Exchange Commission. As long as forex is the only asset traded, an account manager doesn't have to officially provide disclosure documents. That means your research is even more critical when considering a managed forex account.

Documents you can expect to find with other types of SEC–registered products include information about strategy, audited performance, and fees. Even if the information isn't required, be sure to get it anyway. If you can't get the answers you want, run—don't walk—away.

Some brokers who offer managed accounts require at least a $5,000 deposit. Most others require between $10,000 and $50,000 to open an account.

CAPITAL CAUTIONS

You cannot easily move in and out of many managed accounts. Many limit the frequency with which you can enter or exit the system. Others require advance notice when you want to take out funds. Be sure you understand the rules for withdrawal before you deposit any money in a trading system account.

Many also limit access to the account to once a month on a specified day of the month. You may also be required to give a written notice several days before the last trading day of the month in which you want to withdraw funds in order to be allowed to take out your money.

When you read the fine print on a managed account contract, be certain you understand the fees that you will pay, the minimum deposit you must maintain, and any limitations you might have on withdrawing your money. You don't want to be in a position of not having access to your money when you need it.

CURRENCY COIN

The U.S. Commodity Futures Trading Commission (CFTC) announces at least one case of fraud almost every month involving managed forex accounts. Investors can lose millions before anyone notices what is happening.

For example, a case involving a Washington State firm named Sterling forex made headlines in October 2002 for costing forex investors nearly $1.8 million. The firm was charged with "fraudulent misrepresentation."

Sterling began collecting money from investors for its managed forex account in 1998 and reported annual profits in excess of 60 percent between the years of 1999 and 2001, when in fact Sterling hadn't even started trading funds until June 2002. By October 2002, when the CFTC closed them down, all investor money was lost. The CFTC said the firm reported falsely on their website that the performance record was audited monthly by a major accounting firm. By the time the CFTC acted, most of the investors' deposits with the firm were lost.

Trading Systems

Trading systems are a way to put your account on automatic pilot and let the system take over. They can be a good option for traders who may be too busy or overwhelmed to actively trade in the forex market. Trading systems will offer various trading strategies. Be sure you understand the trading strategies that are automatically programmed into the system you choose.

You will find some trading systems offer aggressive trading strategies, which signal you to take on high risk for a higher profit potential. You'll also find others that are more conservative. Although you don't have the potential to make as much with a more conservative system, your losses should also be minimized.

No matter what anyone tells you, no trading system can guarantee profits. Many trading systems signal to you when to buy and sell various forex pairs. Others automatically handle the trades for you. You will find promises of incredible trading wins based on hypothetical results. Hypothetical results are not based on a real portfolio trading with real money. They instead are trading simulations using historical price data.

The trading system promoter can pick the best results using the best part of historical data for his or her system. So don't depend on impressive trading results that are based on hypothetical trading data.

Hypothetical trading results are like depending on 20/20 hindsight. Don't we all wish we could do that sometimes? That would give us the chance to correct mistakes by knowing what we know today. Unfortunately, the world doesn't work that way and neither does forex trading.

You may also see the words that the system is tested using real-time trading. Beware! That doesn't mean that real money was traded. It just means that the system was tested using a live data feed rather than with historical market data.

Fees for trading systems and managed accounts vary greatly, but can be as high as 20 percent on trading gains, as well as an annual fee of 1 to 2 percent of your account value. Be certain to read the fine print before signing any contract for a trading system, and make sure you understand the fees you will be charged for the services you will receive.

Managed forex can be a good alternative if you don't have the time to spend researching the market and learning the trading tools. But you still need to carefully research any of the managers, managed accounts, or trading systems you choose to use. There are many scam artists out there that promise you huge profits with very little risk. Don't believe them. There is no risk-free way to trade forex.

The Least You Need to Know

- You can access professional forex managers through forex brokers or dealers that have arrangements with the manager. Call your broker or dealer to find out more about forex management opportunities.

- Hedge funds that specialize in trading forex give you the opportunity to access professional diversified forex managers, but be ready to put up at least $100,000 to open an account.

- Managed accounts can be a way to take advantage of a professional forex trader's strategies, but these accounts are not regulated, and you must research the account managers carefully.

- Automated trading systems provide a way to use programs developed by professional traders, but be cautious of the promises made by system designers.

Forex Trading Using Options

Chapter 22

In This Chapter

- Understanding options
- Looking at puts and calls
- Reviewing pricing
- Managing risks
- Learning some forex market strategies

Options give you a way to trade forex without actually buying and selling currency pairs. With an option, you enter into a contract with a buyer or seller for the right to buy or sell a currency pair.

Options based on currency pairs are not the only types of options. They have been used in the market since 1982, when the Chicago Board of Trade began trading options on Treasury bond futures. Today they are used to trade physical commodities, securities (stocks and bonds), and real estate. Typically, speculators in the forex options markets are investors seeking to profit from changes in a currency's price on a more leveraged basis.

In this chapter, you learn what options are and how you can use them to speculate and to minimize your forex risk.

What Is an Option?

An option, just as the definition would imply, gives you a choice. The buyer of an option enters into a contract to acquire the right—but not the obligation—to buy or sell an underlying financial product at a specific price on a particular date in exchange for payment for that right (called a premium). The buyer of an option has the right to exercise the option, which means he or she has the right to buy the underlying financial product according to the specifications of the contract.

There are two basic types of options:

- A call option gives the buyer the right, but not the obligation, to purchase a particular financial product at a specific price.

- A put option gives the buyer the right, but not the obligation, to sell a particular financial product at a specific price.

The price at which the buyer of a call option has the right to purchase the financial product or the buyer of a put option has the right to sell the financial product is known as the *strike price* (or exercise price).

The date the purchaser of the option has the right to purchase (call options) or sell (put options) the underlying financial product is known as the *expiration* or *expiry*.

DEFINITION

The **strike price** is the price at which the financial product underlying a call or put option can be purchased (call) or sold (put); also referred to as the "exercise price."

Expiration month for an options contract is the month preceding the contract delivery month. For example, an option on a March contract expires in February but is referred to as a March option because its exercise would result in a March contract position.

Each option has predetermined strike price and expiration dates. Each option contract can only be offset before expiration by trading an identical option (same commodity, month, and strike price call or put). The only variable in the equation is the price paid for this right, or the premium.

To see how these all work together, let's look at an example. Suppose you've done some research and believe that economic events will cause the price of the EUR/USD to drop in the next three weeks. You want to sell the EUR/USD, but you want to get in at a price that you feel is ideal.

Most options brokers provide a listing of available options to trade in their trading platform software. So you view a list of available options for the EUR/USD. You can find the list through your broker. Suppose you choose an option contract for the price of 10 pips with the right to sell EUR/USD at the price of 1.3500 on March 21st.

Now imagine that it's March 21st and the EUR/USD has dropped more than you expected; the market price of the currency pair is now at 1.3400. There's a 100 pip difference between the market price (1.3400) and the strike price of your option (1.3500). Your net profit on this would be 100 pips minus the 10-pip premium you paid for the option, or 90 pips.

As you can see, forex options are similar to trading forex. Both provide traders with an opportunity to find profit through speculation. With forex options, however, you may limit your risk to the premium you pay. To show you how this would work, let's imagine that the market price of the EUR/USD was at 1.3500 on March 21st. The market price of the currency pair and the price on your option are the same. If you bought the option, there would be no reason to exercise it, so you would let it expire. Your only loss would be the cost of the premium that you paid for the option.

Let's back up once more and imagine that on March 21st, the market price rose above 1.3500 at the expiration date. The market price of the currency pair is higher than the price on your option. You wouldn't want to exercise your option because you would be selling EUR/USD at a lower price than the current market. So instead you would let your option expire and your only loss would be what you paid for the option.

Understanding Options Prices

The premium (remember, this is the price of an option) is a function of where the underlying financial product is in relation to the strike price, the amount of time left before the option expires, and the volatility of the underlying financial product.

Let's take a closer look at what these factors mean.

Strike Price

The biggest factor in determining the price of a forex option is where the underlying currency pair is in relation to the strike price. A call option with a strike price below the current price of the currency pair has *intrinsic value.*

DEFINITION

The **intrinsic value** of an option is the amount of money that option would be worth if it were exercised and turned into a financial product today. For example, a 100 call option with the underlying financial product price at 120 would have an intrinsic value of 20. A 100 put option with the underlying financial product at 80 would also have an intrinsic value of 20.

When trading forex options, the intrinsic value as it relates to forex trading is the difference, if any, between the market price of the underlying currency pair and the strike price of the option. A call option has intrinsic value if its strike price is below the price of the currency pair. A put option has intrinsic value if the strike price is above the current underlying price for the currency pair. Any option that has intrinsic value is said to be *in-the-money.* As a general rule, the premium paid for an option will be higher, depending on the amount of intrinsic value that the option has.

If an option has no intrinsic value, it is said to be either *at-the-money* or *out-of-the-money.* An at-the-money option is one where the underlying price for the currency pair is equal to the strike price of the option. If a call option has a strike price higher than the current price for the currency pair, the option is said to be out-of-the-money. If a put option has a strike price below the current price for the currency pair, the put option is said to be out-of-the-money. At-the-money and out-of-the-money options have what is known as extrinsic value or time value.

DEFINITION

In-the-money forex call option means that the price for the currency pair is above the strike price. Put options are considered in-the-money if the currency pair is trading below the strike price of the put.

At-the-money forex option means the strike price of the option equals the price of the currency pair.

Time Value

The second major component of an option price—or premium—is time value. Time value is the amount of money that option buyers are willing to pay for an option in the anticipation that the price of the underlying financial product will change in value over time, causing the option to increase in value. Time value also reflects the amount of money that a seller of an option requires to give up the right to the purchaser.

Generally speaking, the time value of an option depends on the amount of time until an option's expiration: the longer the amount of time, the greater the time value of the option will be. This is because the right to buy or sell something is more valuable to a market participant if they have several months to decide what to do than if they only have several days. Conversely, the option seller has more risk over time that the option will go in-the-money (or stay in-the-money) and thus demands more premium in exchange for selling the right to buy or sell over a longer period of time.

You can look for some parallels between options and insurance policies. For example, the premium charged for term casualty insurance increases as the policy period increases. That's because it's more likely the policy holder will make a claim on the policy over time. Therefore, the policy writer (the insurance company) takes on greater risk and charges a higher premium.

The same general principle applies to options: the longer the time to expiration, the greater the likelihood that the option will be exercised. So the writer of the option takes on more risk and charges a higher premium.

WEALTH BUILDERS

Remember, because the risk and potential reward associated with time impacts the premium of the option, you'll find that the greater the amount of time to expiration of the option, the more expensive the premium will be.

Options with a longer time frame generally carry a higher premium, because the trader has more time for the market to work in his or her favor. As the option gets closer to its expiration date, the time value drops because there's less time in the option. This is called time decay.

Changes in volatility also cause changes to the option premium. Let's take a closer look at how volatility impacts premiums.

Volatility

Another component of extrinsic value—or time value—is the *volatility* of the underlying currency pair. Volatility is the amount of movement in the underlying market over a period of time. Obviously, if prices are jumping up and down by large amounts, the risk and potential reward associated with this market is greater, and hence the price of the option is greater.

DEFINITION

Volatility is the amount of movement in the underlying market over a period of time. Options tend to be more expensive when volatility is high and cheaper when volatility is low.

Volatility and time to expiration have tremendous impact on the price of out-of-the-money and at-the-money options. These factors also affect the extrinsic value portion of an in-the-money option as well. Just because an option is in-the-money does not mean that it doesn't have any extrinsic value. But as an option gets deeper and deeper in-the-money, it loses time value as a component of its pricing.

Because options have extrinsic value, or time value, they are decaying assets. As time passes, the amount of time value decreases. The rate of decay of time value increases as you get closer to expiration, speeding way up close to six weeks until expiration. Hence, for the option purchaser, time is the enemy, slowly eroding the value of an option.

So how does all this translate into forex options? Remember that a forex option is a contract for the right to buy or sell a currency pair at a specific price on a particular date. That means that after you select a currency pair and determine if you want a call or put, you'll specify the expiration date and strike price.

The Expiry or the Expiration Date

This is the date in the option contract when you buy or sell the currency pair at a specific price. In our EUR/USD option example, the expiry for that option was March 21st.

Although you can open or close an option position at any time, your choices will be based on the time periods set by your broker or the options contract. For example, GFT (co-author Gary Tilkin's company) offers expiries ranging from one week to up to six months. The expiry at GFT will usually occur on Wednesdays at 10 a.m. ET.

If Wednesday is not an eligible trade day because of a holiday or other event, expirations will be moved to 10 A.M. ET the first available day prior to Wednesday.

GFT offers European-style options, so they cannot be exercised before they expire. If you want the right to exercise your option at any time before the expiration date, you need to find a broker that offers American-style options.

The Strike or Exercise Price

This is the specific price in the option contract that your buy or sell forex position would be opened at on the expiry if your option had value on the expiry. For example, in the EUR/USD option we talked about earlier, the strike price was 1.3500.

When you want to trade an option, your broker may offer you a range of fixed strike prices. Or you may be able to choose your own strike. The number of available strikes is usually based on a reasonable range of anticipated prices in the underlying market.

To buy the option, you'll pay the option price or premium. When you view a list of options, you'll notice that the value of the premium varies from option to option. That's because many factors have an impact on the price of an option: the price of the underlying currency pair, interest rates, volatility, the strike price, and the amount of time until expiration. These are used to calculate the premium.

The difference between the strike price of your option and the current price of the underlying market is called the intrinsic value, as we discussed earlier. Here are the key points you need to remember about intrinsic value when trading forex options:

In-the-money

Call: strike price is below current price for currency pair.

Put: strike price is above current price for currency pair.

At-the-Money

Strike price equals current price for currency pair.

Out-of-the-Money

Call: strike price is above current price for currency pair.

Put: strike price is below current price for currency pair.

Selling Options

Up to now we've being talking about buying options, so let's take a look at how you would sell a call or put option. Remember, in our EUR/USD option example, you believed that economic events would cause the price of the currency pair to drop in the next three weeks, so you bought a EUR/USD put with a strike price of 1.3500.

As an experienced trader, you know that a lot can happen in three weeks. An economic event may cause volatility in the market, causing the premium of your EUR/USD put to rise. If you sold your put option, you would gain the difference between the new and original premium prices.

Now let's say you're considering opening another option in the EUR/USD. After doing some research, you now believe that economic events will cause the price of the underlying EUR/USD currency pair to rise in the next three weeks. Because of the nature of the market, you decide that you want to sell the put. So from a list of available options for the EUR/USD, you select a EUR/USD put at 1.3600 on April 21st.

Because you are selling the put, the buyer is purchasing the put from you, and you receive a 10-pip premium credit. Remember, as the seller of the put, you are required to honor the terms of the option if it is exercised. As the option approaches the expiration date, you could expect one of three things to happen:

- If the market price of the EUR/USD falls below 1.3600 to 1.3500, the put would be in-the-money. On April 21st, it would be exercised. You would be obligated to buy EUR/USD at 1.3600 and your account would be credited the premium for selling the put. Your overall loss on the trade would be 90 pips; 100 pips on the spot position minus the 10 pips received for selling the put.

- If the market price of the EUR/USD stays at 1.3600, your put would be at-the-money. On April 21st, it would expire worthless and you would be credited the premium for selling the put.

- If the market price of the EUR/USD rises above 1.3600, your put would be out-of-the-money. On April 21st your option would expire worthless and your account would be credited the premium for selling the put.

CAPITAL CAUTIONS

Selling an option has unlimited risk. Be sure you are familiar with the risks and have a basic understanding of forex option trading. Once you do, you'll be able to sell options as part of a larger strategy more easily.

Evaluating Risk

You can evaluate the risks of options most effectively with a set of tools called the Greeks. These tools forecast how much risk an option has over time. As you trade forex options, you may use the Greeks individually or combine them to gauge how well your option will do.

Let's take a closer look at the Greeks and how each can be used to forecast your option outcome. Research from your broker or data service will include this information.

Delta or the Hedge Ratio

Delta gauges how the price of the option changes when the price of the underlying currency pair changes. Expressed as a percentage, the Delta forecasts the likelihood that your option will expire in-the-money, based on the current state of the market.

For example, an at-the-money option has a 50 percent Delta, as it has an equal chance of finishing in or out of the money at expiration. An out-of-the-money option has a Delta close to 0 percent. An option that is deeply in-the-money will have a Delta that is close to 100 percent.

Gamma

Gamma measures the rate that the Delta of an option changes in response to a 1 percent change in the underlying product. Long options will usually have a Gamma with a positive value, while short options will have a negative Gamma.

Vega

Vega gauges how market volatility affects the option premium. You will see Vega change during times of large price movements in a currency pair.

Vega falls as the option gets closer to maturity. Even if there isn't a price change, if the market expects a change in volatility, Vega can change. For example, if the Vega of an option were +92.5 and the implied volatility decreased by 1 percent, then the option value would fall by $92.50

Theta

Theta measures the change of value the option may have over time. If Theta sounds familiar, that's because it represents the time decay. Time decay accelerates as the option approaches the expiration date.

Rho

Rho gauges how the value of an option will change if there are changes in interest rates. For forex options, you need to consider both the interest rate on the base currency (which is the euro for the EUR/USD) and the interest rate on the reference currency (which is the dollar for the EUR/USD). Higher interest rates generally result in higher call premiums and lower put premiums. Rho measures the amount of change in premiums due to a 1 percent change in the prevailing risk-free interest rate.

Option Strategies

You can use options in any market environment. The combination of option purchases and sales using calls and puts is almost limitless. It would be impossible to cover all the strategies here. But you will get a solid appreciation for the power of options and the flexibility they provide, and an appreciation for why put and call options are bought and sold en masse on a daily basis.

WEALTH BUILDERS

When purchasing options, it is very tempting to buy deep out-of-the-money options because they are cheap. Only buy deep out-of-the-money options if you like betting on long shots!

Let's first take a look at strategies for speculating with what we call vanilla options. These have standard expiration dates and strike prices.

Long Call Options

Remember, a call option gives the buyer the right to buy the underlying currency pair at a predetermined price (the strike price) on a specific date (expiration date). In exchange for this right, the buyer of the option pays a premium to buy the option.

Generally you buy a call option to hedge against higher prices. You expect the price for the underlying currency pair will rally, and increase the premium you paid for the option. A forex trader buying a call option anticipates that the price of the currency pair will rise and wants to take advantage of that movement. The profit is unlimited, while the loss is limited to the price of the premium.

As the purchaser of the call option, you have the right to exercise it, sell it on the open market, or hold it until expiration.

In essence, the purchaser of a call option is making a limited risk speculation that prices will rise between the purchase date and the option's expiration date. It can also mean the purchaser plans to make money selling the option and exit the position at a higher premium price. The total risk of the position is limited to the premium paid.

Long Put Options

A put option gives the buyer the right to sell a currency pair at a predetermined price (the strike price) on a specific date (expiration date). In exchange for this right, the buyer of the option pays a premium.

The general logic behind buying a put option is either to hedge against lower prices, or to hope that the market will decrease, increasing the premium one pays for the option. Remember, because put options give the buyer of the option the right to sell the underlying currency pair, put options increase in value when the price of the underlying currency pair declines in value.

If you plan to buy a long put option, it means you expect the price of a currency pair to fall and you want to take advantage of that movement. The profit is unlimited, and the loss is limited to the price of the premium.

As you get closer to the expiration date, you can continue to hold the option or sell it. Remember that a put option only has intrinsic value when the strike price is above the current market price. If it's below the market price, you can just let the option expire, but if it's above the market price you can either hold it and exercise the option, or you may be able to sell the option at a profit prior to the expiration date.

In essence, if you purchase a put option, you are making a limited risk speculation that prices will decline between the purchase date and options expiration, or the time you decide to exit the position by offsetting it. The total risk of the position is limited to the premium paid.

Short Call Position

Short positions are used when you decide to sell the option. In reality the options industry believes that 85 percent of all options expire worthless. Plus options are a decaying asset, which means that options decrease in value the closer they get to expiration. With this in mind, many industry experts believe that option selling is the way to go.

However, selling options can be extremely difficult. A short option position has a limited reward to the premium collected at the time of the sale, while risk is unlimited. Second, the writer of an option has obligations, not rights. He or she must deliver the underlying currency pair only if it is unprofitable for him or her to do so.

CAPITAL CAUTIONS

Unlike options purchases, where the risk is limited to the premium paid, writers of options have unlimited risk. Be sure you understand what your risks and obligations are before you trade options.

Selling options, or short option positions, is slightly akin to writing an insurance policy. Think about life insurance for a minute. Life insurance companies know you will eventually die. However, they write policies because they charge enough in premiums to compensate them for the fact that your beneficiaries will eventually collect on the policy.

Though option sellers do not know for sure whether an option will be exercised or not, they are always faced with the possibility. As such, options sellers will demand a price for their options that they feel compensates them for the risk. As a trader you decide it's worth taking the risk. You anticipate that the price of a currency pair will fall. So you decide to sell the call and collect the premium. The only profit you get is the premium received, but your loss is unlimited.

So as the writer of a call option, which means you initiate a short call position, your profit potential is limited, but you risk unlimited speculation that prices will decline between the purchase date and options expiration date, or the time you decide to exit the position.

The total risk on this position is unlimited, as prices for currency pairs can advance, but the profit potential is limited to the premium collected. However, because options are a decaying asset, meaning that their value declines the closer they get to expiration, call options writers not only benefit from declining prices, but they also benefit from stable, sideways price movement as well.

Short Put Position

If you decide to write a put position, it means you are selling the right to sell a currency pair at a predetermined price (the strike price) on a specific date (expiration date). In return for granting these rights to the purchaser, the writer of an option collects the premium paid.

Selling put options has an unlimited risk. Yet your possibility of reward is limited. You speculate that prices will rise or at least not decline below the strike price by an amount greater than the premium received for the option. As you trade, you expect that the price of a currency pair will rise. You sell the put and collect the premium. Your profit is limited to the premium received, and your loss is unlimited.

In essence, the writer of a put option, which means you initiate a short put position, is making a limited profit potential/unlimited risk speculation that prices will rise between the purchase date and options expiration, or the time he or she decides to exit the position.

The total risk on this position is unlimited, as prices for the currency pair can decline, while the profit potential is limited to the premium collected. However, because options are a decaying asset, meaning that their value declines the closer they get to expiration, put option writers not only benefit from rising prices, but they also benefit from stable, sideways price movement as well.

Option Buying Offers Limited Risk

If you are thinking of using options as a way to try your hand at forex trading, remember the purchase of a long options position (put or call) is a limited-risk endeavor. As the owner of an option, you can lose no more than the initial price—or premium—paid for that option. This is not true for short options positions.

Buying options is the only limited risk/unlimited reward way to speculate in the forex market. However, do not discount the risk of losing your premium. Most long-option purchases expire worthless. This is especially true of the "cheap," out-of-the-money options that are popular for the retail trading public.

Options buyers also pay a time premium for the option. As the option approaches expiration, this premium is removed and can result in financial losses for the option purchaser. Because options are a decaying asset—losing time value—it is possible to be correct on the direction of the market and still lose money on the purchase of an option.

Most options traders use options in conjunction with other options or with the direct purchase of currency pairs to establish option positions that can generate more likely profits or reduced risk in the market.

You may want to use these types of vanilla options in combination with currency pairs and even other options. You can use a number of different strategies to both protect your trade and position yourself in the market.

Some of the most common strategies used today include Vertical, Straddle, Strangle, and Risk Reversal. Let's take a closer look at each.

Vertical

With this strategy, you can open a long and a short call or put on the same currency pair. This is called a multileg order, and each option would be considered a leg. Both option legs have the same expiration date, but different strike prices.

Many traders use verticals when they have an idea which way the market will swing, but they aren't sure how strong the swing will be.

Straddle

With a straddle, you buy both a call and a put on the same underlying currency pair with the same strike price and expiration date.

When traders suspect that the market may be volatile and this may cause the price of the underlying currency pair to swing, but they aren't sure which direction the market will go, they often consider buying a long straddle.

This may provide unlimited profit potential while limiting your loss to the premiums you paid to open the straddle. When you expect a little volatility in the market, you can use a short straddle, which has a profit limited to the premiums received, but unlimited loss potential.

Strangle

A strangle has a similar set up to a straddle. You open both a call and a put on the same currency pair. These must both be going either long (a long strangle) or short (a short strangle), and have the same expiration date. With a strangle, however, your put has a lower strike price than the call.

Risk Reversal

A risk reversal is a strategy often used to protect a long or short currency pair position, but it can also be used to speculate on market volatility.

With this strategy, you sell (buy) an out-of-the-money call and buy (sell) an out-of-the-money put option in the same currency pair. The options have similar Delta value and are set up to have the same expiration date and number of lots as your long (short) currency pair trade. There is no limit on your profit potential, but you also face unlimited risk if the direction of the market changes.

Market Safety

You may think this entire market sounds too risky because you don't know who is selling you the options. The options market has basic safeguards to ensure market integrity. Options sellers are required to post *performance bond margins* to ensure fulfillment of the options contract.

DEFINITION

Performance bond margins are deposits required to ensure that an options writer can cover potential losses with his or her trading positions.

Options margins are assessed only on positions that have unlimited risk and are subject to change at the discretion of the exchange. Long-options positions require no margin to be posted, as risk is limited to the amount paid for the option.

Generally, options provide traders and hedgers another vehicle to either profit from or reduce the risk of currency price movements. The combination of option purchases and sales using calls and puts is almost limitless, but we've given you the basic strategies so you have an idea of the trading possibilities for using options as a way to get into the forex market.

The Least You Need to Know

- A call option allows you the right to buy an underlying currency pair at a predetermined price on a specific date.
- A put option gives you the right to sell an underlying currency pair at a predetermined price on a specific date.
- The buyer of an option (long position) exposes himself to risk limited to the amount paid for the option, but he enjoys potentially unlimited profit potential if he guesses the direction of the market correctly.
- The seller of an option (short position) has unlimited risk potential, but his or her profit potential is limited to the amount someone paid for the option.
- Most options expire worthless and options are a decaying asset, so either a long or short strategy can be profitable if proper risk management is used.

Setting Up Your Trading Business

In This Chapter

- Planning your business
- Office set-up
- Establishing inventory
- Taking profits

If you want to be successful as a trader, you have to start thinking of forex trading as a business rather than just an investment opportunity. When you're ready to take your trading business seriously, you can also enjoy some tax benefits.

In this chapter, we talk about how to set up that business and how the tax code helps you offset gains.

Start by Developing a Business Plan

Now that you've learned the basics of forex trading, you need to make these critical decisions:

How much money do you want to risk?

We recommend that you start trading with no more than about 2 percent of your portfolio assets. When you are confident that you know what you're doing, you may decide to increase that percentage. Even as your confidence grows, you don't want to risk more than 5 percent of your portfolio assets in such a risky business venture. But that's up to you to decide.

What return do you expect to make?

As you decide on your return expectations, don't set unrealistic goals that you have no chance of making. You'll set yourself up for defeat before you even get started.

Remember that even the best money managers aim for a goal of 15 to 20 percent annual return over the long term.

How much time will you be able to devote to the business?

Determine the number of hours you plan to spend trading, researching, and evaluating your trades. Think of it no differently than you would going to your office every day. Set up daily hours for your business and maintain them as you would any other work or business situation. Start thinking of yourself as a business person.

Where will you work on your trading business?

Establish a business office. Determine what physical assets your business will have, including your workspace and computer equipment.

The more structured you make your surroundings, the greater control you will have over your business activities. You can't take your business seriously if it's sometimes in the family room and sometimes at your dining room table.

If you can't afford a dedicated workspace, you're not ready for serious trading. You need a quiet place where you can research your trades, develop your charts, and map out your trading strategies.

How will you manage your inventory?

Think of the currency pairs that you hold as your inventory. They are the "products" you buy and sell. Avoid becoming emotionally involved with your inventory. Just because you like a decision you made to buy a pair, if the pair doesn't perform as expected, sell it and move on.

The biggest mistake many traders make is to hold on to protect their pride. Every business person makes mistakes. That's true for forex traders as well. Don't try to defend a trading mistake. Take your loss and move on. If your choice no longer makes good business sense, make the cold, hard decision to exit the position before a small loss turns into a big one—which can happen in seconds when market conditions are volatile.

When will you take your profits?

When you have a healthy profit and reach your exit point, don't hold on to the inventory. Remember, no one can accurately pick the top or bottom of any trade every time.

Don't push your luck; take your profits and get out. Develop a trading plan for every trade and follow your plan.

Positioning Your Business with the IRS

After you develop your business plan, you should start thinking of yourself as a trader rather than an investor. That definition is critical if you want the IRS to consider you as being in the trading business and offer you additional tax-reduction benefits.

Many people consider themselves investors, but investors don't get the same tax breaks as traders. Investors can get tax savings through the treatment of capital gains on things they buy and sell after a 12-month period. As a forex trader, you won't be holding inventory for that long.

The IRS code does not actually define the business of trading. The definition stems from court cases and decisions in favor of taxpayers who made this claim. As any good businessperson, you should sit down with your tax advisor and determine the best structure for your business and how to best minimize the tax bite.

WEALTH BUILDERS

You can find out more about how the IRS differentiates between traders and investors at the IRS website (www.irs.gov/taxtopics/tc429.html).

When it comes to trading, these have been the key determining factors in court cases:

- How long you hold on to your inventory.

- How frequently you trade.

- The dollar amounts of your trades.

- Whether or not your profits are from short-term trading activities or from long-term gains or dividend interest. Traders must earn their profits primarily from short-term trading activities.

- The amount of time you devote to the activity.

As a currency trader, because your profits will be from short-term trades, you should be able to prove your case with the IRS if questioned, but you must do a good job of record-keeping to prove you are operating a trading business. To be certain your business will stand up to an IRS audit, be sure you establish good record-keeping habits based on advice from your tax advisor.

Initially as a trader you can create a *sole proprietorship* and take your business expenses on a Schedule C; however, because you don't have earned income, you'd report your income or losses on a Schedule D, because they will still be considered capital gains or losses.

DEFINITION

A **sole proprietorship** is any business owned by one person that is not incorporated.

Because you have no self-employment income, your trading losses are limited to $3,000 per year according to tax law. You can carry forward your losses indefinitely to future tax years, so if you have a bad year, you'll be able to write off those losses the next year—provided your next year is a good one. You also can write off any losses from forex trading against any stock trading gains or vice versa.

As your business grows you may want to consider creating your own trade corporation. This would become the legal entity under which you conduct your trading. There are some extra costs for setting up your business and maintaining it, but you'll quickly see that advantages far outweigh the costs if you are developing a serious trading business.

Organizing as a corporation will definitely establish your status as a trader. You will be able to deduct all your trading expenses against your trading gains and they won't be limited to $3,000 per year.

These expenses can include:

- Your trading education

- Your financial software

- Accounting fees

- Brokerage fees and commissions

- Office costs, such as computers, Internet connection, dedicated phone line, and others (review this list with your financial advisor)

- Tax advice related to your business

- Legal advice related to your business

- Travel to seminars, trade shows, and other business-related trips

- Subscriptions to newspapers and magazines related to trading and investing

- If you have dedicated a room in your home for your office, you can write it off as a home office

- Expenses for the use of your car related to your trading business

Check with your tax advisor to see if other expenses not mentioned here will be appropriate for your new business. Also note that tax laws and regulations are subject to change at any time. The information provided should not be taken as tax advice, and you should seek guidance from your local advisors.

In addition to these write-offs, the advantage of separating your trading business into a separate legal entity enables you to protect your family and your personal assets from some creditors. Talk with your legal advisor about how best to structure this new business to protect your personal assets and family.

Understanding Corporate Structure

When you do sit down to discuss forming your own corporation, you need to consider three types of entities: a C Corporation, a Subchapter S Corporation, and a Limited Liability Company.

Limited Liability Companies

You can limit your liability as a sole proprietor by establishing your trading company as a limited liability company or LLC. This designation falls somewhere between a corporation and a sole proprietorship. An LLC is a state entity organized under state laws.

How limited your liability is under this organizational structure depends on the laws in your state. Most states give LLCs the same protection from liability as they give corporations.

The IRS can treat LLCs as sole proprietorships, but you can ask to have them treated as a corporation for tax purposes if you file Form 8832. LLCs do enjoy limited liability when it comes to claims, but owners frequently have to take on debt by giving personal guarantees to financial institutions that make loans to the LLC, especially if the business is new. Owners of a new corporation could be faced with the same problem when debt is needed for the new business.

Corporations

A corporation offers you the greatest liability protection because it is a separate legal entity. As an individual, you are protected from getting sued or facing collections because of actions taken by the corporation. This may sound attractive to you as a trader.

You must form a board of directors when you start a corporation, even if you include only your spouse and children. (Imagine what those family meetings will be like!) The board of directors can be made up of owners and nonowners. The board members who are not owners may receive directors' fees for serving on the board.

You also must divvy out ownership shares in the form of stock. You don't have to sell that stock on the stock exchange, though. Most small businesses do not trade their stock on an open exchange.

Corporations are a separate tax entity and must file tax returns. The two types of corporate structures are C and S. You can avoid corporate taxation by filing with the IRS as an S corporation.

The S corporation is purely an IRS designation that does not affect the legal status of the corporation. S corporations do not pay taxes. For tax purposes, they are treated primarily as a partnership with profits and losses passed through to the owners. All income and expenses are passed through to the owners/shareholders, even if they include you, your spouse, and your children.

CAPITAL CAUTIONS

The biggest disadvantage of establishing your business as a C corporation is that you must pay taxes on your dividend income twice: once at the corporate level and again at an individual level for any distributions to the company's stockholders. In other words, as a small business owner, you could end up paying taxes twice on the same money.

A big disadvantage of an S corporation is that you have less flexibility in how you pass through the profit and losses. Whereas a partnership can determine its own distribution formula, an S corporation must distribute its profit and losses based on percentage of corporate ownership of each of its shareholders.

C corporation dividends are taxed twice—once at the corporate level and once at the individual level—at least for now. Business owners can avoid the corporate level tax on this money by paying themselves and their employees (even if the employees are their spouse and children) a reasonable salary.

Generally, C corporations are for public companies with multiple shareholders. Most likely your tax advisor will recommend that you set up as an S corporation or limited liability company.

Now that you have a trading plan and established your trading business, you're ready to make those profits. Don't get overconfident and start second guessing your business plan or your trading strategies.

As you become more experienced, you'll likely find you want to revise those plans and strategies. Don't be afraid to do so. Nothing is carved in stone. But do revisit those original strategies and write down new ones before making any significant changes.

Finding the best sources for information about currencies is critical to your success. In the final chapter, we identify reliable news sources for trading currencies. Good luck with your trading business and may your profits grow each year.

The Least You Need to Know

- Establish the risks you're willing to take and the returns you expect and put that in writing in your business plan.
- Know where and when you'll work on your trading business if you plan to be a serious trader.
- Understand the tax differences between being a trader and investor. Know how to establish yourself as a trader for tax purposes.
- As your trading business grows, you may want to incorporate your business to protect your assets and improve your tax write-offs.

Finding Information About Forex

Chapter 24

In This Chapter

- Getting up-to-date news
- Finding forecast data
- Comparing forex to other financial instruments

When trading forex, you need to know a lot more than just the exchange rate between the two currencies you want to trade. You also need to know about the economic and political conditions of the countries whose currencies you plan to trade.

In addition, you want to watch for any dramatic moves in the value of either currency in a given pair that might impact the value of that trade. You should also be aware of any upcoming economic announcements that could affect the volatility or the relative value of the currency you are considering trading, so that you can determine the best times to trade.

You might wonder whether currency trading is the best market for you to trade, or if some other market such as stocks or futures would be better. This chapter examines the best places to get news about the currencies you are trading and compares forex to other trading opportunities.

Getting the News About Money

When it comes to finding news about the financial markets, you may already be aware of the three top news sources:

- *The Wall Street Journal* (www.wsj.com) is the most respected daily business newspaper. You do need to buy a subscription to read the articles online, but you can get one for as low as $155 per year. We feel the expense could help improve your research and ultimately your trading success.

- Bloomberg (www.bloomberg.com) is the leading global provider of financial news. It does have a radio and a television station, which is great if your local cable provider includes it in your package; but if not, you can always access its information online.

- *The Financial Times* (www.ft.com), based in London, provides an excellent overview of the financial news from a European perspective. When trading foreign currency, it's critical to understand the news from a global perspective.

In addition to these key financial newspapers, one excellent website that focuses entirely on forex news is FX Street (www.fxstreet.com). There you can find breaking news about various currencies as well as upcoming economic events and economic indicators.

Co-author Gary Tilkin's company, GFT, provides resources on its website to help you trade. The website includes commentary and forecasts from some of the leading experts in the forex market and an economic calendar. You can find information about the most actively traded pairs and their spreads at www.gftforex.com/Markets-And-Pricing/Forex-Spreads/Default.aspx.

You should also read the key newspapers for whichever country's currency you plan to trade. Many times it will take days and sometimes weeks to learn about key news stories that impact only one country. If that country happens to be one in which you are trading its currency, you want to know the breaking news as soon as possible. The best way to do that is to read the national newspapers for the countries whose currencies you trade.

Staying Alert to Breaking Currency News

Coverage of breaking news regarding currency and other financial issues is best found on one of the top two financial cable networks:

- Bloomberg Television is a 24-hour news channel that reports on key financial news. The station has 750 reporters and editors in 79 bureaus around the world that focus on money and the markets.

- CNBC is a world leader for covering business news stories and broadcasts financial news highlights throughout the day. You can find more in-depth coverage of contemporary business issues during its evening programs.

FX Street, which we mentioned previously, also provides news alerts about currency in the "Exclusive Currencies Forecast" section on its home page.

Getting Forecasts on Major Currency

To make money trading foreign currency, it's helpful to read the forecasts about what is likely to happen to the value of the currency in the future. You can visit a number of excellent websites that give you forecasts from key foreign exchange analysts:

- London's *Financial Times* (news.ft.com/markets/currencies) provides excellent coverage in its "Currencies" section.

- FX360.com provides news and analysis on key currencies including the U.S. dollar, the euro, the Japanese yen, the British pound, the Canadian dollar, the Australian dollar, and the New Zealand Dollar at www.fx360.com.

- FX Street (www.fxstreet.com) provides forecasts on key currencies from numerous analysts at www.fxstreet.com/technical/forex-forecasts/experts-forecast-currencies-poll/2010/12/24. You can find forecasts and commentary about the U.S. dollar, the euro, the British pound, the Japanese yen, the Australian dollar, the Canadian dollar, the Swiss franc, and the Chinese renminbi.

- Consensus Economics publishes monthly analysis of the key world currencies based on a comprehensive survey of over 250 forecasters at /www.consensuseconomics.com/forex_major.htm.

The Least You Need to Know

- Reading key financial newspapers daily is important for whatever type of trading you plan to do.
- Read the analyst forecasts regarding the currencies you trade or plan to trade. Foreign currency analysts cannot move markets the way stock market analysts can; instead, they provide an excellent overview of the key factors that do influence the price of the currencies they follow.

Glossary

American terms Phrase used in the United States that refers to a direct quotation for U.S. dollars per one unit of the foreign currency.

arbitration Involves a process during which an impartial third party hears the arguments between two parties and reviews any supporting evidence. He or she then decides how the matter should be resolved.

ask Price at which the forex market maker is willing to sell a currency pair, and at which a customer can buy the pair.

at-the-money With forex options, means the strike price of the option equals the price of the currency pair.

balance of payments Measures the flow of money into and out of a particular country to other countries. Pieces of this calculation include a country's exports and imports of goods and services, as well as the transfer of financial capital. The balance of payments is basically the summary of all economic transactions between a country and all other countries during a particular period, usually a quarter (three months) or a year.

Bank for International Settlements (BIS) International organization based in Basel, Switzerland, that serves as a bank for the world's central banks. It fosters international monetary and financial cooperation by promoting discussion and policy analysis among central banks and the international financial community. It also conducts economic and monetary research.

Bank of Japan Financial Network System (BOJ-NET) BOJ-NET processes transactions involving the Japanese yen and the Bank of Japan and other Japanese financial institutions through its online network. The Bank of Japan started developing BOJ-NET in 1982 and began its foreign exchange yen settlement service in 1989.

bar chart Shows the highs and lows for the currency during the time period selected. Each bar on the chart represents one time period.

base currency   The underlying or fixed currency. For example, in European terms, the U.S. dollar is the base currency because it is the currency in the transaction that is fixed to one unit. When you hear a quote, the base currency is stated first.

bear market   Type of market in which the overall market is trending down.

bid   Price at which the forex market maker would be willing to buy a currency.

Bretton Woods Accord   Established a system of international monetary management with rules for commercial and financial relations among the world's major industrial nations after WWII in July 1944. The accord died in 1971 when then-President Richard Nixon single-handedly closed the gold market and made the dollar no longer convertible to gold directly.

bull market   Type of market in which the overall market is trending up.

candlestick charts   Charts originated in Japan over 300 years ago. In these charts, a little box forms representing the time periods instead of just bar lines. The top of the box is the opening price for the period; the bottom of the box is the closing price. On most candlesticks, you'll also see a line above and below the box. The line above the box shows you the high during the period, and the line below the box shows you the low.

carry trade   Foreign exchange strategy where a trader sells a certain currency with a relatively low interest rate and uses the funds to purchase a different currency yielding a higher interest rate. The trader attempts to benefit from the difference in the two rates.

CHAPS   Electronic system for settling same-day transactions involving the British pound sterling with the United Kingdom Clearing Banks. Payments are individually and continuously processed through CHAPS throughout the day, in real time.

CHIPS   Private bank-owned settlement system for clearing large value payments of the U.S. dollar. CHIPS processes over 285,000 payments a day with a gross value of $1.4 trillion. It serves the largest banks from around the world, representing 19 countries worldwide. CHIPS has been processing payments for U.S. corporate and financial institutions for over 35 years. Today it processes over 95 percent of the U.S. dollar cross-border payments.

CLS   Group founded in 1997 to create the first global settlement system with the goal of eliminating settlement risk in the foreign exchange market. The CLS service, offered by CLS Bank International, is supported by over 70 of the world's largest banking and financial institutions. CLS is a unique real-time process enabling simultaneous FX settlement across the globe, eliminating the settlement risk caused by delays arising from time-zone differences.

Commodity Futures Trading Commission (CFTC)   U.S. government entity that protects market users and the public from fraud, manipulation, and abusive practices related to the sale of commodity and financial futures and options. The Commission's mission also includes fostering open, competitive, and financially sound futures and options markets. The CFTC has a new role as part of the Dodd-Frank bill, passed in 2010 to bring comprehensive regulation to the swaps market. Swaps dealers will be subject to new oversight.

counterparty   Party such as a dealer or brother who is willing to trade with you; necessary for every foreign currency exchange involving a pair of currencies traded between two parties. For example, if someone wants to trade U.S dollars for euros, one party needs to be holding the euros and one party needs to be holding the U.S. dollars in order to trade.

DAX 100   Index of the 100 most heavily traded stocks in the German stock market.

derivatives   Type of financial instrument that's value is dependent upon another instrument, such as a commodity, bond, stock, or currency. Futures and options are two types of financial derivatives.

Dow Jones Industrial Index (DOW)   Most widely used indicator of the overall condition of the stock market, but it only tracks 30 actively traded blue chip stocks. The stocks tracked are picked by the editors of *The Wall Street Journal*. The DOW index was founded in 1896 by Charles Dow.

economic indicators   Any variable that gives you an idea of where the market may be headed, such as new employment statistics or trade balances.

electronic funds transfer (EFT)   System where money is transferred from one bank account directly to another without any paper money changing hands. If you use direct deposit for your paycheck, that is a form of an EFT. Most forex trading is done using an EFT.

EURO 1   Large-value payment system for euro payments managed by the EBA Clearing Company, which was set up by the Euro Banking Association (EBA). The EBA is a cooperative undertaking between EU–based commercial banks and EU branches of non–EU credit institutions. Currently more than 70 participating banks from the 15 member states of the European Union (EU) and five non–EU countries participate in the system. EURO 1 handles credit transfers and direct debits. Payments are processed throughout the day. Balances are settled at the end of the day via a settlement account at the European Central Bank.

European terms   Refers to a direct quotation for someone in Europe from their currency per one unit of U.S. dollar.

expiration month   Month preceding the contract delivery month for an options contract. For example, an option on a March contract expires in February but is referred to as a March option because its exercise would result in a March contract position.

Federal Open Market Committee (FOMC)   This committee of the U.S. Federal Reserve is a group of 19 people plus about 40 staffers. The 7 members of the Federal Reserve Board and 12 presidents of the Federal Reserve Banks make up the committee. When the committee takes a vote only 12 of the people can vote: the 7 Federal Reserve Board members, the president of the Federal Reserve Bank of New York, and 4 of the other 11 Federal Reserve Bank presidents. Voting rights rotate among the bank presidents.

Fedwire   Provides a real-time gross settlement system (RTGS) to the more than 9,500 participants in the Federal Reserve System that maintain a reserve or clearing account with a Federal Reserve bank. You must have an account with a Federal Reserve bank to use Fedwire. Participants use Fedwire to handle large-value, time-critical payments, such as payments for the settlement of interbank purchases and sales of federal funds; the purchase, sale, and financing of securities transactions; the disbursement or repayment of loans; and the settlement of real estate transactions. Payment instructions can be given online or by telephone.

fixed exchange rate   Type of exchange rate regime where a currency's value is matched to the value of an individual country's currency or a basket of other countries' currencies.

floating exchange rate   Type of exchange rate regime where the value of a currency fluctuates according to the foreign exchange market, rather than being pegged to a specific commodity (such as gold) or a specific currency (such as the U.S. dollar).

forex   Shortened version of foreign exchange. Commonly used to refer to the foreign exchange trading market.

forward transaction   With this transaction, you trade one currency for another on a pre-agreed date at some time in the future, but it must be three or more days after the deal date. The forward transaction is a straightforward single purchase or sale of one currency for another.

FTSE 100   Stock index that tracks the top 100 stocks on the London Stock Exchange and is similar to the S&P 500. The index is co-owned by the *Financial Times* daily newspaper of London and the London Stock Exchange.

fundamental analysis   Type of analysis interpreting data collected about what is happening in the economy and then using the results to understand how these economic conditions impact the current value of a particular currency, as well as predicting what might happen to the currency's future value. Many things can impact the state of the economy, including monetary policy set by government agencies, capital and trade flows, production, and employment (or unemployment). Understanding these key economic indicators and how they impact the value of money is critical for currency traders.

GDP or **Gross Domestic Product**   Market value of all final goods and services produced within a country during a specified period of time.

International Bank for Reconstruction and Development   Bank that initially served as a vehicle for the reconstruction of Europe and Japan following WWII. Today it fosters economic growth in developing countries in Africa, Asia, and Latin America, as well as the post-Socialist states of Eastern Europe and the former Soviet Union.

International Monetary Fund   Oversees the global financial system. It monitors exchange rates and balance of payments for foreign exchange transactions, and provides technical and financial assistance when requested by individual member counties.

in-the-money   Forex call option that indicates the price for the currency pair is above the strike price. Put options are considered in-the-money if the currency pair is trading below the strike price of the put.

intrinsic value   Amount of money that an option would be worth if it were exercised and turned into a financial product today. For example, a 100 call option with the underlying financial product price at 120 would have an intrinsic value of 20. A 100 put option with the underlying financial product at 80 would also have an intrinsic value of 20.

laws of supply and demand   The law of supply states that as price rises, the quantity supplied rises; as price falls, the quantity supplied falls. The law of demand states as price falls, the quantity demanded rises; as price rises, the quantity of demand falls. When supply and demand are in balance, that means at a certain price and quantity, the amount the buyer wants to buy is equal to what the seller wants to sell.

limit order   Allows you to specify a price at which you want to buy or sell the currency. If you are looking to buy a currency, you would place a limit order specifying that you will buy the currency at a specific price or lower. If you are looking to sell a currency, you would place a limit order specifying that you will sell the currency at a specific price or higher.

line chart   Created by plotting one price point of a currency over a specified period of time. The line is made by connecting the dots of each of these plotted points.

managed float regime   Currency regime in which the exchange rates fluctuate from day to day, but a central bank attempts to influence the country's exchange rates by buying and selling currencies, a practice commonly referred to as a "dirty float."

margin   Amount of money that is required to be deposited by a customer to the broker or dealer. Margin is a percentage of the forex position value.

margin call   Broker or dealer's demand on a customer to deposit additional funds into his or her account. Margin calls are made to bring a customer's account up to a minimum level.

mark to market   Indicates the value of the option is set at the end of the trading day based on the value of the underlying currency pair.

market maker   In the foreign exchange world, a bank or forex dealer that provides publicly quoted prices for specific currency pairs. Market makers add liquidity, and provide a two-sided market. International banks serve as market makers for more than 70 percent of the foreign exchange market. Retail or individual customers typically go through licensed forex dealing firms that act as market makers, because these firms can access the prices and liquidity of the international banks, while providing individuals with market access.

market order   Simplest and most basic order you can place. It is an order to buy or sell a financial instrument immediately at the best possible price.

market sentiment   Reflects the general mood surrounding the currency market. Understanding this general mood helps you develop a plan based on the expected behavior of the market, which is critical to developing a good trading plan.

mediation   Involves a process where two parties try to come to a mutually acceptable agreement with the help of a third party.

mini account   Type of forex account that allows you to buy a smaller amount of currency using a mini lot. A mini lot is 10,000 units of currency, which is just a tenth of the size of a standard lot of 100,000 units. Mini accounts typically have smaller minimum deposit requirements and offer higher leverage.

Nasdaq Composite Index that tracks primarily technology stocks, so it is not a good indicator of the broader stock market, but is a good indicator of what is happening in growth stocks. The index dates back to 1971, when the Nasdaq stock exchange was first created.

National Futures Association (NFA) Industry-wide, self-regulatory organization for the U.S. futures industry that develops rules, programs, and services to safeguard market integrity, protect investors, and help its members meet regulatory responsibilities.

Nikkei index Most respected index of Japanese stocks. The index is calculated using Japan's top 225 blue-chip companies on the Tokyo Stock Exchange. Many think of the Nikkei as the equivalent of the Dow index in the United States. It was even named the Nikkei Dow Jones Stock Average from 1975 to 1985. The index was started by Japan's leading business newspaper, *The Nikkei*, in 1950.

payment When carrying out a foreign exchange transaction, the payment involves giving instructions regarding the value of the transaction.

performance bond margins Deposits required to ensure that an option writer can cover potential losses with his or her trading positions.

pip Smallest amount that a currency pair can move in price. This is similar to a "tick" on the stock market.

PNS A hybrid settlement system. Participants can set bilateral limits. Transactions are settled in real time if there is sufficient liquidity in the participant's account and if bilateral limits are met. Otherwise, transactions are queued.

POPS Real-time system operated by the participating banks on a decentralized basis in Finland. It is the Finnish TARGET component BoF-RTGS. At the end of the day a settlement is made, thereby zeroing any remaining bilateral obligations.

position Amount of currency you own or owe in your trading account.

real-time gross settlement system (RTGS) Continuous settlement of payments on an individual order basis. RTGS is a system for large-value interbank funds transfers. Settlement risk is minimized because interbank settlements occur throughout the day rather than just at the end of the day.

resistance Used in technical analysis, resistance is a price point above the current market price at which sellers decide to sell. It is always the upper trading range boundary. When a currency pair hits the resistance point, buyers are losing interest in buying because the price is too high, and sellers must lower their price in order to find buyers.

settlement   When carrying out a foreign exchange transaction, the settlement involves the actual clearing of the funds based on the payment instructions.

Smithsonian Agreement   International agreement made in 1971 when the Group of Ten devalued the dollar to $38 per ounce of gold with trading allowed up to 2.25 percent above or below that value. U.S. dollars could not be used to convert directly to gold.

spot forex market   Market in which the currency is bought and sold for cash and delivered immediately.

spot rate   Current market price, also known as the benchmark price.

spot transaction   Simplest type of transaction in the world of foreign exchange. It is simply the exchange of one currency for another.

stop order   Type of order that will automatically be executed when your price is hit. When the price is hit, the order becomes a market order and will be executed immediately.

stop-limit order   Type of order that utilizes the benefits of both a stop order and a limit order. If you place a stop order, but are worried that the market may move too quickly for the order to be executed in time, then you can include a limit order as part of the stop order. When you use a stop-limit order, the stop becomes a limit order rather than a market order and won't be executed unless your broker or dealer can get the price you specified or better.

strike price   Price at which the financial product underlying a call or put option can be purchased (if a call) or sold (if a put). Also referred to as the "exercise price."

support   Used in technical analysis, it is the price point below the current market price where buying occurs. It is always the lower trading range boundary. When the price drops to the support level, then buyers start to buy in order to stop the price from dropping any lower.

swap   Allows you to exchange one currency for another and then re-exchange back to the currency you first held.

TARGET   RTGS system for the euro that was created by interconnecting two key settlements systems—the national euro real-time gross settlements system and the European Central Bank payment mechanism. It is used for the settlement of Central Bank operations, large-value euro interbank transfers, and other euro payments. It provides real-time processing and settlement in central bank money. TARGET stands for **T**rans-European **A**utomated **R**eal-time **G**ross settlement **E**xpress **T**ransfer system.

technical analysis   Looks at the historical price movements and patterns of currencies. Technical analysts believe that by tracking a currency's historical price movements, you can spot trends and predict future price movements.

terms currency   Foreign currency that is being quoted as a pair to the base currency.

UK gilt   Government bond similar to U.S. treasury bonds.

volatility   Amount of movement in the underlying market over a period of time. Options tend to be more expensive when volatility is high and tend to be cheaper when volatility is low. Options buyers should look to buy in quiet markets and sell their options when prices become volatile.

World Bank   Provides financial and technical assistance to developing countries around the world. The bank is owned by 184 member countries and works to reduce global poverty and improve the living standards of people in developing countries. The bank provides low-interest loans, as well as interest-free credit and grants to developing countries for education, health, infrastructure, communications, and other purposes.

Websites

Key Regulatory Agencies

The two primary forex regulators are as follows:

Commodity Futures Trading Commission (www.cftc.gov) is a U.S. government entity that protects market users and the public from fraud, manipulation, and abusive practices related to the sale of commodity and financial futures and options. The Commission's mission also includes fostering open, competitive, and financially sound futures and options markets.

National Futures Association (www.nfa.futures.org) is a self-regulatory body for the futures industry that was given its authority by the Commodity Futures Trading Commission (CFTC). All forex dealers and market makers must be registered with the NFA. You can find out if your broker is affiliated with the NFA by using the National Futures Association's Background Affiliation Status Information Center at www.nfa.futures.org/basicnet.

In addition to these two primary forex regulators, you can get help at the state or local level:

National Association of Attorneys General (www.naag.org) provides links to your state attorney general's consumer protection bureau. In the middle left of the page you'll see a U.S. map that you can use to locate the attorney general for your state. You'll then be able to get to his or her information page where you will find a link to the attorney general's consumer protection website.

North American Securities Administrators Association (www.nasaa.org/ QuickLinks/ContactYourRegulator.cfm) provides links to your state's securities commissioner.

Better Business Bureau (www.bbb.org) can help you research any business you plan to work with. On the national Better Business Bureau website you will find links to access the national database of businesses, as well as information to contact your local Better Business Bureau or to access its website.

Key News Sources About Currency

Here are the major currency-related news media outlets:

Bloomberg (www.bloomberg.com) is the leading global provider of financial news. It does have a radio and a television station, which is great if your local cable provider includes it in your package, but if not, you can always access its information online.

Business Week (www.businessweek.com) is an excellent weekly business news magazine.

CNN Money (money.cnn.com) is a good source to find information about investment waves to locate your next best trading opportunity.

Financial Times (www.ft.com) provides an excellent overview of the financial news from a European perspective (based in London). When trading foreign currency, it's critical to understand the news from a global perspective. You can find excellent coverage of currency trends in the *Financial Times* currency section (news.ft.com/markets/currencies).

The Wall Street Journal (www.wsj.com) is the most respected daily business newspaper. You do need to buy a subscription to read the articles online, but you can get one for as low as $155. We feel the expense could help you improve your research and ultimately your trading success.

In addition to the major news media, several key forex websites can help keep you informed about money trends:

Consensus Economics publishes monthly analysis of the key world currencies based on a comprehensive survey of over 250 forecasters at www.consensuseconomics.com/forex_major.htm.

Daily FX provides a weekly forecast for key currencies including the U.S. dollar, the euro, the Japanese yen, the British pound, the Canadian dollar, the Australian dollar, and the New Zealand dollar at www.dailyfx.com/forex_market_news/forecasts.

FX Street (www.fxstreet.com) focuses entirely on forex news. There you will find breaking news about various currencies as well as upcoming economic events and economic indicators. FX Street provides forecasts on key currencies from numerous analysts. You can find forecasts and commentary about the U.S. dollar, the euro, the British pound, the Japanese yen, the Australian dollar, the Canadian dollar, the Swiss franc, and the Chinese renminbi.

Global Forex Trading provides resources on the most actively traded pairs and their spreads at www.gftforex.com/Markets-And-Pricing/Forex-Spreads/Default.aspx.

U.S. State Department (www.state.gov/r/pa/ei/bgn) provides a good summary about the political conditions and the economy of countries in the "Background Notes" section.

Exchanges for Options on Foreign Currencies

Chicago Mercantile Exchange (www.cme.com)

New York Board of Trade (www.nybot.com)

Philadelphia Stock Exchange (www.phlx.com)

U.S.–Based Forex Settlement Systems

CHIPS (www.chips.org) is a private bank-owned settlement system for clearing large value payments of the U.S. dollar. It serves the largest banks from around the world, representing 19 countries worldwide. Today it processes over 95 percent of the U.S. dollar cross-border payments.

Fedwire (frbservices.org) provides a real-time gross settlement system (RTGS) to the more than 9,500 participants in the Federal Reserve System that maintain a reserve or clearing account with a Federal Reserve Bank.

European Forex Settlement Systems

CHAPS (www.bankofengland.co.uk/markets/paymentsystems) is an electronic system for settling same-day transactions involving the British pound sterling with the United Kingdom Clearing Banks.

EURO 1 (www.abe.org) is a large-value payment system for euro payments managed by the EBA Clearing Company, which was set up by the Euro Banking Association (EBA).

PNS (www.banque-france.fr) is a hybrid settlement system. End-of-day balances are credited to the participants' settlement accounts at the Banque de France.

POPS (www.bof.fi) is a real-time system operated by the participating banks on a decentralized basis in Finland. It is the Finnish TARGET component BoF-RTGS. At the end of the day a settlement is made, thereby zeroing any remaining bilateral obligations.

TARGET (www.ecb.int/paym/t2/html/index.en.html) is the RTGS system for the euro and was created by interconnecting two key settlement systems—the national euro real-time gross settlement system and the European Central Bank payment mechanism.

Other Forex Settlement Systems

BOJ-NET (www.boj.or.jp/en/index.htm), the Bank of Japan Financial Network System, processes transactions involving the Japanese yen and the Bank of Japan and other Japanese financial institutions through its online network.

CLS Group (www.cls-group.com) was founded in 1997 to create the first global settlement system with the goal of eliminating settlement risk in the foreign exchange market.

Central Banks

The following is a list of central banks around the world:

- Reserve Bank of Australia (www.rba.gov.au)
- Bank of Canada (www.bankofcanada.ca/en/monetary/target.html)
- Czech National Bank (www.cnb.cz/en/index.html)
- Bank of England (www.bankofengland.co.uk)
- European Central Bank (www.ecb.int/home/html/index.en.html)
- Hong Kong Monetary Authority (www.info.gov.hk/hkma/eng/currency/link_ex/index.htm)

- Bank of Japan (www.boj.or.jp/en)

- Reserve Bank of New Zealand (www.rbnz.govt.nz)

- South African Reserve Bank (www.resbank.co.za)

- Swiss National Bank (www.snb.ch)

- Central Bank of the Republic of Turkey (www.tcmb.gov.tr/yeni/eng/index.html)

- U.S. Federal Reserve (www.federalreserve.gov)

Other key web sources of the U.S. Federal Reserve include:

- Federal Reserve activities related to foreign exchange are handled at the Federal Reserve Bank of New York (www.newyorkfed.org/markets/foreignex.html).

- The Fed's Beige Book (www.federalreserve.gov/FOMC/BeigeBook) summarizes economic conditions in the United States.

- The Fed's Fred (Federal Reserve Economic Data) (research.stlouisfed.org/fred2) database is an excellent resource with all current economic indicators.

Money Forums

Elite Trader (www.elitetrader.com) provides an online community for discussion about not only forex, but also stock, options, and futures trading.

MoneyTec Traders (www.moneytec.com) is a discussion forum that serves as a resource to help forex traders become better traders. You can meet fellow traders from around the world and learn more about forex trading, as well as discuss trading ideas, techniques, and strategies.

Trading Platforms

In addition to co-author Gary Tilkin's DealBook® 360, which you can download at gftforex.com/Software/Default.aspx, here are some other reputable trading platforms you can try out:

- **Capital Market Services** (www.cmsfx.com). You can open an account with US$200. Languages available are Arabic, Chinese, English, Japanese, Russian, and Spanish.

- **Forex Capital Markets** (www.fxcm.com). You can open an account with US$2,000. Languages available include Arabic, Chinese, Dutch/Flemish, English, French, German, Italian, Japanese, Portuguese, Russian, and Spanish.

- **Forex.com** (www.forex.com). You can open a mini account with US$250, but a standard account is US$2,500. Languages available include Chinese, English, and Russian.

Note: The information listed for these forex firms was taken from each company's website. This information can change, so please conduct thorough research prior to trading with any firm.

U.S. Regulatory Agencies

Forex can be a very risky way to trade. Luckily, some of that risk is minimized by the regulatory agencies involved in monitoring the world of forex. Here are some of the top agencies that you should get to know.

Commodity Futures Trading Commission (www.cftc.gov)

The Commodity Futures Trading Commission (CFTC) has the jurisdiction and authority to investigate and take legal action to close down a wide assortment of unregulated firms offering or selling foreign currency futures and options contracts to the general public. In addition, the CFTC has jurisdiction to investigate and prosecute foreign currency fraud occurring in its registered firms and their affiliates. Significant new responsibilities will fall under the CFTC under the Dodd-Frank Wall Street Reform bill passed in 2010. The CFTC will develop comprehensive regulations for the swaps marketplace. Swap dealers will be subject to robust oversight. Standardized derivatives will be required to trade on open platforms, and be submitted for clearing to central counterparties.

Under the Dodd-Frank bill, the CFTC also developed new rules for retail forex that included regulations for registration, disclosure, record keeping, financial reporting, minimum capital, and other business conduct and operational standards. Specifically, the regulations require the registration of counterparties offering retail foreign currency contracts as either futures commission merchants (FCMs) or retail foreign exchange dealers (RFEDs), a new category of registrant. Persons who solicit orders, exercise discretionary trading authority, or operate pools with respect to retail forex also will be required to register, either as introducing brokers, commodity trading advisors, commodity pool operators (as appropriate), or as associated persons of such entities. "Otherwise regulated" entities, such as United States financial institutions and SEC–registered brokers or dealers, remain able to serve as counterparties in such transactions under the oversight of their primary regulators.

The final rules include financial requirements designed to ensure the financial integrity of firms engaging in retail forex transactions and robust customer protections. For example, FCMs and RFEDs are required to maintain net capital of $20 million plus 5 percent of the amount, if any, by which liabilities to retail forex customers exceed $10 million. Leverage in retail forex customer accounts will be subject to a security deposit requirement to be set by the National Futures Association within limits provided by the Commission. All retail forex counterparties and intermediaries will be required to distribute forex-specific risk disclosure statements to customers and comply with comprehensive record keeping and reporting requirements.

To find out more about its consumer-protection programs, go to www.cftc.gov/cftc/cftccustomer.htm.

You can write the CFTC at the following address:

Commodity Futures Trading Commission
Division of Enforcement
Three LaFayette Centre
1155 21st Street, N.W.
Washington, D.C., 20581

You can ask a question, report information, or file a complaint by calling 1-866-366-2382.

The CFTC's e-mail address for complaints is enforcement@cftc.gov, or you can file a complaint online at www.cftc.gov/enf/enfform.htm.

National Futures Association

National Futures Association (NFA) is the regulatory organization for the U.S. futures industry, which also registers many of the brokers and dealers who serve forex traders. Its mission is to safeguard market integrity, protect investors, and help its members meet their regulatory responsibilities.

Membership in NFA is mandatory for everyone that conducts business with the public on the U.S. futures exchanges—more than 4,200 firms and 55,000 associates—must adhere to the same high standards of professional conduct. NFA is an independent regulatory organization with no ties to any specific marketplace.

It operates at no cost to the taxpayer. NFA is financed exclusively from membership dues and from assessment fees paid by the users of the futures markets.

The NFA maintains the Background Affiliation Status Information Center (BASIC), where you can find information about a forex firm's CFTC registration and NFA membership. You can also find regulatory and nonregulatory actions by the NFA and the CFTC. You can access BASIC online at www.nfa.futures.org/basicnet.

You can also file a complaint about a broker, dealer, or his or her firm at www.nfa. futures.org/basicnet/Complaint.aspx.

You can contact the NFA at one of its two offices:

Chicago Headquarters
300 S. Riverside Plaza, #1800
Chicago, IL, 60606-6615
312-781-1300
312-781-1467 (fax)

New York Office
120 Broadway, #1125
New York, NY, 10271
212-608-8660
212-964-3913 (fax)

Or you can call the NFA at 1-800-621-3570.

Other Regulatory Entities

The CFTC and NFA do regulate the majority of forex firms, but it's possible that firms you are dealing with, or may deal with, are registered or regulated by other institutions or entities not under the CFTC's jurisdiction. The following are the key regulatory entities that also may be able to help you if you are having a problem with a forex trade involving one of their regulated entities.

Federal Deposit Insurance Corporation (www.fdic.gov)

If the bank you are dealing with is a chartered bank that is not a member of the Federal Reserve, then its chief regulator is the FDIC. This includes commercial and savings banks that are not in the Federal Reserve System. You can find resources for consumers at the FDIC website: www.fdic.gov/consumers/consumer/index.html. You can call the FDIC for information about a chartered bank at 1-877-275-3342. Or you can file a complaint or inquiry online at www2.fdic.gov/starsmail/index.asp.

If you want to reach the FDIC by mail, you need to write one of five office addresses in Washington, D.C. For a directory of key contacts in Washington, go to www.fdic.gov/about/contact/directory/index.html.

Federal Reserve Board (www.federalreserve.gov)

If you are dealing with a state-licensed bank that is a member of the Federal Reserve or a financial holding company, your best source for regulatory information is the Federal Reserve. You can research any enforcement actions against a bank at www.federalreserve.gov/boarddocs/enforcement.

You can contact the Federal Reserve Board of Governors as follows:

Board of Governors of the Federal Reserve System
20th Street and Constitution Avenue, NW
Washington, D.C., 20551
202-452-3000

Or you can find the nearest Federal Reserve Bank at the board's website at www.federalreserve.gov/FRAddress.htm.

National Credit Union Administration (www.ncua.gov)

The National Credit Union Administration is the regulatory agency you should contact if you are having a problem with a federal- or state-chartered credit union. You can contact the Washington office as follows:

National Credit Union Administration
1775 Duke Street
Alexandria, VA, 22314-3428
703-518-6300

The Office of the Comptroller of the Currency (www.occ.treas.gov)

The oldest of the financial regulators is the Office of the Comptroller of the Currency, which was founded in 1863 as a branch of the U.S. Department of

Treasury. Today its role in the financial industry is to charter, regulate, and supervise all national banks, including their domestic and international activities.

If you have a complaint about a national bank, call the OCCC at its Consumer Assistance Group, 1-800-613-6743.

You can also contact the Consumer Assistance Group by mail:

Customer Assistance Group
1301 McKinney Street
Suite 3450
Houston, TX, 77010

U.S. Securities and Exchange Commission (www.sec.gov)

If you are working with a firm that also trades securities, it is probably regulated by the U.S. Securities and Exchange Commission. You can file a complaint or send in a tip online at www.sec.gov/complaint.shtml.

You can call for consumer assistance on its information line at 1-800-732-0330.

You can contact the SEC's Washington headquarters as follows:

SEC Headquarters
100 F Street, NE
Washington, D.C., 20549
Office of Investor Education and Advocacy
202-551-6551

Or you can e-mail them at help@sec.gov.

The SEC also has 12 regional offices. You can locate their contact information online at www.sec.gov/contact/addresses.htm.

State Regulators

You may also find additional information at your state attorney general's office and state banking, insurance, and securities regulators. You can find state websites on the Internet at www.statelocalgov.net.

Prime Trading Times

Because you make money trading forex on just fractions of a cent called pips, it's critical that you know the best times to trade each day. That differs for every currency depending upon the key market movers for that currency, which involve the releases of market-moving economic news.

In the following tables, we list the currency, the most actively traded currency pairs for that currency, and the market movers. The tables are developed by the most active trading hours by currency.

The currencies included in the tables are:

>AUD: Australian dollar

>CAD: Canadian dollar

>CHF: Swiss franc

>EUR: Euro

>GBP: British pound

>JPY: Japanese yen

>NZD: New Zealand dollar

>USD: U.S. dollar

Trading Time: 1:45 A.M. ET, 5:45 GMT: Swiss Economic Releases

Currency	Pairs	Market Movers
CHF	CHF/JPY EUR/CHF GBP/CHF	Consumer prices GDP (gross domestic product) KOF leading indicators (Swiss business expectations) Retail sales Swiss National Bank interest rate decision UBS consumption index

Trading Time: 2:00 A.M. ET, 6:00 GMT: London Open

Currency	Pairs	Market Movers
CHF	CHF/JPY EUR/CHF GBP/CHF	Consumer prices GDP KOF leading indicators Retail sales Swiss National Bank interest rate decision UBS consumption index
EUR	EUR/CHF EUR/GBP EUR/JPY	European Central Bank rate decision German consumer prices German GDP German IFO (business confidence) German unemployment Manufacturing and service sector PMI (Purchasing Manager's Index)
GBP	EUR/GBP GBP/CHF GBP/JPY	Bank of England rate decision Claimant count Consumer prices GDP Industrial production Retail sales

Currency	Pairs	Market Movers
USD	AUD/USD EUR/USD GBP/USD USD/CAD USD/CHF USD/JPY	Consumer and producer prices Consumer confidence Fed interest decision GDP Non-farm payrolls Retail sales Service and manufacturing ISM (Institute for Supply Management) Trade balance Treasury international capital flow report (TIC)

Trading Time: 4:00 A.M. ET, 8:00 GMT: European Economic Releases

Currency	Pairs	Market Movers
EUR	EUR/CHF EUR/JPY EUR/GBP	European Central Bank rate decision German consumer prices German GDP German IFO (business confidence) German unemployment Manufacturing and service sector PMI (Purchasing Managers' Index)

Trading Time: 4:30 A.M. ET, 8:30 GMT: UK Economic Releases

Currency	Pairs	Market Movers
GBP	EUR/GBP GBP/CHF GBP/JPY	Bank of England rate decision Claimant count Consumer prices GDP Industrial production Retail sales

Trading Time: 7:00 A.M. ET, 11 GMT: Canadian Economic Releases

Currency	Pairs	Market Movers
CAD	AUD/CAD CAD/GBP EUR/CAD	Bank of Canada rate decision Consumer prices Employment change GDP IVEY PMI (Purchasing Managers' Index) Retail sales

Trading Time: 8:30 A.M. ET, 12:30 GMT: U.S. Economic Releases

Currency	Pairs	Market Movers
AUD	AUD/CAD AUD/JPY AUD/NZD	Consumer and producer prices Employment change GDP Reserve Bank of Australia rate decision Retail sales Trade balance
CAD	AUD/CAD CAD/GBP EUR/CAD	Bank of Canada rate decision Consumer prices Employment change GDP IVEY PMI (Purchasing Managers' Index) Retail sales
CHF	CHF/JPY EUR/CHF GBP/CHF	Consumer prices GDP KOF leading indicators Retail sales Swiss National Bank interest rate decision UBS consumption index
EUR	EUR/CHF EUR/GBP EUR/JPY	European Central Bank rate decision German consumer prices German GDP German IFO (business confidence) German unemployment Manufacturing and service sector PMI (Purchasing Manager's Index)

Currency	Pairs	Market Movers
GBP	EUR/GBP GBP/CHF GBP/JPY	Bank of England rate decision Claimant count Consumer prices GDP Industrial production Retail sales
JPY	AUD/JPY CAD/JPY CHF/JPY EUR/JPY GBP/JPY NZD/JPY	Bank of Japan rate decision Consumer prices Corporate goods price index GDP Retail sales Tankan report (Survey of business sentiment)
NZD	AUD/NZD EUR/NZD NZD/JPY	Consumer prices Employment change GDP Reserve Bank of New Zealand rate decision Retail sales Trade balance
USD	AUD/USD EUR/USD GBP/USD USD/CAD USD/CHF USD/JPY	Consumer and producer prices Consumer confidence Fed interest decision GDP Non-farm payrolls Retail sales Service and manufacturing ISM (Institute for Supply Management) Trade balance Treasury international capital flow report (TIC)

Trading Time: 7:00 P.M. ET, 23:00 GMT: Tokyo Open

Currency	Pairs	Market Movers
AUD	AUD/CAD AUD/JPY AUD/NZD	Consumer and producer prices Employment change GDP Reserve Bank of Australia rate decision Retail sales Trade balance
JPY	AUD/JPY CAD/JPY CHF/JPY EUR/JPY GBP/JPY NZD/JPY	Bank of Japan rate decision Consumer prices Corporate goods price index GDP Retail sales Tankan report (Survey of business sentiment)
NZD	AUD/NZD EUR/NZD NZD/JPY	Consumer prices Employment change GDP Reserve Bank of New Zealand rate decision Retail sales Trade balance

Trading time: 7:30 P.M. ET, 23:30 GMT: Australian, Japanese, and New Zealand Economic Releases

Currency	Pairs	Market Movers
AUD	AUD/CAD AUD/JPY AUD/NZD	Consumer and producer prices Employment change GDP Reserve Bank of Australia rate decision Retail sales Trade balance

Currency	Pairs	Market Movers
JPY	AUD/JPY	Bank of Japan rate decision
	CAD/JPY	Consumer prices
	CHF/JPY	Corporate goods price index
	EUR/JPY	GDP
	GBP/JPY	Retail sales
	NZD/JPY	Tankan report (Survey of business sentiment)
NZD	AUD/NZD	Consumer prices
	EUR/NZD	Employment change
	NZD/JPY	GDP
		Reserve Bank of New Zealand rate decision
		Retail sales
		Trade balance

Index

N

O

T

CHECK OUT
THESE BEST-SELLERS

More than 450 titles available at booksellers and online retailers everywhere!

ALPHA   idiotsguides.com